T0373456

The Urban Roots of Democracy and
Political Violence in Zimbabwe

Rochester Studies in African History and the Diaspora

Toyin Falola, Senior Editor
The Frances Higginbotham Nalle Centennial Professor in History
University of Texas at Austin
(ISSN: 1092–5228)

A complete list of titles in the Rochester Studies in African History and the Diaspora, in order of publication, may be found at the end of this book.

The Urban Roots of Democracy and Political Violence in Zimbabwe

Harare and Highfield, 1940–1964

TIMOTHY SCARNECCHIA

 University of Rochester Press

First published 2008
Reprinted in paperback and transferred to digital printing 2013

University of Rochester Press
668 Mt. Hope Avenue, Rochester, NY 14620, USA
www.urpress.com
and Boydell & Brewer Limited
PO Box 9, Woodbridge, Suffolk IP12 3DF, UK
www.boydellandbrewer.com

ISSN: 1092-5228
hardcover ISBN: 978-1-58046-281-5
paperback ISBN: 978-1-58046-363-8

Library of Congress Cataloging-in-Publication Data
Scarnecchia, Timothy.
    The urban roots of democracy and political violence in Zimbabwe : Harare
and Highfield, 1940–1964 / Timothy Scarnecchia.
        p. cm. — (Rochester studies in African history and the diaspora,
ISSN 1092-5228 ; v. 35)
    Includes bibliographical references and index.
    ISBN 978-1-58046-281-5 (alk. paper)
    1. Zimbabwe—Politics and government—1890–1965. 2. Harare (Zimbabwe)—
Politics and government. 3. Highfield (Zimbabwe)—Politics and government. 4.
Mzingeli, Charles. 5. Democracy—Zimbabwe—History. 6. Political violence—
Zimbabwe—History. 7. Political culture—Zimbabwe—History. I. Title.
    DT2972.S28 2008
    968.9103—dc22

                                                                2008010459

A catalogue record for this title is available from the British Library.

This publication is printed on acid-free paper.

Contents

Illustrations

Acknowledgments

There are many people to thank for their assistance in the research, writing, and publication of this work. Frederick Cooper deserves special thanks for all the time and effort he devoted to developing my skills as a researcher and a historian. I would also like to give special thanks to Luise White and Terence Ranger. Over the years Luise has dedicated a great amount of effort to keep me going and engaged and has continued to challenge me. Terence Ranger has also played an important role in helping me to understand the complexities of Zimbabwean and southern African history. His openness to my attending his seminars in the early 1990s helped in shaping my work, while his personal commitment to building Zimbabwean historiography, particularly urban history, has encouraged me to continue to develop my own projects in new and challenging ways.

I also received a great deal of advice and assistance from individuals in England. Trevor and Christina Gadsby in Woodstock, Oxfordshire, deserve special thanks for their generous hospitality and wonderful meals, which made long days at the Rhodes House Library easier. The staff at the Rhodes House Library were quite helpful, even if I had to use my noisy laptop in the damp basement. More recently, Lucy McCann of Rhodes House Library was quite helpful locating the photos of Mzingeli that appear in chapter 3.

In Zimbabwe I was fortunate to have the support of the Department of Economic History in the early 1990s. Victor Machingaidze, as department chair, was quite generous of his time and efforts to make my affiliation there pleasant. There were a number of honors economic history students who also helped to conduct an initial oral history survey in Mbare and Highfield. Similarly there were a large number of people living in Highfield and Mbare who assisted me in my research, in particular Joseph Seda and Simba Handeseni were essential to making the many hours spent interviewing in Highfield and Mbare so successful. The staff at the National Archives of Zimbabwe were also quite helpful.

I would also like to thank the rest of the expat scholars in Harare at the time, especially Timothy Burke, Lynette Jackson, David Maxwell, Mario

Zamponi, Heike Schmidt, Randal Smith, Blair Rutherford, and Laura Farquharson, for their camaraderie and sharing of housing and expenses. After leaving Harare, scholars of Zimbabwe including Teresa Barnes, David Johnson, Allison Shutt, and Brian Raftopoulos provided support and an intellectual engagement in each other's works. Todd Leedy and David Leaver also deserve my appreciation and thanks for their collaborations in our ChiShona language training. Albert and Erica Natsa also deserve special thanks for all their patience with us as students. Michael O. West has been particularly supportive of this book, helping with files on Charles Mzingeli and also with locating the photos of Mzingeli that appear in the book. I would like to thank Rita Aggarwal, Wendy Urban-Mead, and Blair Rutherford for their helpful comments on earlier versions of sections of this book. I would also like to thank Judith Todd for sharing a personal photograph, which appears in chapter 7.

Having taught at a number of universities in the past ten years, I owe many former colleagues and staff my gratitude. The staff and faculty in the Department of History and Center for AfroAmerican and African Studies at the University of Michigan were quite helpful during the two years I taught as a visiting professor there. The staff and faculty in the Department of History and the African Studies Department at the University of North Carolina–Charlotte were also quite supportive of my work. Similarly, the efforts of the staff in the History Department and the African Studies program at Georgetown University made my time there quite productive. It would be a long list of all the colleagues who helped me at these schools, but I would like to give special thanks to Gwendolyn Mikell, director of Georgetown's African Studies program, and John Tutino, chair of the History Department at Georgetown, for their professional support during my four years as a visiting professor and professorial lecturer. I would also like to thank the many students in my African history and African Studies seminars for their insights into the type of questions university students might ask of this period and material, their encouragement of my work with their intellectual curiosity, and their genuine eagerness and dreams to improve the world. I'm sure the same is true of Zimbabwean students, wherever in the world they may be studying, and I hope they will find this book useful in their own explorations of Zimbabwean history.

It has been my good fortune more recently to benefit from the generous support of the staff and faculty in the Department of History at Kent State University. Their support in the final stages of completing this book is very much appreciated. The Kent State University Research Council's funding to assist with photographic permissions is also appreciated. I am grateful to Yukihiro Suzuoki of the Kent State Geography Department for his careful and talented design of the two maps used in this book.

I would also like to thank the editors at University of Rochester Press for all their work in moving this book forward. In particular, I would like to thank series editor Toyin Falola for recognizing what this book seeks to achieve. Editorial director Suzanne Guiod, managing editor Katie Hurley, and copyeditor Bob Fullilove have been extremely supportive and efficient in overseeing this project. I would also like to thank one anonymous reader, as well as Jocelyn Alexander, who both provided extremely useful criticisms and suggestions on an earlier version of this book.

Last but not least, I would like to thank my family for their support, especially Rita Aggarwal for all her effort to make it possible for me to work on this book, and Mira and Sean for providing so many helpful distractions. As academics with families know, the ability to stay focused and in the Zen-like state necessary to write a book is all but incompatible with family life. But as most people are apt to agree, having a family and a network of students, friends, and colleagues around the world is a price worth paying for the noticeable gaps between what we would wish to produce and what is possible.

Lastly, I would like to dedicate this book to individuals who have passed away since this project began: Marvin Becker, Reuben Jamela, Masipula Sithole, Simba Handiseni, and Tsuneo Yoshikuni. They would most likely have enjoyed reading this book, and all of them contributed to it in their own ways. Others who have known them will hopefully appreciate their spirit in this work.

Kent, Ohio
February 2008

Abbreviations

AFL-CIO	American Federation of Labor–Congress of Industrial Organizations
FCB	Fabian Colonial Bureau
HRP	Harare Residents' Party
ICU	Industrial and Commercial Workers Union
ICFTU	International Confederation of Free Trade Unions
NDP	National Democratic Party
N(UA)ARA	Native (Urban Areas) Accommodation and Registration Act
PASU	Pan-African Socialist Union
PCC	People's Caretaker Committee
RICU	Reformed Industrial and Commercial Workers Union
SCYL	Salisbury City Youth League
SRANC	Southern Rhodesian African National Congress
SRATUC	Southern Rhodesian African Trade Union Congress
SRLP	Southern Rhodesian Labour Party
SRTUC	Southern Rhodesian Trade Union Congress
UFP	United Federal Party
ZANU	Zimbabwe African National Union
ZAPU	Zimbabwe African People's Union
ZNP	Zimbabwe National Party

Notes to the Reader

Note on Name Changes

For non-Zimbabweans, locating Harare and Highfield may be a bit confusing. Prior to the 1980 independence, when Zimbabwe replaced Rhodesia, the name of the capital city was also changed from Salisbury to Harare. Prior to independence Harare had been the name of the oldest African township in Salisbury. After independence, it was renamed Mbare high-density suburb. Harare (now Mbare) was/is located southwest of Salisbury's city center. Divided from the city center by a railway track and marsh areas near the Mukuvisi River, the area was first called the "Native Location"; its name was later changed to Harari Location, and then Harare African Township by the 1950s. For consistency, I refer to it as Harare township throughout. Highfield began as a residential area for married government workers to live with their families. It was sometimes known as five-mile village because of its distance from the city center, but in the early 1950s it was expanded into a much larger residential area known as the New Highfield African Township, while the original area of houses became known as Old Highfield.

Cities and towns with new names after 1980

Previous Name	Current Name
Fort Victoria	Masvingo
Gwelo	Gweru
Que Que	Kwekwe
Salisbury	Harare
Sinoia	Chinhoyi
Umtali	Mutare
Wankie	Hwange

Note on Southern Rhodesian Currency

Southern Rhodesia, during the period covered in this book, used the British pound sterling currency system. The system consisted of pounds (£), shillings (s), and pence (sing. penny) (d). For example, a reference in the text to a monthly cost of living for an African urban worker as £14/8s/2d (or 14/8/2) means 14 pounds, 8 shillings, and 2 pence. There were 20 shillings to a pound, 12 pennies to a shilling, and 240 pence to a pound.

Note on Charles Mzingeli's Writing in Quotations

There are examples in the following text of longer quotations from Charles Mzingeli's writings, either from his letters sent to supporters in England or the minutes of political meetings sometimes typed by Mzingeli and sometimes by the RICU secretary. Rather than placing a "[*sic*]" at each grammatical or spelling error, I have left them verbatim in order to show how effective he was as a communicator in written English, even though he had only a basic education in English. His writing examples also help to capture his gift for oration in English and his ability to use the rhetoric of democracy and equality voiced in the laws of Southern Rhodesia—although rarely meant to include Africans—to make strong claims for the recognition of African rights.

Note on Sources

This book is based primarily on official papers and publications found in the archives in Zimbabwe, the United Kingdom, and the United States. It is also based on interviews conducted in Harare in 1991–92. Although some of these interviews are used in this book, the evidence collected during those years helped to shape the larger questions framing the narrative. In addition, the majority of the research on the earlier section on Charles Mzingeli came from archival sources found in the Records section of the Zimbabwean National Archives, a section that at the time had not been extensively used by researchers. In these files, as well as in the files located in the Harare Town Hall, I was able to find Mzingeli's minutes of meetings and his correspondences. He also sent many of his records to the Fabian Colonial Bureau in London, and their papers are in the Rhodes House Library in Oxford, U.K. As I carried out interviews in Mbare and Highfield, Charles Mzingeli's political career came to life, allowing me to investigate further the political setting in which he lived and worked. A series of interviews with Tobias and Fidelis Nhapi helped to identify the transition from Mzingeli's Reformed Industrial and Commercial Workers Union to the Salisbury City Youth League in the 1950s, and then the shift to the Southern Rhodesian African National Congress. Interviews with former trade union leaders Reuben

Jamela and Shato Nyakauru were also fundamental in shaping the story of the conflict between trade unions and nationalist parties.

Once I returned to the United States, I had hoped to investigate some of the claims made in the interviews, particularly Jamela's story of support from the United States for his trade union congress in the early 1960s. I began with the U.S. State Department files in the National Archives in Washington, D.C., which contain detailed accounts by the American diplomats in Salisbury concerning the struggle between Jamela and the ZAPU leadership over the control of the trade unions. I then investigated the issue further at the George Meany Memorial Archives of the AFL-CIO. The papers in the AFL-CIO archives relating to Jamela and Southern Rhodesia, along with the careful work already done by Yvette Richards in her excellent book *Maida Springer: Pan-Africanist and International Labor Leader* (University of Pittsburgh Press, 2004), allowed me to further verify Jamela's account of events. The most surprising evidence I found in the National Archives, and in the AFL-CIO archives, however, was the extent to which ZAPU and later ZANU leaders courted financial assistance from the United States government at the same time they were publicly lambasting Jamela as an "imperialist stooge." Much of the narrative reconstruction of events is based on reading accounts in the African press during this period. The U.S. Library of Congress holds many of the original volumes of these papers in its African Newspaper Collection, while the interlibrary loan departments of Georgetown and Kent State Universities were very helpful in obtaining microfilm versions of the *Central African Daily News* for the 1960s up to the point it was banned in 1964.

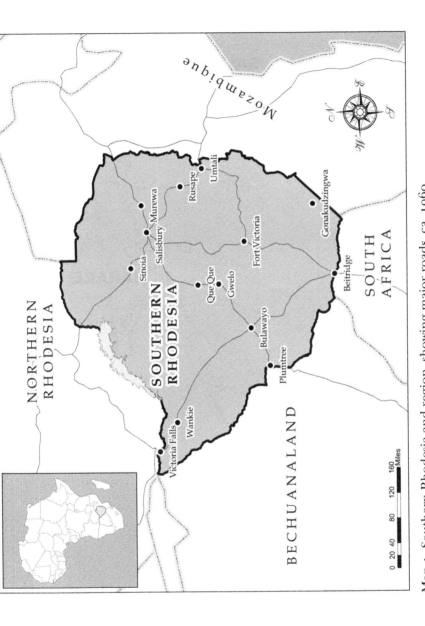

Map 1. Southern Rhodesia and region, showing major roads, ca. 1960.

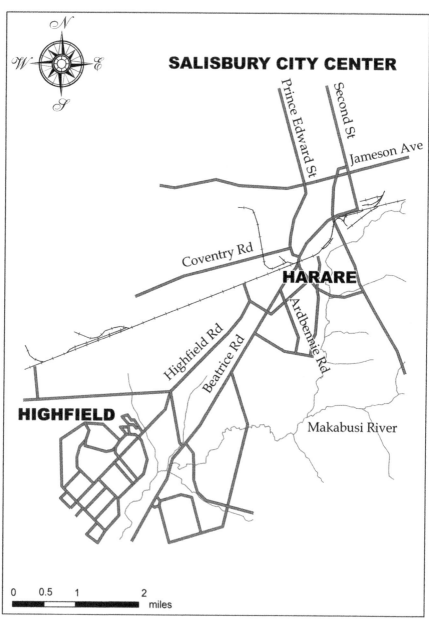

SALISBURY CITY CENTER

Prince Edward St

Second St

Jameson Ave

Coventry Rd

HARARE

Ardbennie Rd

Highfield Rd

Beatrice Rd

HIGHFIELD

Makabusi River

0   0.5   1   2
miles

Map 2. Harare and Highfield, 1960.

Introduction

The primary goal of this book is to provide an account of a democratic tradition that was present in the African townships of what was Salisbury, Southern Rhodesia, and to show how that tradition was cut off by the political violence associated with the leadership struggles and factionalism of the early 1960s. The setting for this story is primarily centered in two places, Harare township (now Mbare) and Highfield township, although the narrative also follows nationalist leaders to London, Dar es Salaam, and Washington, D.C. Zimbabwean scholars, writers, and journalists, have written fondly of their own memories of the cultural and political life in these former African townships of Salisbury.[1] Others have written about the creative music scene produced from the mixing of cultures and working-class life in the townships, helping to show the unique culture and style produced in Harare and Highfield over the years.[2] In addition, historians have written extensively on the labor, gender, and social history of Salisbury's African townships and have developed a strong historiography of the townships' political and social life.

Given the rich body of literature on township life that already exists, the intent of this book is to concentrate on a specific aspect of township history: the development of a democratic political tradition created in the 1940s that survived into the 1950s. The first half of the book concentrates on the political career of Charles Mzingeli and the creation of a democratic politics primarily defined by his cosmopolitan and international connections to larger political currents and movements, including the Pan-African politics of Clements Kadalie's Industrial and Commercial Workers Union (ICU) in South Africa, then the British Labour Party and the Fabian Socialists, and also certain borrowings from the American political tradition. The nature of township life, including the high prevalence of male migrants and a high turnover rate for workers, made the establishment of an urban political tradition extremely difficult for Mzingeli.

The urban democratic tradition established in the 1940s and 1950s was to fall victim to a particular style of political violence that developed out of the peculiarities of township life and the demands of a more radical nationalist politics by the 1960s. Just as townships were designed to contain and control first workers and later entire African urban populations, the township design and structure eventually lent itself to internal control by political factions using harassment, intimidation, and violence to instill discipline and mobilize support. The argument made in this book, however, is that the decisions to use political violence were not predetermined by the spatial structure of township life. The goal of this book is to show how particular leaders and political parties made decisions to accept political violence as they sought to attain political control of township populations. Obtaining such control became an integral part of nationalist strategy in the 1960s as large sums of international financial support were resting on the claims of competing groups to greater grass-roots support. Violence became the most "efficient" short-term means of creating support, even if its long-term effects were disastrous.

Some readers may question the emphasis on the urban roots of Zimbabwe's political violence. After all, there was plenty of violence in the rural areas during the 1960s and there was certainly a very strong nationalist sentiment and organization in the rural areas during these years. As Jocelyn Alexander, JoAnn McGregor, and Terence Ranger argue in *Violence and Memory*, "Although the ideas of urban-based movements were critically important, to build a rural movement, local leaders had to establish a rural social base and redefine issues of local concern within the frame of a nationalist project."[3] Additionally, the violence in the urban townships in the early 1960s was often eclipsed by the violence in rural areas where sabotage was used against state institutions and those African civil servants working for them. As important as it is to keep in mind the rural nature of much of Zimbabwean nationalism, it was, however, the urban areas that played the pivotal role in defining who would lead and how leaders would interact with their supporters. Apart from the physical presence of the nationalist leadership living in Harare and Highfield, the influences of urban cultures had already helped to establish a political style and, more importantly, urban institutions necessary for addressing urban issues and sensibilities in nationalist politics.

Similar to the European and American experiences, African townships were meeting places for Africans of different classes and cultures where a history of political and economic protests had allowed intellectuals to mobilize township residents over local issues and concerns. Urban life offered the possibility to seek out greater democratic participation for a broad cross-section of African men and women. Also, in contrast to most rural nationalisms, the urban areas produced a more "Jacobin" tradition of radical democracy in which demands for African rights and citizenship were also demands to challenge the inequalities of the prevailing economic system.[4] Although this definition of a radical democracy comes from European history, it serves well as a definition of the urban democratic tradition developed as a major theme in this book. As Alexander, McGregor, and Ranger suggest, an ideal approach to the history of nationalism in this period would combine these various rural and urban nationalisms in order to convey the interaction of diverse trajectories into one history. Such a synthesis is outside the scope of this work, but hopefully my concentration on the urban story can contribute to the eventual understanding of the broader history of these diverse nationalisms.

In order to develop the argument of this book over seven linear and chronological chapters, there are three main questions linked throughout: (1) how definitions and representations of gender differences become part of nationalist rhetoric as well as part of the mobilization and uses of violence; (2) how the changing relationship of leaders and led was reflected in the transformation of the public sphere; and (3) why the logic of "sellout" politics would eventually become the central political strategy used to confront real and potential rivals within the nationalist movement.

Gender Relations and Nationalism

The extensive literature on gender and nationalism generally defines nationalism as a male domain established to create a notion of the state and citizenship modeled after the patriarchal family. As Cynthia Enloe succinctly puts it: "Nationalism has typically sprung from masculinized memory, masculinized humiliation, and masculinized hope."[5] Scholarship on Zimbabwean nationalism and gender has worked from a similar notion of this relationship.[6] To drive this analysis further, however, it is important to explore how different categories of women and men experienced, contributed, and at times avoided nationalist projects.[7] Teresa Barnes's work has most significantly moved beyond narrative treatments of either an oversimplified category of "African women" or an exaggerated notion of nationalist unity.[8] Women in the urban areas, according to Barnes, had a separate social and political world in which they carefully and selectively chose which battles to fight—oftentimes sacrificing their own status in order to help mediate the relationship between African men and their children within the highly stratified urban social setting.[9] So while many women did in fact participate in both township and nationalist politics, their presence does not in itself provide evidence of a more inclusive or progressive politics from the standpoint of women's demands or a more egalitarian vision of a future community or nation.

Barnes's work also confronts the difficult issue of how to connect African women's involvement in social welfare organizations with the creation of a democratic political tradition. Tsuneo Yoshikuni summarized this problem, suggesting that "self-help and protest may appear to have little in common, but, nevertheless, it is worth asking whether protest somehow presupposes self-help, if not vice versa."[10] An element of the earlier democratic tradition in the townships was therefore the result of the work of women such as Mai Musodzi, Mai Sondayi, and Ms. Eleanor Solomon, all of whom were community leaders in their own right. In the late 1950s, the new generation of women who became prominent leaders took on very visible roles as community organizers, teachers, and nurses, as well as in less visible roles as community leaders and organizers of street-level support. Instead of looking for the moment when women were "permitted" to participate in politics, it may be more realistic to see how community politicians tried their best to incorporate the issues most important to the existing female leadership in the community. At the same time, by the mid-1950s, the shift from a more reciprocal nationalism to a more elitist conception of nationalism dramatically affected gender relations both in the nationalist movement and between leaders and led.

Masculinity and Violence

Since the early 1990s, the study of masculinity has become more prominent in Southern African studies. William Beinhart's 1992 article in the *Journal of Southern African Studies* opened up the discussion by questioning the foundations of historical works about men and violence in southern Africa.[11] He criticized the functionalist explanations that linked young men to violence. The dominant Marxist historiography of the 1970s and 1980s had developed a reasoning in which the exploitative mining industry in southern Africa, in particular the *chibaro* system developed in Rhodesia, became the basis for organizing the control of men in southern Africa's capitalist economy. The use of residential hostels for men, the compound system, and the urban township were all portrayed as having had the same goal and same results. These confined spaces produced a highly regulated and violent exploitation of mostly young African male migrants who in turn expressed their experience of capitalist exploitation and alienation through their own cultures of violence. Beinhart questioned the explanatory power of this argument, and many excellent studies have since shown the complexities of the impact of this system on masculinity in southern Africa.[12] Still, in a manner similar to the early works on African working-class history and women's history, there has been a tendency to allow the concept of "masculinity" to do "too much."[13] It cannot explain everything or even anything outside of a broader contextualization of other social, cultural, and political factors. In this book, for example, I concentrate on the ways masculinity is inscribed in the rhetoric and strategies of nationalist leaders, while avoiding explanations of events based on notions of masculinity among the nonelite men who acted out much of the violence in the townships. In the process, there is a danger of overstating the importance of masculinity as the *cause* of violence, as if the men caught up in a violent labor system that existed in southern Africa were naturally prone to violence. In order to remain on firm analytical ground and to avoid such sweeping generalizations, I prefer to examine the context of decisions made by leaders to deploy violence or to avoid using it. In this context, appeals to "acting like a man," as part of nationalist rhetoric, need to be examined as part of an ongoing debate over gender relations within the townships that had developed over a number of years. Such an analysis, however, cannot in itself exonerate leaders from having acted in support of violence, particularly against women, through their lack of criticisms or at times acceptance of violence against women as part of party discipline. No matter how seductive the social psychological explanations of masculinity may be, violence is not something to be rationalized through, or contained within, notions of masculinity.

As in the case of ethnicity, the role of masculinity in nationalist mobilization required active intervention by leaders who operationalized a sort of hypermasculinity to serve their own goals. Many of the leaders themselves were from the educated, elite urban classes who had very little in common with the men who fought in the streets, but they used a language of nation and manliness that appealed to those who carried out violence against the state and against potential rivals. Understanding this process is an essential part of challenging nationalist historiography and its preoccupation, at least in Zimbabwe, with "liberation war heroes." Such a narrow glorification of past violence as part and parcel of national history only serves to justify current violence in defense of the state or ruling party.

The Changing Nature of the Public Sphere: The "African Voice" and Radical Nationalist Rhetoric

One way of conceptualizing the history of nationalism in Zimbabwe is to picture a political space that was becoming increasingly viable for democratic participation during the 1940s and 1950s but was then, by the 1960s, abruptly closed down. Benedict Anderson's influential conceptualization of colonial nationalism is useful for visualizing the historical contours of Zimbabwean nationalist politics. Anderson's argument about the nature of anticolonial nationalism emphasizes the leading role of a group of bilingual intellectuals demanding recognition of their own rights as global citizens, as well as increased rights for the majority of less educated colonial subjects.[14] Anderson's formulation in turn recalls Habermas's idea that the "public sphere" helps to emphasize the role of public intellectuals in exerting their influence, notably through newspapers, to openly criticize political leadership, and above all to express a new discourse of public supervision—making public what had previously been the private "behind closed doors" relations between capitalists and politicians. The editorial staff of newspapers therefore became essential to a liberal definition of the "public sphere," as editors became the voice of "public opinion."[15]

This notion of the public sphere is a helpful way of understanding the very active African press that developed after 1940 under the editorial guidance of important African intellectuals across the period covered in this book. Public intellectuals such as B. J. Mnyanda, Jasper Savanhu, Michael Hove, Lawrence Vambe, and Nathan Shamuyarira all made use of the African press to challenge white minority rule while at the same time advocating for reforms within African society. There were, however, important shifts in the arguments used by such men between the 1940s and 1960s. While intellectuals in the earlier period, such as Mzingeli, Savanhu, and Mnyanda, had utilized the rhetoric of imperial citizenship and workers rights to gain state recognition for better living conditions, or better wages through collective bargaining, the new nationalists of the 1960s claimed rights based on notions of African sovereignty and historical solidarity that were not necessarily a direct response to the immediate needs of urban township residents.

This radical rhetoric helped to legitimate nationalist politicians' claims to political power without requiring the new generation of leaders to prove their leadership to any particular constituency. It had a millennialist quality, promising a better future for those willing both to sacrifice materially and, increasingly, to risk their own lives in order to succeed. As with other millennialist movements, when the date of promised independence passed, the followers were told to increase their sacrifices and, more importantly, directed to wage a battle against nonbelievers, the "collaborators" and the "sellouts." African politicians who had previously proven their capacity to lead effectively within existing township institutions were often characterized as sellouts for their continued cooperation with state institutions or multiracial organizations.

The earlier rhetorical strategies of African politicians and nationalists can be roughly divided into two camps before 1960. The more elite politicians utilized an older argument that went back to the liberal tradition of the Cape Colony in South Africa, namely that education and wealth were more important than race as markers of "the civilized." The Southern Rhodesian Bantu (later "African") Congress—referred to generally as "the Congress"—represents this elite position up until the 1950s. These men defended their elite position, particularly their educational and property qualifications for voting, against the majority of Africans who could not qualify based on education or wealth. Charles Mzingeli and his colleagues in township political organizations and trade unions represented a second position. Unlike the mission-educated elite in the Bantu Congress, these men saw themselves as the representatives of township residents and were quite clear in their criticisms of racial segregation and economic exploitation as the root cause of the problems facing township residents. For Mzingeli in particular, the struggle involved increasing educational and employment opportunities so that a greater number of urban residents might, at some point, even in another generation, achieve acceptance as citizens within Southern Rhodesia. Mzingeli not only took on white politicians in his quest for political recognition; he also struggled with the leaders of the African Congress, whom he viewed as too elite and too far removed from township life to represent adequately the interests of urban Africans.

By the mid-1950s, the Salisbury City Youth League (SCYL) and the Southern Rhodesian African National Congress (SRANC), organizations led by young professionals faced with racial discrimination in white-collar occupations, began demanding immediate educational rights and employment opportunities for the majority of Africans. No longer satisfied with incremental opportunities, this new generation of leaders challenged the notion that full citizenship required educational or property qualifications. After 1947, in particular, when the Southern Rhodesian government had increased urban segregation, it became clearer that elite status for qualified Africans was not in itself a guarantee of economic and social equality. In one of the SRANC's first publications an editorial states this antielitist populism: "Nationalism does not recognize the privilege of the lucky few who claim that they are here to rule perpetually, disregarding the legitimate aspirations of others."[16] It is worth quoting the more detailed definition of "African Nationalism" presented by the author:

> Nationalism, therefore is substantially that a nation is composed of a number of human beings who reciprocally regard one another as a part of the whole. Secondly, this implies that the concept of oneness of a people must be consistent with freedom and liberty for all.
>
> Freedoms are inspirable [*sic*] from rights because, otherwise, their realization is hedged about with uncertainty which destroy their quality. If for instance the utterance of an opinion is followed by persecution, we shall cease to express or minds.
>
> This means ceasing to be a citizen and the state for us ceases to have any meaning. For if we cannot embody our experience in its will, it ceases, to be a state we are required to owe allegiance.
>
> Nothing therefore is likely to maintain a condition of liberty as the knowledge that the invasion of rights will result in protest, and, if need be, resistance.[17]

Declarations such as these, which were common in the 1950s, displayed a new level of defiance and an optimism that defiance combined with democratic notions of rights and freedoms would produce the desired liberation of the majority from the tyranny of the minority. The following chapters will describe how short lived this optimism would be, as the political violence of the early 1960s destroyed the very basis of democratic participation that such rights and principles require. The battles over leadership within the nationalist movement and the practices used to silence and discredit opponents seriously challenged any sense of "freedom and liberty for all." At the same time, the reciprocal relationships among individuals and between leaders and led were to break under the strain of conflict, making the democratic claims of African nationalism very difficult to imagine, let alone achieve.

From the mid-1950s on, the public sphere became less about competing visions of a political future and more about immediate confrontations between a more consciously "authentic" nationalism and those African politicians who still held out—at least until 1962—for a possibility of a peaceful negotiated transfer of power to majority rule. In order to fully appreciate the dilemmas political violence created for more democratic notions of nationalism, it is important to understand the achievements made prior to the 1960s to link demands for citizenship and rights within a more democratic political tradition. The impossibility of a compromised future between white politicians and African nationalists was not something that came all at once or in a decisive manner; it was a realization that came slowly and in stages.

The Violent Logic of "Sellout" Politics

The argument put forth in this book is that nationalist rhetoric after 1957 represented a shift away from local demands for citizenship and toward a nationalist position more in keeping with the anticolonial struggles going on elsewhere in the world during that period.[18] As the southern African region became part of a larger revolutionary epoch, nationalist leaders had a new vocabulary to use in their claims to the nation. Younger leaders used this rhetoric as ammunition against the older generation or those their same age with more experience in trade union and political organizations, mobilizing support against the "sellout" or, by the early 1960s, the "imperialist stooge." Once the Southern Rhodesian state started on the course of banning political parties and arresting leaders, political critique of the "sellout" became an even more effective way for leaders to assert their radical credentials and deal with potential rivals. A necessary challenge faced in writing this book is, therefore, to re-create the political narrative of these years to show just how much the strategy of sellout politics weakened the effectiveness of the nationalist movement and, along the way, sapped the strength of the movement in many key areas, in particular, strong trade union leadership and effectiveness.

The use of radical rhetoric and accusations of sellout politics to destroy more progressive democratic elements in a revolutionary setting has been a major theme in the history of modern nationalism. Robespierre's "terror" during the French Revolution, the rise of fascism in Europe, Stalin's murderous purges in the Soviet Union, and Chairman Mao's Cultural Revolution in China all shared at different stages a similar violent logic aimed at "enemies of the people."[19] The lack of interest among historians in comparing these processes within Zimbabwean nationalism has been, in part, a reflection of a general hesitancy to criticize the historical development of political parties and liberation movements in southern Africa.

A key area of investigation in this book is therefore the complex mix of rhetorical strategies that were active in the early 1960s. Although much of the rhetoric seems on the surface to resemble that of Mzingeli and other populists, the actions of the leaders and the purpose of their rhetoric no longer has the same meaning as it did in the 1940s and early 1950s. In this regard, Charles Mzingeli's earlier rhetoric of fighting for the rights of township residents changed in the 1960s to rhetoric from different groups of leaders fighting *over* the allegiances of township residents, as factions presented contesting claims to be the authentic representatives of township and national interests.

Structure of the Book

This book is divided into two sections. The first three chapters cover the political career of Charles Mzingeli, the unofficial "mayor of Harare" for many years. The first chapter examines Mzingeli's transition from a representative of the Industrial and Commercial Workers Union (known by its acronym, ICU, as in "I see you, white man") in the 1930s to his creation of the African Headquarters Branch of the Southern Rhodesian Labour Party during the World War II. After the war, inspired by the railway workers' strike of 1945, Mzingeli formed a new organization, the Reformed ICU. For the next ten years, Mzingeli was omnipresent in African politics in Salisbury and nationally.[20] Chapter 2 examines his role in defending poor women's rights to live in the township and his successes as an elected official on the township advisory board. Chapter 3 focuses on how gender relations changed in the township, and how Mzingeli further championed women's demands into the early 1950s.

The second half of the book covers the transition to what is usually viewed as a more modern nationalism. More linear interpretations of African nationalist history tend to divide into distinct periods of development. These are the initial phases of resistance to colonialism, the "protonationalist" "awakenings" of political consciousness among elite Africans, then a period of constitutional negotiations for greater citizenship. This linear development culminates with the "birth" of a modern movement of "mass nationalism" comprising mobilization of protests, strikes, and rallies aimed at convincing the colonial powers to grant self-rule. A problem with this linear conception of African nationalism is the assumption of a natural progression toward unity and a "growing" consciousness and commitment among working people and peasants that becomes "ripe" for mobilization by a more sophisticated and "mature" leadership. Such "Whiggish" nationalist historiography is ideologically self-serving for those who eventually attain power, but such histories are not extremely helpful in sorting out the many compromises, defeats, instances of victimization, and lost chances that occurred along the way. The strategy used in this book is to retain a measure of linear storytelling for the sake of continuity and clarity while consciously avoiding the trope, or master narrative, or metaphor, that lies at the basis of political history, where nations and nationalisms, like living creatures, always contain a discernible life cycle.

But even if the life cycle of nations and ideas is open to question, the reality of political biography must confront the limits of human generations. Given this reality, the second half of the book sets out to examine how a new generation of leaders were shaped by the urban political setting of Harare and Highfield in the 1950s, and how they challenged the existing leaders, especially Charles Mzingeli, in order to actualize their own nationalist visions. Chapter 4 therefore introduces a new generation of urban-based African leaders, particularly George Nyandoro and James Chikerema, who forged ahead to establish the SCYL in 1956 and the SRANC in 1957.[21]

Trade union leader Reuben Jamela's story is elaborated in chapter 5. Jamela, a builder and trade unionist based in Harare, took over as the main leader of the Southern Rhodesian Trade Union Congress (SRTUC) in the 1950s and early 1960s. His power as a trade union leader was perceived as a threat by the increasingly powerful nationalist leadership. Reuben Jamela's political career therefore reflects the debate over the role of independent trade union movements during the nationalist period. Jamela briefly received relatively large sums of American money for use at his discretion. This created unintended problems for him and for the nationalist political leaders as Jamela began to use the SRTUC and his own popularity to criticize their policies and strategies. In 1962 Robert Mugabe and others in the Zimbabwe African People's Union verbally attacked Jamela as a "sellout" and "imperialist stooge" based on his links to American and European funding. Jamela was removed from his leadership role in 1962 and was almost killed by ZAPU youth. In the process the ability of African trade unionism to protect workers' rights and negotiate wages with employers was weakened.[22] The relationship between Jamela and the Americans turned out to be relatively brief but intense, as it came at a time when the AFL-CIO's strategy of supporting anticommunist trade unions was about to be severely tested and ultimately abandoned.

The roles of Irving Brown, the American representative of the AFL-CIO and at times the ICFTU in Southern Rhodesia, and of the American diplomats in Salisbury are also quite revealing and complex. The failures of

Brown's African anticommunist strategies in the early 1960s meant that Jamela and others, in particular Tom Mboya in Kenya, found themselves on the losing end of a Pan-African struggle for the control of trade unions by nationalist parties.[23] Jamela's contact with Americans, however, goes beyond the historical question of trade union autonomy and the United States' influence because the tactics used in the battle between his trade union congress and the nationalists ushered in a new style of politics. This "sellout" politics, investigated in chapter 6, demanded loyalty and discipline among both leaders and followers and became the dominant form of township politics during the nationalist leadership split in 1963. The resulting factional violence, described in chapter 7, ultimately proved costly to everyone involved and helped to destroy the possibilities of a more reciprocal nationalism.

Frederick Cooper's formative research and writing on the issues of nationalism and decolonization provide the overall structure for the arguments put forth in this book. Cooper emphasizes just how "contingent and partial" the efforts of African nationalists were in creating a unified nationalist movement, in which the nationalist party attempted to dominate competing social movements such as trade unions and women's groups. According to Cooper,

> The forms of power in Africa after decolonization—the institutions through which it is exercised and the idioms in which it is represented—reflect not so much the all-consuming thrust of the national order of things but the fragilities, the compromises, and the violences of insecure leaders that emerged in the process of ending colonial rule.[24]

The first half of this study therefore investigates the earlier social movements in Harare and Highfield during the 1940s and 1950s, while the second half examines the "contingent and partial" mobilization of these movements, as well as the violence and compromises that were part and parcel of the consolidation of nationalist politics before the Rhodesian Front (RF) government banned the African political parties and imprisoned the movement's core leadership in 1964. It is hoped that this study will help to shed light on how these contradictions have, in turn, created practices and styles of urban and national politics that continue to remain resistant to change.

1

Charles Mzingeli's Leadership and Imperial Working-Class Citizenship

Charles Mzingeli's historical legacy is complex, but one aspect of it is in serious need of revision. The notion that he was a "sellout" needs to be put in the context of what came before the 1960s, and of how he felt a betrayal by the younger leaders, particularly after the original decision to boycott the African seats in the Federation Parliament was ignored in 1952. A more realistic view of Mzingeli might be that he consistently did his best to counter any attempts by European authorities to deny African politicians a space to govern themselves. His strategy was to look for opportunities to take over "rubber-stamp" organizations such as the township advisory board and the African Welfare Society, making sure that he and members of his organization, the Reformed Industrial and Commercial Workers Union (RICU), dominated these groups until the late 1950s. Mzingeli's notion of imperial citizenship was therefore significantly different than that of the mission-educated elite—the groups of men who lived outside of the township and saw themselves as the most qualified to represent African interests. Mzingeli sought to provide protection for a wider range of individuals living in the township through his rhetoric around the dignity of labor. For him, formal education was not the only thing that gave a person value, and his distrust of the more educated elite was shared in the township. Shato Nyakauru, the founder of the oldest trade union in Harare—he had founded the Waiters and Caterers' Union in 1938, and was a longtime ally of Mzingeli's—summed up this attitude many years later in an interview: "I knew that almost all educated people are not straight; they are all cheats, who use one hand to write with, and the other for stealing." Even Mzingeli was not immune from Shato's suspicions in this regard, as Shato never gave up control of his union's finances to Mzingeli, but this style of antielite rhetoric was a cornerstone of Mzingeli's successes over the years. Mzingeli defended the rights of access of township residents to the city, while also urging them to gain more education in order to obtain greater respect so that they could in turn make greater claims to an imperial working-class citizenship.[1]

Charles Mzingeli's unique political style and reciprocal nationalism found its greatest success in the late 1940s and early 1950s, but to start the story there would fail to appreciate the many previous years of public life he spent experimenting with different approaches and tactics. The political space for Africans Mzingeli encountered in the 1930s and early 1940s was very limited. First of all, there were no African politicians in the Southern Rhodesian parliament. Direct political representation for Africans by African politicians was to be denied until the early 1950s when the Federation of Rhodesia and Nyasaland made provisions for the first elected Africans to the federal parliament. Before this time, the only elected African politicians were at the local level, as members of the urban township advisory boards established in 1946.

In much of southern Africa, the idea of imperial citizenship was rooted in the "Cape Liberalism" of the Cape Colony in South Africa. The mission-educated elite who saw it possible to obtain equality through education, cultural affinity, and material wealth accepted Cecil Rhodes's famous dictum "Equality for all civilized men." Imperial citizenship also resounded with those Pan-Africanists in the British colonies arguing for equal rights for those Africans capable of attaining the same educational status and property wealth as European colonists. When Southern Rhodesia was granted Crown Colony status in 1923, the white settler government gained control over all legislative issues except those pertaining to African interests. The latter were theoretically protected by Britain's imperial veto power, meaning that the Southern Rhodesian government was required to submit all legislation pertaining to the governing of Africans to the British Parliament for approval. As Michael West has pointed out, the imperial veto was used only once, and that was to protect the rights of elite Africans who met the economic and educational qualifications to vote. This allowed a very small percentage of African men and women to qualify for the vote in Southern Rhodesia based on their education and wealth.[2] These African elites naturally looked for leadership from among themselves, including cultured leaders such as the Reverend Thomas Samkange, or men such as Aaron Jacha, who formed the "Bantu Congress" in Salisbury in 1936. The Bantu Congress had organized to be the voice of the elite as well as to represent all Africans, but the elitist and paternalistic overtones of the Congress's rhetoric left it open to criticism from African populists such as Mzingeli who would argue that its members were more concerned with protecting their privileged status as "civilized men" rather than with helping the working class and township residents. Like their counterparts in Europe and North America, elite Africans defended their privileged participation on traditions "in liberal theory," by which "access to political rights required possession of property, education, and a less definable quality of moral standing."[3] Mzingeli's goal of expanding imperial citizenship to those without property and without much formal education therefore faced opposition from European and African elite opinion.

From the perspective of white governing officials, African interests were relegated through two main legal bodies, the Native Affairs Department and the Federation of Native Welfare Societies. European men led both of these groups, and although the welfare societies had African representatives, their leader, the Reverend Percy Ibbotson, jealously guarded his role as the voice of African interests. So in addition to competing with the more elite Congress leaders, Mzingeli also had to contend with white men such as Ibbotson who saw Mzingeli and his associates as outsiders and troublemakers, and ultimately as competitors. Mzingeli's political contemporaries and the white "Native Affairs" experts were not too kind to him, nor was he to them, as he was viewed as insufficiently cultured and educated to stand among "civilized men." Terence Ranger and Michael West have both written histories of African politicians in this period who were more eloquent and articulate than Mzingeli.[4] Unlike many of these more elite African leaders, however, Mzingeli fought for the rights of the poor and the working class in order to protect them both from the gross injustices of a settler racist society and misrepresentation by elite African politicians.

Another key to Mzingeli's politics was just how jealously he guarded the achievements of the African community, the very "local" that is so often juxtaposed with the national. This was frustrating to the more elite nationalists who saw him as a stumbling block to national unity, but it was also an important aspect of his nationalist vision. It is also noteworthy that the rhetoric Mzingeli used was surprisingly nonsexist given the paternalistic tone of both African and European rhetoric in the 1940s and 1950s.

Mzingeli's Local Roots and Populist Identity

Charles Mzingeli began his political career in Harare while still only in his twenties, and even earlier as a teenager he had been attracted to the politics of Clements Kadalie's ICU in Bulawayo.[5] Bulawayo, situated on the rail line between Salisbury and South Africa, always seemed to import South African political influences and currents before they reached Salisbury's African townships. But Salisbury also belonged to the greater network of southern African urban areas, and word would have spread about tough-talking African politicians in South Africa, Nyasaland, and Northern Rhodesia. Politically minded township residents would have heard of Kadalie and perhaps have heard him speak as they traveled along the main railway lines and roads from the north and to the south. These more activist residents therefore likely welcomed the arrival of their own ICU leader to the Salisbury

African Township (referred to at the time as the "Harari Native Location"), and they were fortunate to get, in 1929, a talented twenty-four-year-old organizer named Charles Mzingeli.

Mzingeli was born in 1905 at the Embakwe Roman Catholic Mission in the Plumtree District.[6] He was not able to attend school beyond Standard IV (fourth or fifth grade in North America), but this did not stop him from developing an impressive speaking style in English. In 1952 Mzingeli described his background in an interview with American geographer Edwin Munger. Munger summarized Mzingeli's account as follows:

> Mzingeli's father, who is still living at an age estimated between eighty-five and ninety, was born in the days of the great Matabele chief Mzilikazi in a little kraal south of present day Bulawayo. He was a warrior—Mzingeli's grandfather had commanded an *impi*, or regiment—and as a young man fought under Lobengula when the Europeans began coming to Rhodesia in numbers.[7]

According to Munger's account, Mzingeli's father then settled near the "Roman Catholic Mission at Empandine near the Bechuanaland border which had been given to the missionaries by Lobengula in more peaceful days." Mzingeli's father sent him to Durban at the age of eight to attend school. According to Munger, "It appears that Mzingeli had a happy childhood although he was never robust. As Mzingeli described it, he had a bad chest and returned in 1914, after one year, to Empandine, where he went through primary school."[8] That he stopped attending school at age fourteen corresponds with Lawrence Vambe's account of how Mzingeli ran away from home when he was only fourteen and went to work as an assistant on the railways. After leaving home and the Catholic mission school, he traveled to Bulawayo, as well as Livingstone and Broken Hill in Northern Rhodesia. Vambe tells of Mzingeli's mental state as a young man: "For a time he lived in what he described as intellectual bewilderment, where he saw things clearly when his fellow men seemed too stupid and ignorant to be roused into a common effort to ameliorate their position."[9] His role in the Southern Rhodesian branch of the ICU was to spread the ICU message and trade union organizational structure to Salisbury. Mzingeli, along with S. Masosha Ndlovo and Job Dumbutshena, was trained by Robert Sambo, Clements Kadalie's representative sent to Southern Rhodesia to expand the ICU northward from South Africa. Although Sambo was quickly deported back to South Africa by the Southern Rhodesian authorities as an "undesirable" foreigner, Mzingeli, Ndlovo, and Dumbutshena could not be deported because they were native-born Rhodesians. It is truly remarkable, given the levels of police harassment these men experienced, that they even managed to establish ICU branches in the major towns and on the mines and farms of Southern Rhodesia.[10]

The ICU had achieved remarkable success in South Africa by combining race-pride populism with an attention to local grievances. The message of the ICU had succeeded in South Africa in the 1920s, particularly through organizing rural protests against the increasingly segregated economic and social world of South Africa.[11] This was the organizing strategy Mzingeli brought with him to Salisbury. He achieved immediate notoriety in Salisbury as a brave and eloquent speaker. Large crowds attended ICU gatherings in the township on Sunday afternoons. Mzingeli was not afraid to call European officials thieves and would use the popular play on words that mocked the supposed authority of European native commissioners who expected Africans to refer to them as "chief" and whose ultimate authority resided with the office of the Chief Native Commissioner. Mzingeli referred in his speeches to the "Thief Native Commissioner" to the delight of the crowd. Mzingeli's early successes also included rural issues, such as a campaign against a native commissioner in the Mwera District accused by locals of confiscating their cowhides. Mzingeli publicized this scandal and successfully stopped this practice. His success in standing up for African interests increased his popularity in rural and urban areas as news spread of his bravery. Urban workers brought back stories of his courage against the white police and government.

Tobias Nhapi, who was to become one of Mzingeli's main supporters in the 1940s and 1950s, had first seen Mzingeli in 1934 when Nhapi arrived as a teenager to work in Salisbury. Mr. Nhapi's father, a domestic worker for a wealthy miner, had told his sons about Mzingeli and the campaigns he waged in the early 1930s against the laws of the white police. "We were told that in Harare there was an American "Negro" by the name of Mzingeli who was quite a good English speaker, and he was a threat to the '*Majoni*' [white police officers]."[12] In this fashion Mzingeli embodied, at least in the early 1930s, the confident ICU message that had its roots in the Pan-Africanism, Garveyism, and Ethiopianism that had previously empowered many southern African political organizers under the influence of Kadalie's ICU. This confrontational but nonviolent approach was in contrast to the conciliatory language of elite Southern Rhodesian African leaders trained at the mission schools.[13] His approach also made him a unique character in the 1930s and 1940s in Salisbury.

Even though he became well known and respected, Mzingeli had a difficult time as a union organizer since the majority of workers saw little need to pay dues for a union that had not proven its ability to negotiate directly with employers on their behalf. European employers warned their African employees to stay away from Mzingeli and the ICU, threatening to fire those associated with it. Government workers and African teachers, categories of township residents most likely and most qualified to join a protest movement, were officially banned from joining the ICU.[14] This left Mzingeli in a predicament; without a solid base of dues-paying workers to sign up with the

ICU, he was unable to make a career simply as a trade unionist. After some initial enthusiasm, the union's only supporters remained a small group of community leaders, mostly self-employed entrepreneurs who were looking for an organization to protect their rights in the city. Tsuneo Yoshikuni has described the main organizing barrier in the 1930s to be the division between "long-term residents," who took an interest and a civic role in the township, and migrant workers, who saw the township as their temporary home away from their rural homesteads.[15] These long-term residents put a great deal of effort into protecting themselves and their children (particularly their daughters) from the majority of male migrants. This strong division made political mobilization difficult, as the interests of the long-term residents rarely coincided with those of the migrants.[16] The ICU membership was therefore dominated by self-employed entrepreneurs, men and women in the few job categories open to Africans at the time, including shopkeepers, furniture makers, drivers, traders, and other self-employed individuals. It would be a mistake, however, to think that Mzingeli's support was only limited to the dues-paying, officially registered membership; many others supported him but were careful not to join in fear of losing their positions with European and state employers.

In the early 1930s, Mzingeli had worked as a musician in the local "Native Eating Houses"—a name given to government-licensed but African-owned restaurants and nightclubs that did a great amount of business on Rezende Street in the southern part of the city near the township. Mzingeli played guitar and also helped to organize weekend dance parties. He eventually went into a business partnership to open up a "Native Eating House" in 1935, but the business partnership soon soured as Mzingeli was pushed out of the very lucrative "hop beer" business by his partner and evidently by his partner's "strongmen." The "negotiations" over who owned what in the partnership turned violent and a man was killed. Mzingeli was arrested in 1936 and charged with "assault to do grievous bodily harm" and served one month in jail. A friend of his was later charged with the murder, but the charges were dropped.[17] Mzingeli brought his partner to the magistrate's court in Salisbury and sued him for damages, but it is not clear if he managed to recover any of his lost investment or profits.

The authorities harassed and arrested him on several occasions, usually in relation to Eating House violations related to hop beer regulations. "Native Eating Houses" were popular restaurants and profitable because they sold a form of beer that was not extremely strong (some people remember it disparagingly as weak "like Coca-Cola"). In order to avoid fines and arrest, the proprietors' hop beer could not exceed the official specified maximum alcoholic content. The authorities, knowing that Eating House managers competing for customers increased the alcoholic content of their hop beer, often harassed and arrested the proprietors. Mzingeli was arrested on such hop beer violations in 1940. After serving two months of his sentence he was called back to court to face perjury charges, for which he served an additional six months in jail. Mzingeli told Munger that while in the Umtali prison, he "suffered terrific physical torture" and "was not allowed to wear boots or a hat," adding, "One day I dropped unconscious due to the hot sun."[18] No doubt the authorities and the Central Investigation Division (CID) tried their best to harass Mzingeli from the time he set foot in Harare and after he had gained a reputation as an outspoken critic of European policies. The experience also made him an advocate for better conditions for prisoners in later years.

Mzingeli's very protective attitude toward his leadership role, and his growing distrust for coalitions and partnerships with other Africans, was likely shaped by these experiences with the law and African businesses in the township. His experiences as a musician and eating house proprietor also had a positive side, as it caused him to be less dogmatic about the general presence in the township of drinking, gambling, and prostitution. Having a reputation as a fair-minded businessman also made him more acceptable to those who had no trust in the more aloof educated "elite" Africans. His approach to township life differed from the mission-educated Christian elite in other ways as well. His business ventures with untrustworthy partners likely influenced the strong personal animosity he would show toward those elite Africans who held their superior educational achievements over him in public and private discourse. These men used to say that Mzingeli had "only known the mission schools from the outside," and that he did not have the educational credentials to lead township residents.[19] Mzingeli, by contrast, was not afraid to speak for those township residents whom these missionary educated elites thought to be below their standing. He used this intimacy to his advantage, creating a populist identity that was to gain him a loyal following for most of the 1940s and early 1950s.

True to his earlier ICU experience, when an issue developed in the interests of workers living in the township, Mzingeli took on the challenge without the moralistic overtones of the elites who tended to blame township residents for bringing on hardships because of their "lower" status and lack of civility.[20] Mzingeli fought petty segregation laws from the beginning, including laws that fined Africans for walking on the pavement reserved for whites in Salisbury's central business district.[21] Another example of Mzingeli's interest in the welfare of the disenfranchised sections of the population was his campaign to get proper uniforms for African men in prisons. Before then, they were often only given a simple "pajama," a long shirt to wear when transported to the European sections of the city or in the township to perform gang labor on roads. Mzingeli was embarrassed for these men, as they were often seen "half-naked" working on roads or traveling in trucks. He managed to convince the authorities to provide more modest attire for prisoners. Part of his concern for the welfare of workers must have come from his experiences as a railway worker on the rail lines from South Africa to the Northern Rhodesian Copperbelt. Such experiences led him to interpret the notion of the "dignity of labor" to mean that even the "lowest" categories of workers should be afforded dignity, including groups such as night soil removers or prisoners.

The motivating factor of the ICU, according to Mzingeli, was to build the character and dignity of urban Africans, "to form up an opinion and slogan which will assist the African to have the feeling of belonging." He was also quite conscious of the undignified way Europeans cast Africans as inferiors, where a "man is a boy, a woman is a nanny and whiteman is baas."[22] Mzingeli would later tell Munger in 1952 about the personal humiliation he experienced when young white women called him "boy": "When I go into a shop and a young girl says to me, 'yes, boy'—I hate it. I know she doesn't mean to hurt my feelings but she has been told to keep up European supremacy. Sometimes I write a note to myself. They are usually polite if they think you're doing an errand for a European."[23] Mzingeli's rhetoric worked toward restoring the dignity of African manhood but within the ideological and social constructs of European ideas around masculinity, labor, and respectability. When the ICU failed to survive into the 1940s, and with his business dealings in the eating house finished, Mzingeli applied for and received a general dealer's license allowing him to open a grocery shop in a building owned by an Indian landlord. Once his business was established, however, another African shop owner offered the landlord a higher rent and Mzingeli was given notice to vacate the property. He ended up relocating his store within the Harare township, where he leased a store from the municipality in the area known as Maggio's plot. It was from this store that Mzingeli began a new phase of his political career, a phase that would occupy his efforts during World War II, as he entered a political alliance with white politicians within the Southern Rhodesian Labour Party (SRLP).

Fighting Racist Legislation: The African Headquarters Branch of the Southern Rhodesian Labour Party

After the Salisbury branch of the ICU had dwindled to little more than the union's letterhead, Mzingeli continued to champion township causes through various means until he entered into an alliance with a group of white politicians. These years brought him into contact with Gladys Maasdorp, an influential member of the Southern Rhodesian Labour Party, and onetime mayor of Salisbury. It may seem incongruous for Mzingeli to have joined with white politicians given his strong race-pride message. But as with much of Mzingeli's political career, when he saw a chance to advance his cause, he seized the opportunity. Mzingeli recalled the relationship with

Maasdorp having begun when he approached her with the letter he had received from Prime Minister Godfrey Huggins's Federal Party asking for his vote in the next elections.

Mzingeli would later explain how the letter from Huggins so offended him that he showed it to the few white politicians he knew in the SRLP to discuss an appropriate response. He eventually met with Maasdorp and she suggested that since the Labour Party had no color bar it would be possible to have African members. Mzingeli agreed but also told Maasdorp, "I don't agree with the policy of the Labour Party—it's white labour. But to spite this gentleman [Huggins] I am going to join."[24] For the small group in the SRLP leadership, the Headquarters Branch represented their commitment to giving Africans more of a voice in Southern Rhodesian politics.[25] Mzingeli did not want the African Branch to become simply an auxiliary to the white SRLP, and he would use the legitimacy of the branch to reach an international audience. He founded the African Headquarters Branch of the Southern Rhodesian Labour Party in 1941 and served as its general secretary until 1946, tirelessly petitioning government and colonial officials to improve the political and economic conditions for Africans in the country.

The peculiar position of the African Branch can best be understood in relation to the constricted nature of political influence in Southern Rhodesia. D. J. Murray's account of Southern Rhodesian politics emphasizes Prime Minister Huggins's ability to rule through "representative economic associations." With such a relatively small and privileged electorate, Huggins maintained his base by allowing the special interests of mining, agriculture, and manufacturing groups to dictate legislation.[26] According to Murray, white labor was never seen as a particularly important political voice, as witnessed by the marginal role of the Southern Rhodesian Labour Party. For much of the 1930s and 1940s, African interests were only "officially" represented through two state-recognized bodies: the Federation of African Welfare Societies and the government's own Department of Native Affairs.[27] Mzingeli had become involved with the Welfare Society but was in constant disagreement with the European chair of the society, the Reverend Percy Ibbotson, who saw himself as the sole "expert" on African interests. Because of this, Mzingeli made use of the slight opening of political space offered by the African HQ Branch. In 1947 Ibbotson mentioned this feud in a letter to Godfrey Huggins after Mzingeli and B. J. Mnyanda had called for Ibbotson's resignation as the organizing secretary of the Federation of African Welfare Societies in Southern Rhodesia. Ibbotson wrote,

> Mzingeli and Myanda [*sic*] had it in for me because I publicly defended certain discriminatory legislation; they created a fuss, but I have refused to move from the position, and in this I have received strong backing from Africans and Europeans. Myanda [*sic*] and Mzingeli are now licking their sores![28]

That Prime Minister Huggins shared Ibbotson's paternalist view toward Africans is expressed in the debate over the future of "Natives in Urban Areas," a parliamentary debate in November 1944 that eventually led to more restrictive segregation legislation. Huggins argued for legislation that would require African men working in town to give up their rights to land in the African reserves—the areas set aside by Europeans for Africans to reside legally. Huggins argued that whites had to "realize that a permanent urban class is arising and is bound to grow in the future."[29] This view was shared throughout much of British colonial Africa, and therefore Huggins and Ibbotson believed they were in charge of the destiny of Southern Rhodesian Africans. If Mzingeli and Mnyanda shared one thing, it was the belief that they should push Ibbotson and Huggins to recognize the rights of urban Africans to lead their own communities, without having to defer to those Mzingeli often referred to as "our so-called experts" on African affairs.

The call for higher wages for urban workers was never a popular suggestion with the mining and farming interests that feared higher wages in industry would attract workers away from the mines and farms, resulting in the need to raise wages in those sectors as well. The solution, as will be discussed in the next chapter, was legislation that extended to the cities the bureaucratic control over workers' housing and mobility, similar to the control that had originated in the *chibaro* system of the mines. The government's claim to control the movement of African workers from one area to another was at the heart of Southern Rhodesian "Native Administration," and like settler policies toward indigenous peoples elsewhere, particularly in the United States, the power to move people from their lands onto reservations was a fundamental aspect of white settler rule. While the intention was to dominate and control, the "success" of these policies from the standpoint of the state was always in question.[30] By attempting to gain some level of real political power, Mzingeli and his associates were willing to confront Huggins and Ibbotson and were then forced to appeal to Britain's imperial veto power over legislation designed to further restrict and criminalize much of African economic, political, and private life.

Mzingeli's Meeting with Prime Minister Huggins

Mzingeli had sent letters of protest against the segregationist land policy found in the 1945 Land Apportionment Act directly to the prime minister. As none of his letters received a reply, Mzingeli approached the SRLP member of Parliament George H. Macintyre and asked him to help arrange a meeting with Huggins.[31] A meeting was agreed upon with Prime Minister Huggins in October 1945. At the meeting, Mzingeli presented a copy of a letter he had previously sent outlining six proposals for amending the act. For Mzingeli and other township residents, the most important proposed changes were the new limits on Africans' ability to purchase land in urban areas. Mzingeli complained to Huggins that his letters had not been answered. Huggins apparently took offense at Mzingeli's direct approach and responded by telling the delegation "that there was a Native Welfare Society looking after the interest of native people in the Colony: 'But who are you?'" Mzingeli responded by saying that the SRLP African HQ Branch was "a constitutional organization formed for the purpose of voicing African opinion; that it would certainly be against the interests of the Welfare organizations if the Government would attempt any pressure in favour of the Welfare Societies, and the African Branch would maintain its organization in spite of everything."[32]

The meeting seemed to go from bad to worse, at least insofar as one can tell from the African HQ Branch's minutes, as Huggins showed little patience for the meeting and was obviously trying to intimidate Mzingeli and the others for not going through Reverend Percy Ibbotson's Native Welfare Society. Huggins delivered a veiled threat by suggesting that they, as "enlightened Africans," should "realize that Europeans were to-day taking more interest in the welfare of Africans than they did in the past. Therefore, any action similar to that of the deputation would do great harm to the cause of African progress, the deputation must be careful that they are not rubbing Europeans on the wrong side."[33] Mzingeli replied with his own veiled "threat":

In thanking the Minister for the interview, Mr. Mzingeli added that the deputation did not regard the matter as closed; that the Minister's statement with regard to the Branch's organisation is very serious. African people are quite entitled to look on democracy as a symbol of freedom and not as a mere name. The Branch will regret to have to resort to the Colony's Letter Patent [veto powers], instead of presenting matters before the Minister of Native Affairs.[34]

Mzingeli had come a long way from his early days as an assistant on the railways, or as an entertainer in one of the township's restaurants. Here he was face to face with the prime minister who had insulted his sensibilities back in 1939 by sending him a request for his vote. Mzingeli did not have many more meetings at this level, except, ironically, when Prime Minister Huggins would seek out Mzingeli's assistance in negotiating with African workers during the 1948 General Strike.

The African Headquarters Branch of the SRLP had a formal membership of nearly one hundred people throughout Southern Rhodesia. During this time, Mzingeli's office—a room connected to his shop located in Maggio's plot—became a center of activity. His shop served as a political library where young students home for their school holidays from mission schools were able to read literature Mzingeli had obtained from British and Southern

Rhodesian socialists, trade unionists, and Pan-Africanists, as well as the South African political papers.[35] Mzingeli mentored many young people, some of whom would grow up to challenge his leadership, and he remained a community leader to whom people brought their problems for representation.

Doris Lessing, the novelist, was a member of the SRLP and a close friend to both Maasdorp and Mzingeli. Her observations of Mzingeli point to a different interpretation of the alliance between Mzingeli and the Labour Party, particularly in the friendship that developed between Mzingeli and Gladys Maasdorp. On the one hand, he presented himself around Maasdorp as the congenial soft-spoken intellectual, known for his recitations of the English poets. On the other, Lessing describes another side of his personality that came out in the township and particularly at meetings where his sarcastic and cutting wit was put to use in challenging the injustices of Rhodesian racism and whites' hypocrisies. The meetings Mzingeli attended in Gladys Maasdorp's office were illustrative of the different political styles he possessed. He and his companions would cycle in the early evenings to the city center but would need to return home to the township before the onset of the curfew. They were required to petition the township authorities to give them special passes to meet with whites in the city center.[36] Lessing describes how Mzingeli was the only African who would attend Labour Party meetings and discussion groups, although sometimes he would bring an associate. Then, a few hours later, just as the political discussion began to heat up, Mzingeli and his African companions would have to excuse themselves from the meeting in order to ride back to the Harare township before curfew. Lessing describes how she and others in the group felt after this departure:

> When they had gone we might burst out in frustrated rage, hating so much what we were part of, or sit depressed, because of our impotence, hardly able to look at each other. We knew that these men would, once they reached the Location borders, separate and go carefully to their homes where they would hide whatever books and papers we had given them, because of the Location police. . . . When Charles remarked he had more than once been beaten up by these men, or told how they had invaded his little house and torn up his pamphlets, knocking him about in front of his wife and children, and we were indignant, he found us funny, like sheltered children being told of the wicked world. "Yes, that is so, that is how things are with us," he might remark, patiently, smiling.[37]

Lessing and the others in the small group of Maasdorp supporters were clearly impressed with Mzingeli's bravery in the face of harassment and injustice. She would later write a short story, "Hunger," that involves a young African man who recently arrives in the township and finds himself torn between a life of petty crime or joining the township political organization led by a "Mr. Mizi." Lessing no doubt had Mzingeli in mind when she created Mr. Mizi, and the story does a nice job of capturing the dilemmas confronting Mzingeli—for example, his need to maintain an impeccable reputation with the European authorities while at the same time trying to help those who, given the many petty laws and regulations, were often in trouble with the authorities.[38]

As a city councillor, and later Salisbury mayor, Maasdorp was a brave woman who stood upon matters of principle and was one of the few white politicians to continue to fight for these principles despite the privileged status segregation afforded them. Lessing suggests that Maasdorp had wanted the assorted white leftists in Salisbury to join the Labour Party in order to help "vote on her side about the African Branch."[39] Both groups were trying to make the most of the alliance, and it seems Mzingeli and Maasdorp took certain risks to advance what both held as an ultimate goal—greater political rights and freedoms for Africans in Salisbury.[40] Lessing describes how Maasdorp agreed to go to Harare township and address an informal "educational" meeting on Mzingeli's request. Mzingeli, not satisfied with simply having Maasdorp appear as a guest, turned the meeting into the first Labour Party Congress in the Township in February 1944. As Maasdorp's initial wariness had predicted, the racist town councillors on the city council, led by Charles Olley, jumped at the chance to use her presence at this interracial political meeting—the first of its kind in Harare township—to ban all political meetings in the township.

In retrospect, it may seem naive for Mzingeli to have spent as much effort as he did in writing to the British groups involved in colonial and African politics, particularly the Fabian Colonial Bureau (FCB). It may be hard to understand the value in Mzingeli's campaigning for the British to use their veto power when they had only made use of it once. But from Mzingeli's particular perspective, the situation after World War II presented the possibility for a new group of sympathetic British politicians finally to change course and challenge Prime Minister Huggins and his colleagues on segregationist legislation. The main source of that optimism was the landslide victory of the British Labour Party in the 1945 elections and the eventual selection of Arthur Creech-Jones as Britain's Secretary of State for the Colonies. It was assumed by Mzingeli and others on the Left in Rhodesia that the members of the FCB would now be able to translate their previous sympathies into direct action to stop further repressive laws. Creech-Jones was a key player in the FCB and the British Labour Party, a representative of the more progressive elements in the British Colonial Service and a key architect of changes in British colonial policy after the war.[41] In 1946 Mzingeli wrote Creech-Jones a strongly worded letter stating how

Africans are aware that there is no difference between our segregation and that of which we persecuted and destroyed Hitlerite for and the question is this: If Hitler did not have the right to maintain *Herrenvolk* principle of race supremacy, where does Southern Africa Dominions get their rights from? Failure by the British Government to veto Southern Rhodesia Land Apportionment Act and Native (Urban Registration and Accommodation) Act, would seriously defeat the influence of those provisions in Colony's Constitution reserving the interest of native people and not only among Africans Southern of Zambezi but the civilized world as well as the United Nation's organization.[42]

Rita Hinden, the leading Fabian socialist expert on Africa and a close associate of Creech-Jones, replied to one of Mzingeli's similar requests suggesting that although the Labour Party government was opposed to "color discrimination," without the support of British public opinion there was little Creech-Jones could do. Now that the Labour Party was in office, according to Hinden, the Fabians were experiencing difficulties in "finding the ways and means of carrying their principles into practice." Hinden then told Mzingeli, "We must not deceive ourselves into thinking that this is going to be an easy battle. The trouble is that these things have been allowed to happen for so many years without anybody effectively protesting, and once one is sliding quickly down a slippery slope, it takes a great deal to stop the fall."[43] Hinden's reasoning must have been small comfort to Mzingeli, in whose opinion his allies in London were capable of intervening to stop new racist legislation in Southern Rhodesia after the war.

The historical record shows that Rita Hinden and Marjorie Nicholson did in fact attempt to influence key British politicians, such as Lord Addison and Lord Farington, to veto Southern Rhodesian segregation legislation. They came close to pushing for a veto, or at least Lord Farington had originally put forth a motion that a specific segregation law should receive further scrutiny before the British allowed it to pass without veto, but he withdrew his motion once it became clear that Lord Addison and Lord Hailey supported the Rhodesian government's position. This reversal caused Rita Hinden to send a diplomatic yet rather direct response to Addison questioning his abrupt change of heart after he had met with Godfrey Huggins. Hinden complained to Addison, pointing out how "particularly under a Labour Government, which has on so many occasions expressed its abhorrence of racial discrimination, a firmer stand should be taken on matters of this nature, if we are not to be accused of hypocrisy and weakness."[44] Although Hinden and the FCB had achieved their goal of gaining influence in the Colonial Office, they were ultimately unable to challenge the entrenched ties among British MPs and Lords with financial and land interests in Rhodesia. Such men were not about to take the views of Africans and their small group of white allies seriously. Instead, they simply parroted the language of the Southern Rhodesian government, as each subsequent piece of segregation legislation was portrayed by Huggins to be in the "best interest" of Africans.[45] Mzingeli's understanding of how successfully Huggins's

REFORMED
INDUSTRIAL AND COMMERCIAL
WORKERS UNION of AFRICA
(REFORMED I.C.U. HEAD QUARTERS)

P.O. BOX 679
SALISBURY, S.R.
AFRICA

All Correspondence to be
addressed to the Secretary

RESUSCITATED
APRIL 1946

Head Office :

MAGGIO PLOT
LOCATION ROAD

SALISBURY S.R.

Figure 1.1. Mzingeli's Reformed ICU letterhead.

propaganda worked in Britain made him all the more vigilant to keep the Southern Rhodesian government from appointing African "yes-men" to the institutions and boards it developed to project a rosy picture of a "benevolent Native Administration."

By 1946 Mzingeli's efforts spent petitioning sympathetic British allies had proved a disappointment, as Britain failed to use its imperial veto against the segregationist laws of the Rhodesian government in the 1940s. Additionally, Mzingeli's growing disillusionment with the abilities of his British contacts to intervene on his behalf was combined after the war with the realization that certain leaders in the SRLP, some of whom had been supportive of the interracial political alliance during the war, were now coming out against the African Branch in order to guarantee white working-class votes and support. The main example of this was Col. George Walker, who originally supported Mzingeli but after the war left the SRLP to reform the Rhodesian Labour Party along with other prosegregation trade unionists. Following World War II, many of the pro-Mzingeli members of the SRLP had left Rhodesia, including Doris Lessing and Gladys Maasdorp, so the little support that remained for the African Branch within an already marginalized SRLP became inconsequential.[46]

Mzingeli therefore drifted away from an interracial politics in 1946 and concentrated his efforts on forming a new African political organization, the Reformed ICU (RICU). The transition from the SRLP African HQ Branch to the RICU did not, however, stop him from continuing to correspond with Rita Hinden and the Fabian Colonial Bureau. On the contrary, he continued sending copies of meeting minutes and RICU memorandums on a regular basis. After the inaugural meeting of the RICU in February 1946, Mzingeli sent a copy of the minutes to Hinden with a cover letter asking for her to help by giving "publicity of the activities of our Trade Union as we should like to make our work known; such would confound those whose excuses for suppressing our Trade Unions is that we are not yet efficient to organize ourselves into a Trade Union—they are careful to see that their oppositions receive broad publicity from our daily press with favourable comments while our reply is completely ignored." Mzingeli understood quite well by the end of the war the importance of international support; he closed his letter by stating, "We are convinced that given help overseas by way of publicity to begin with, such would discourage any shameless attitude hitherto adopted by our so-called students of Native Affairs."[47] These "so-called students" referred to European "experts" on African affairs, especially Percy Ibbotson of the Welfare Society, and members of the government's Native Affairs Department, who continued to claim the authority to speak on behalf of African interests.

Mzingeli's contacts with the FCB did not go unnoticed by Ibbotson, who made a special effort to discredit Mzingeli both to the FCB and to Prime Minister Huggins. In November 1946 Ibbotson met with Rita Hinden in London to lodge a complaint against the "undesirable influence of the Fabian Colonial Bureau." In his letter to Huggins, Ibbotson listed the points he raised with Hinden, including the following:

> No matter what the Fabian Colonial Bureau thought or said, a certain amount of racial discrimination was necessary in Southern Rhodesia considering the backward state of the vast majority of the African population. . . .
>
> The African population was not to be judged by so-called and self appointed African leaders, some of these whom I know were in touch with the Bureau. . . .
>
> The drift to urban areas had created problems and an understanding of this was possible on the part of those people living in Rhodesia, but was not possible from academic knowledge gained in London. . . .
>
> The Bureau was giving to certain Africans, particularly Charles Mzingeli and his friends, a false impression of their own importance. . . .
>
> Southern Rhodesia did not need the help of the Fabian Colonial Bureau in a solution of its problems, particularly those concerning the African population.[48]

Ibbotson's letter to Huggins would appear to affirm the effectiveness of Mzingeli's correspondences with the FCB in starting a dialogue with those in London who could voice, however ineffectively, his antisegregationist message in the British Parliament and the British press on behalf of the urban African population. Ibbotson, already finding himself in competition with Mzingeli at home, seemed determined to challenge Mzingeli's ability to bring the injustices of Southern Rhodesian segregation and discrimination to a wider audience.[49]

By 1946 Mzingeli and the others within the African Branch began articulating a cynical analysis of the use of racist rhetoric by white politicians as they competed with each other for white votes at the expense of expanding the rights of Africans at the end of the war. Politicians such as Charles Olley, for example, or members of the Labour Party were notorious for using racist arguments to further their political ambitions. Mzingeli and the RICU saw the infusion of racism in politics as unnecessary and dangerous:

> We deny that segregation is necessitated by the general attitude of Europeans in the Colony; we submit that the incentive of race prejudice has been injected into the minds of Europeans in the Colony by politicians whose chief aim is to attain self satisfaction even at the cost of any progress. Records of debates on the introduction of segregation dating back to 1930 reveal a fanatical deliberation in the creation of race hatred.[50]

After the demise of the African Branch of the SRLP, Mzingeli and his associates would operate outside of white politics, existing as a township political group, but they continued to bring international attention to the hypocrisies and injustices of segregation policies as they applied to African urban populations. His combination of an imperial working-class citizenship and his interest in improving the rights and conditions of all Africans he knew had been given a raw deal by the settler state and society put Mzingeli in a position to define a new type of reciprocal nationalism.

2

Township Protest Politics

The period of demobilization after World War II was a crucial one for Pan-African politics, as soldiers, workers, and intellectuals found common ground through their demands for better treatment and representation. Mzingeli's contacts with other Pan-Africanists may not have been extensive beyond his reading of Pan-African newspapers and pamphlets, but his politics suggest that he was working within the ideological framework of other African and African Diaspora political movements of this period.[1] The RICU had taken shape by September 1946, and Mzingeli was trying his best to call attention to the government's hypocrisy in sending African troops to fight the Japanese in Burma while failing to recognize Africans at home as "workers" under the Industrial Conciliation Act. Mzingeli told the RICU meeting:

> If the legislator saw fit in 1934, that African is not fit to be included in the Conciliation Act, they also saw it fit in 1940, that an African is capable of defending democracy against Nazis and Fascist horders whose doctrine was oppression of the working classes. The democracies armed themselves not only with forces of all nations irrespective of colour or creeds, but also with eight points from the Atlantic Ocean. The points include provision of freedom for all persons that include Africans as well. Also we have entered [a] New World so much promised during years of hostility therefore to deny an African a recognition as an employee is not only undemocratic but is committing suicide of social and economic justice.[2]

At a time when the British found themselves confronted by the power of African labor throughout their African and Caribbean colonies, a series of strikes shook the complacency around African–colonial labor relations after the war. The Southern Rhodesian government was also given its own "wake-up call" in the form of a powerful and effective railway strike in 1945.[3]

The Southern Rhodesian railway workers' strike began after higher-wage-earning workers, who organized into a union in 1944, were told by European management that their demands for better overtime pay would not be heard. As Ian Phimister describes it, this small group of elite workers turned to the rank and file and soon found they had the support of two thousand railway workers in Southern Rhodesia and eventually eight thousand workers throughout central Africa who shut down the vital railway lines in Southern Rhodesia.[4] Ken Vickery's narrative and analysis of the strike shows that the October 1945 strike leaders did not coordinate with the existing African political leadership either in Bulawayo or Salisbury, although leaders in both cities tried afterward to claim responsibility for it.[5] Vickery summarizes the attitude of European employees toward railway workers before the strike: "African railwaymen's demands for compensation when sick or injured, for paid leave, and for benefits when leaving the service, can all be seen as their response to the Railways treating them rather like a sponge, to be squeezed tightly when actually productive, but hung out to dry when not."[6]

The European administrators responsible for agreeing on a new wage scale after the strike expressed their respect for the strikers' organization and discipline. They were, however, concerned about the extent to which strikes were likely to become a feature of African labor now that African workers had shown themselves capable of shutting down the railways, the key means of exporting profitable raw materials from the landlocked country. As Vickery argues, the success of the strike in obtaining wage increases for railway workers led to intense pressure for further wage increases from other categories of African workers.

Mzingeli jumped at the opportunity to make the most out of this new worker solidarity to promote his RICU. No longer having to use British or South African trade unions as historical examples, he now had evidence right in Southern Rhodesia of the potential success a disciplined and strong trade union could achieve. But Mzingeli's optimism was quickly tempered by his competitive nature, as he remained wary of the successes of one Bantu Congress leader, Jasper Savanhu, who had quickly formed an African trade union movement in Bulawayo in the wake of the strike. Mzingeli wrote to Mrs. Kabell, the acting general secretary of the SRLP in November 1945 suggesting that the SRLP should publish the remarks "Mr. Sawanhu" made while addressing a crowd of five thousand workers located in Bulawayo. Mzingeli had already approached the *Bulawayo Chronicle* with the quote, but they had refused to print it. Given the radical message of Savanhu's quote, it is easy to understand why the *Chronicle* would have turned it down. Mzingeli quoted Savanhu as having told the crowd the following:

> The Railway strike had proved that Africans have been born. The old African of tribalism and selfishness has died away. Africans realize as never before that united

they stand and divided they fall. The reason is not far to seek. We have found ourselves faced by a ruthless foe—exploitation and legalised oppression by the white man for his and his children's luxury. "Applause."

The days when a white man could exploit us at will are gone and gone forever. The employer who ill treats one of the least of African workers does it to all of us. We must not fail in our duty to suffer with him. "Cheers." We have called you here tonight not only to explain the strike situation and to appeal for funds but also to start what might be called the AFRICAN TRADE UNION OF BULAWAYO. These A.T.U.'s will take the place of the ICU, which failed because we were then less informed.[7]

Savanhu's skillful use of populist rhetoric is evident here. The appeal to unity against a common enemy was to become the centerpiece of African populism. The call to unity around the protection of fellow workers from exploitation sought to link leaders such as Savanhu, himself from a more privileged background, with the political mobilization of thousands of Bulawayo's township residents. He linked their desires for better treatment by employers with protection for all Africans from the racist laws of their communities and workplace.

Mzingeli, however, by sending the full text of Savanhu's speech to the SRLP, was not simply showing his solidarity with Savanhu; he was also questioning Savanhu's motives. He told Kabell that since Savanhu's statement represented the views of both the Bulawayo Native Welfare Society and the Bantu Congress of Bulawayo, his comments were "more deserving of suspicion than otherwise." He explains somewhat sarcastically how organizations such as the Welfare Society and the Bantu Congress existed "to cooperate with the Government" and "to exhort, guide, lead, the Africans in way of purity, peaceful advancement, good and right living in their homes, chiefly to lead them to become law-abiding people and obedient to Government authority, Etc etc." Here Mzingeli was chastising the Congress because he saw its members as elites who wanted to maintain their privileged positions without having to deal directly with the day-to-day problems of the townships. Many of them, such as Savanhu, were successful farmers and businessmen who lived in the "Native Purchase Areas," where elite Africans were permitted to farm.

Terence Ranger has contextualized this quote of Savanhu's and argues Savanhu's strategy was to align the previously more elitist Congress movement with the railway workers. When the text of the speech was finally published in the *Bantu Mirror*, the African paper in Bulawayo, it included an additional quote from Savanhu advising workers to "let no device separate you from enlightened African leaders; they will not mislead you."[8] For Mzingeli, the enlightened African leadership of Savanhu and other Congress leaders could never achieve the same relationship as he had managed to develop with township residents. Mzingeli had a deep mistrust of the

Congress and did not believe that it truly represented the interests of African workers and township residents in the same way he did. He concluded his letter to Mrs. Kabell by criticizing Savanhu and the Congress, stating that his African HQ Branch would not "tolerate any one claiming the right to monopolise the championing of the African cause."[9] This attitude was Mzingeli's trademark response, a style of public posturing and intransigence that would become a central element of nationalist politics in the future.

Forming the Reformed ICU (RICU)

Mzingeli's defense of his right to fight for township residents did not stop him from making the most of Savanhu's popularity in order to promote the launching of the Reformed Industrial and Commercial Workers Union (RICU) in February 1946.[10] Given the restive mood of township workers after the railway strike, Mzingeli organized a meeting to be held near the Ndaba Tree just opposite the Native Dutch Reformed Church outside Harare township. The meeting was held on Sunday, February 10, with the intention of discussing the formation of an African trade union in Salisbury. A group of sixty township residents gathered at the Ndaba Tree at "3:15 in the afternoon" to hear Mzingeli, Shato Nyakauru, and Jasper Savanhu. Shato spoke first to the crowd in ChiManyika, carrying his bull's tail wisp as he often did at such occasions. Shato, the longtime leader of the Salisbury Waiters' Union (he was popularly referred to by his first name, which translates as "the python"), encouraged the crowd to form a new trade union that could unite all "employees and professional workers" to avoid the confusing "multiplicity of organizations" that were in existence at the time.[11] Shato represented the Waiters' Union, but there were also representatives of the railway workers, builders, drivers, and leaders of various burial societies, all organizations that had a longer history in the township and were interested in hearing what Mzingeli's new organization might hold in store for them.

Jasper Savanhu, speaking in English with an occasional passage in ChiShona for added emphasis, stressed the need for an African trade union to represent African interests and gave examples from British trade union history. Savanhu told the small crowd that already in Bulawayo the African Trade Union meetings had attendance in the range of three thousand to seven thousand people. He also congratulated Shato for having organized the Waiters' Association into a trade union in Salisbury and congratulated the railway workers on their successful 1945 strike "because through their solidarity they proved to the world that the Africans have reached the stage where they should organize themselves into Trade Union on the same basis as those of Europeans."[12]

The forty-one-year-old Mzingeli addressed the crowd in English, and Savanhu translated what Mzingeli had to say into ChiShona. Mzingeli praised Savanhu for having formed a trade union in Bulawayo and stressed the need for both funds and leadership if a trade union was to be created in Salisbury. Mzingeli told the audience of his many years' experience since his youth with African organizations that had failed because of inadequate financial support and poor leadership. He suggested that there were "good and well educated Africans who could lead them, but for the fear of difficulty they were not prepared to risk." He elaborated on the meaning of a trade union, pointing out that trade unions did not exist simply to call strikes but that strikes were a matter of last resort: "No strike should be called until every means had been exhausted." The corollary to this, Mzingeli continued, was the need for negotiations that would require "skilled experts such as lawyers," all of which would require "funds and strong moral support from members of the Trade Union."[13]

He concluded the meeting with a reference to the Atlantic Charter, telling the crowd that they should "keep themselves abreast with current events; they should study [the] Atlantic Charter, particularly 'Point Four,'" which states as follows: "Fourth, they will endeavor, with due respect for their existing obligations, to further the enjoyment by all States, great or small, victor or vanquished, of access, on equal terms, to the trade and to the raw materials of the world which are needed for their economic prosperity." After reading Point Four to the audience, Mzingeli stated

> that as far as he understood it, it declared a freedom for all persons, Victor or Vanquished, and it must be clearly understood that while he was addressing the meeting our Africans were returning from Asia and some were still there awaiting repatriation. They had gone up to teach Japan civilization. Therefore We in Rhodesia . . . cannot afford to permit any idea calculated to deny us the human rights annunciated in the Charter already referred to.[14]

Mzingeli had not only managed to lay out the possibility of a more inclusive trade union; he continued to use the human rights rhetoric that linked the gaining of imperial working-class citizenship for those Africans who had supported the war effort, either as soldiers in Burma or as workers in Salisbury. Even in the township, he was making links to a wider, more cosmopolitan world by linking the experiences of Africans in the townships to those of the "victor or vanquished" in World War II, as they faced increased segregation and economic discrimination. Mzingeli, like his counterparts throughout sub-Saharan Africa, hoped to mobilize workers and residents in their collective claims for imperial citizenship and human rights.

The Wider Context of Township Politics

Political organizations, however, were not the only visible public gatherings in the townships as large elite weddings and dances also used the township's recreation hall. The elites in Harare township displayed their class distinctions through impressive shows of wealth and consumption. The main arena for this was the wedding reception, and the *African Weekly* never missed reporting on a big one. In January 1947, for example, the wedding between Benjamin A. Dhliwayo of Mount Silinda and Effa David, daughter of James D. David, the "proprietor of No. 12 Store, Harare Township" included "a chain of about 8 cars—six V8 taxis and two private ones belonging to Mr. Dannie Mhlanga, proprietor of No. 1 Butchery, Harare Township."[15] The groom wore a "new Chicago pitch black suite [*sic*]" and "the bride looked charming in 1947 model silk gown." B. J. Mnyanda, now the general secretary of the African (formerly Bantu) National Congress, was the "chairman" at the reception, and gifts included "£19.17s.1d" in cash and "expensive plates, cups, spoons, forks, sugar basins, trays, table cloths, and other articles." The wedding guests were entertained by no less than six choirs, including the "Salisbury Bantu Actors and the Mt. Silinda Humming Bees."[16] Mnyanda's more elite status most likely irked Mzingeli at such events, although they were occasionally reported as guests at the same elite event in the "Who's Who" column of the *African Weekly*. As Jamela remembered it, eventually the competition between Mnyanda and Mzingeli became so intense that it was best not to mention Mnyanda's name within earshot of Mzingeli. Much of this rivalry had to do with their competing for elections to the newly established township advisory board.

The Native (Urban Areas) Accommodation and Registration Act, or N(UA)ARA, had included a provision for the creation of a new native advisory board for Harare township. The township advisory board system was already operating in South Africa's major cities by this time, and there too they had been designed to offer Africans input into the running of the township but without significant decision-making power of their own.[17] Earlier, Reverend Percy Ibbotson, the leader of the African Welfare Society, had suggested to the government that advisory boards would "act as a 'safety valve' for the ventilation of native feelings and opinions." He thought it would be a good idea for the municipality to elect a few members and that voting by ballot should be used unless it led to "selection of undesirable people of the worst agitating type," in which case, "other steps must be taken" as "everything depends on securing the right type of person."[18] Mzingeli, always suspicious of the government's intentions, also understood this to be the intended use of the advisory boards, so he took it upon himself to be elected along with as many RICU members as possible so that the advisory boards would not serve as yet another African "rubber-stamp" organization created by the government. As in the past, particularly with the Native Welfare Society, Mzingeli had gone into the organization to make sure it did not become a European vehicle to falsely represent African interests.

As a testament to his tenaciousness, Mzingeli would go on to dominate the township advisory board for ten years. Once again he walked a fine line between collaborating and protesting, as he managed at times to take advantage of the government through the office of the advisory board—to the constant dismay of Ibbotson, who served as the European adviser to the board for many years. Likewise, while people in the township voted for Mzingeli more than any other candidate, it was not his role as leader of the advisory board that people remember Mzingeli most. As Reuben Jamela later recalled, members of the advisory board received some respect, "but not a whole hell of a lot of respect."

The first township advisory board elections were held at the recreation hall on October 25, 1947. Ibbotson and other Europeans had most likely hoped that Bradfield Jacob (B. J.) Mnyanda would have been elected, along with his colleagues Rex Moses and Dominico Valente Joseph. But these three men were to receive the least number of votes in the election. The voting was open to all residents with proof of occupancy. In the first election only 119 registered occupiers voted, and voting was carried out in an "open voting" style, with each candidate moving to one side of the stage and those who supported him moving to the corresponding side of the room. Mzingeli received seventy-six votes compared to Mnyanda's four votes. Ibbotson, annoyed with the success of the RICU candidates, made more of an effort the next year to get Mnyanda and other more cooperative township residents elected.

In the 1948 election, Mzingeli was again the top vote getter with sixty-nine votes, but Mnyanda was not far behind with sixty-three. The list of elected board members was a veritable who's who of the township elite. In addition to Mnyanda and Mzingeli, there was Francis Joseph, Benjamin Zulu, M. Hove, D. Samuriwo, and E. Rakgajane. The voting was more contested in 1948, as the Native Commissioner decided to switch to a secret ballot in following years. A question arose whether the wife of a man with a certificate of occupation had the right to vote. The Native Commissioner decided only wives with their own occupation certificates in their own names were entitled to vote. This would have limited the female voters to the group of African nurses who had their own houses and a few other socially important women. Mzingeli was upset about the Native Commissioner's decision, which was likely taken to handicap Mzingeli in the next elections.

Some in the RICU disagreed with Mzingeli's strategy to control the advisory boards and the Welfare Society. Men such as Moses Ayema and Francis Ayema, both of whom had previous problems with Mzingeli, spoke out against the strategy at the December 7, 1947, RICU meeting. Moses Ayema said he had no confidence in the Welfare Societies and was also "doubtful whether the Advisory Board would do any better than those Advisory Boards in the Union of South Africa which have created most unenviable conditions of race relations." B. Zulu agreed with this criticism, saying that the RICU leaders "were wasting time talking and asking people to wait for fair justice when the native Urban Area Act is being enforced without any regard to human feelings." Francis Ayema brought up the historical precedents of "India, Palestine and Burmer [sic]" that had recently proven there was no way peaceful negotiations could lead to a settlement between "the ruling British people and those under them." But Mzingeli and his closest associates remained steadfast, defending their strategy to dominate the advisory board and the Welfare Society:

> At this stage, the Chairman [D. B. Ntuli] pointed out to the meeting that RICU leaders follow the principle of democracy and believe that negotiations carried out reasonably would certainly be of great benefit to both sections of the community rather than any other methods. . . . You must guard yourself against provocators [sic], continued the Chairman. He was well aware of such people."[19]

Ntuli and Mzingeli worked as a close team in the leadership of the RICU, and Ntuli often took the role of defending Mzingeli's views at meetings and in the press in order to protect Mzingeli, although Mzingeli was never one to avoid a confrontation when challenged. The next test for Mzingeli and the RICU was its response—or lack of response—to the powerful General Strike of 1948.

The 1948 General Strike

In the midst of Mzingeli's attempts to channel residents' protests against the N(UA)ARA through the "proper channels," the mood of African workers in the urban areas had moved beyond his patient combination of threats of action with negotiation and consultation. The government's Native Labour Wage Boards moved very slowly after the 1945 railway strike and were in no way concerned with keeping minimum-wage requirements in line with the increased postwar cost of living. The African railway workers, having won recognition by the government as workers, received a pay raise determined by the National Native Labour Board (NNLB). Subsequently, other groups of African workers demanded similar wage determinations but the NNLB's officials were notoriously slow in making a wage determination. As Ngwebe Bhebe shows in the Bulawayo case, there were many mass meetings in the township where public demands were voiced that an across-the-board wage increase be enacted for all African workers or else there would be a strike. The spark for the strike came on April 7, 1948, not from a call to strike by the established leaders, but by the newspaper headline in the *Bulawayo Chronicle*. The headline referred to a meeting of the Federated Chamber of Commerce, an association of white employers, who were debating the need to raise wages but were not an official government body empowered with the task of determining minimum wages. The headline read: "National Talks on Africans Basic Pay, Suggested Monthly, Urban 30sh Rural 25sh."[20] As Bhebe explains, it was the misinterpretation by Bulawayo township residents of these wage rates as the new minimum and maximum wages that sent people into the streets and was the catalyst for the strike.

According to Mzingeli's own account of the strike, a joint conference of African organizations was held at Gwelo (Gweru) on April 10 to discuss the possibility of a strike. The leaders attending that meeting were informed that the Bulawayo workers were planning to strike on April 14. Mzingeli relates how the Bulawayo delegates were advised (presumably by Mzingeli) to "postpone the strike until the present Native Labour Advisory Board machinery is fully used and that when there is no other machinery and as the last resort if demands were not granted, a general strike would then be organised throughout the colony."[21] A few days later, on the fourteenth, the General Strike began after a dramatic evening rally in Bulawayo attended by an estimated twenty thousand to thirty thousand people. The strike then moved to Gwelo, and by the following Monday, the strike reached Salisbury.

The April 1948 General Strike lasted two days in Salisbury, but as it followed immediately after the Bulawayo and Gwelo strikes, it was of major importance in showing the power of African labor.[22] More importantly, it confirmed European fears that Africans could in fact "close down" the city. There was, however, a circular logic to this confirmation of African protest power, as it was in part the overreaction of the police to the strike that helped to shut the city down. As news came of the potential spread of the strike from Bulawayo and Gwelo to Salisbury, the municipal administration and the police decided to use the Harare Location as a detainment area, which was cordoned off and "protected" using mostly young white volunteer "troops." Africans working in the city, many of whom did not even live in the township, were rounded up, put on lorries, and brought to the township for the duration of the strike. A complaint after the strike by elite Africans who testified to the Strike Commission was that they had been harassed by European police or by the European youth in the hastily conscripted militia who would not allow them to proceed into town for work. African leaders argued that it was the action of the police and those European employees who sent their domestics to the Location that had in fact contributed to the success of the strike.[23]

Gladys Maasdorp, Mzingeli's friend and ally in the SRLP, provided an account of the strike from her perspective in the city center where she witnessed patrol vans picking up Africans and taking them to the township. Maasdorp described to Rita Hinden how one of her domestic servants had been picked up by the police and taken to the township, where, according to Maasdorp, he "was badly beaten for having worked at all." She then described, secondhand, the conditions in the Location: "There was little food there, what there was in the small open air market was looted, and no food came in. There was a great deal of hooliganism, exacerbated by the lack of food."[24] Inside the cordoned-off township many African residents were fearful of the violence. Witnesses remember three days of violence and looting, with people locking themselves inside their homes for fear of attack. According to the Hudson Commission Report following the strike, young men from the township who took advantage of the strike, calling it a "holiday," were behind the "hooliganism." Groups of strikers set up picket lines and threatened anyone trying to leave the Location. In the morning of the second day of the strike, "gangs of young hooligans armed with sticks were in evidence at the location, chasing and assaulting African females and carrying out looting of firewood owned by Africans."[25] Businessmen and civil servants such as the postmaster Patrick Pazarangu, a close associate of Mzingeli's, had their houses stoned because they refused to stop working. The RICU leadership was unable to exert any control over the striking young men, a situation that was disappointing both to the RICU leaders and the European administrators.[26]

The impression that the majority of the male migrant population was out of the control of both the state and the strike leaders during the General Strike was not, however, substantiated by the subsequent testimony to the Hudson Commission. Instead, the spatial organization where migrants lived in hostels based on who they worked for allowed the authorities to use violence to put down any such threat. On April 21, according to the Hudson Commission Report,

> on two occasions mobs of strikers became unruly and threatened to use violence. They were dispersed on each occasion by a baton charge carried out by a comparatively few European police. Immediately after the second charge which was directed against municipal employees at their hostel, numbers of Africans came forward and offered to return to work. They were separated from the main body of strikers and given police protection. Thereafter most of the inhabitants of the hostel came forward and offered to resume work. They were taken to their employment on Lorries.[27]

According to the Hudson Commission Report, workers from the main sections of the township also began to return to work at this point. In 1948, then, it took only "a comparatively few European police" to force migrants out of their hostels and back to work.

The 1948 General Strike had been a spontaneous action on the part of frustrated and disgruntled urban workers and residents subjected to high prices, low wages, food shortages, and a severe drought in the rural areas.[28] Mzingeli had not been able to control or predict this strike, and his main task was to negotiate with the authorities and to ask workers to return to work. He and the other leaders in 1948 were responding to mass action rather than leading it. Maasdorp described how African leaders had "found themselves between two fires, suspected by Europeans on the one hand and attacked by the Africans on the other. Some were in actual physical danger, also their wives and families. I am told that Charles Mzingeli's papers have been impounded by the Central Intelligence Division (C.I.D.) and that he is in hiding from his fellow Africans."[29]

Mzingeli's account of the strike that he sent to Rita Hinden suggests that he was not completely unaware of the impending strike. He confirms their interpretation of events in the morning of the nineteenth when workers at the Dairy Co-op went out on strike and the police response—sending "all strike minded Africans to [the] location while a Police Corridor had been spread along all lines leading to the City"—had, in Mzingeli's opinion, "organised the strike to a point in Salisbury." But his account suggests that he and others were not so completely caught by surprise. After a large crowd had gathered on Monday morning in the Location, George Ballenden sent a message that "the Government had decided on that Afternoon, to expand the present native Labour Advisory Board granted to Bulawayo Municipal African employees, into a National Native Labour Advisory Board to cover the whole colony of Southern Rhodesia." This was an impressive concession, but one the "unmanageable" crowd rejected. The following afternoon, on Tuesday, Mzingeli and other leaders met with the prime minister and the minister of justice at the Chief Native Commissioner's office. Describing that meeting Mzingeli writes: "Obviously some of the leaders knew something about the strike but were not prepared to explain the fact other than that African people have gone on strike for a high wages." On the contrary, as general secretary of the RICU, Mzingeli told government officials that he and his union "knew nothing of the strike as his Union had accepted Gwelo decision and this was made clear to those organizations affiliated and those in co-operation with the Union." He went with the Chief Native Commissioner to the township, and he and other leaders interpreted the CNC's message about the new Native Labour Board.[30]

Reuben Jamela's recollection of the strike corroborates Mzingeli's more positive account of his role and his ability to make the most of the strike for workers and the RICU without making the tactical mistake of claiming any knowledge of the strike. Jamela, then a young graduate of Domboshawa School, was starting his career as a builder. He was a member of the RICU and recalled how Mzingeli used the strike to gain legitimate recognition from the government. Jamela's account shows Mzingeli's remarkable ability to make the best of situations confronting him:

The then Prime Minister [Huggins] asked for a meeting with us. We went to see him, and told him that the people were not satisfied with their wages. He then told us that it was illegal to call for strike action, and threatened us with arrest. He even said we had no right to call for meetings, and that all the organizations that we represented (the RICU, the Builders' Association, etc) were not recognized by his government. Mzingeli was told to go and break the strike. Mzingeli reiterated by saying how could he call off the strike when he was a nonentity in their eyes. He claimed he was leading the rest of us out of the office, so that the white government could address those picketing. The Prime Minister refused, and then persuaded us to ask the strikers to go back to work while their grievances were looked into. We got our first recognition there.[31]

The results of this meeting between Mzingeli and Huggins were quite different than the previous one. The power of the strikers had so turned the tables that Mzingeli was able to gain a modicum of respect from Huggins during that critical moment. After the strike was over, the government encouraged the National Native Labour Board to investigate wage and working conditions for the various industries in order to set minimum wages, with the ability to force employers to comply. The strike may not have originated with Mzingeli and the RICU, but for a brief time the RICU's position as mediator earned it a greater level of legitimacy. It is also quite possible and likely that Mzingeli was aware of the strike organization in Salisbury but given the strict laws against organizing, he had to keep a low public profile.

Once again, Mzingeli and other African leaders tried in vain to organize a unified movement after the strike. After two meetings organized by the Bantu Congress failed to move forward, Mzingeli organized a meeting for July. Before the meeting he wrote a letter to the *African Weekly* to explain his views on leadership:

> We wish to assure our African leaders that it does not need any protest for any leader to tell whether he is agitator or no agitator, political minded or non political minded, anti-white or Government or not. While it is true that leadership want educated men and women it is also true that such leaders must possess long experience of the leadership. In these days of atomic age and Western civilization, it is dangerous to have uninformed leader whatever experience he may have had, to deal with present day diplomacy.[32]

This statement sums up many of the fissures making any alliance difficult between Mzingeli and other leaders. The contrast between agitators and nonagitators likely had to do with accusations and counteraccusations concerning who had been more "radical" during the recent General Strike. Additionally, the political identities of being trade unionists versus politicians may also have surfaced, as did the question whether certain leaders should work alongside whites and the government or act independently. All of these issues were to remain fault lines for cooperation in forming viable political alliances, and they suggest, as will be shown throughout this book, there were greater difficulties than Mzingeli's personality and intransigence to overcome.

After the strike, Harare township settled back into the contrasting images of poorer workers compared with elite social gatherings at the Township Recreation Hall, such as the function held on August 10, 1948, attended by "140 ladies and gentlemen," many from the outlying areas— "from Epworth Mission, Highfields, Waterfalls, the British South Africa Police Camp, and as far away as Domboshawa. What could be described as the cream of society was present at the function."[33] This contrasted with the violence of "gangsters"—stories about men who assaulted beer drinkers in the "Jo'burg lines" section of Harare township.[34] The violence associated with the strike started a debate in the African press about the threat of violence more generally in the township. George Ballenden, Salisbury's director of Native Administration, downplayed the strike as an actual labor action, and played up the youthful "hooligan" nature of those most visibly involved: "There was a certain amount of violence which took place in the location between Natives and Natives, but it was principally committed by the youngsters..., and our Native population is an extremely youthful population."[35] The *African Weekly*'s editorial of April 28, 1948, was much more critical of the lack of discipline shown in the township. According to the editors, the strike "was not a strike at all. Rioting, looting, and assaulting went on absolutely unchecked, reaching its climax on Tuesday when a number of people were brutally assaulted, outrages were perpetrated on women, much damage was done to property, and most of the rioters indulged in an orgy of madness."[36] Even after discounting the paternalistic nature of the early African press editorials, the impact of the strike on this elite section of the African population brought out the frustrations of those in the "respectable class" who hoped to define an urban respectability but who were faced with the "dangerous classes" whom they could neither control nor avoid. The difficulty was made all the worse in the struggle over the public sphere, where African journalists worked so hard to establish their credentials for democratic participation, while the European press used the public violence and unruly crowds as a representation of township life. The conduct of certain groups in the township during the strike worked against their own campaigns advocating for rights and freedoms comparable to their own levels of respectability and civility.

By the end of 1948, Mzingeli and other members of the Harare township advisory board were losing patience with the way the Salisbury's Native Administration Department and the Salisbury Municipal Council ignored most of their requests and recommendations. At a November 1948 meeting, the advisory board passed a resolution calling for the Salisbury Municipal

Council "to give great weight" to the board's views, expressing, in words that sounded trademark Mzingeli:

> This Board wishes it to be clearly understood that in its opinion, in the event of the Municipal Council assuming an attitude which implies that the Advisory Board is a "dummy" and a medium through which native people "let off steam," co-operation and mutual understanding between the Harari Township Residents and the Council will become impossible.

The impact of the General Strike and the considerable amount of verbal abuse with which Mzingeli and his RICU colleagues on the township advisory board must have had to contend led to a strongly worded resolution. The resolution resulted in a special meeting between the advisory board and the director of Native Administration for Salisbury, George Hartley. Hartley summarized the list of grievances in his report to the Municipal Council. The first grievance included the lack of electricity and the city council's failure to provide it after promising to do so in 1947. Other grievances included the lack of space between the new houses being built, the ongoing eviction of township tenants found in possession of liquor—it was felt this was an injustice given that it did not apply to "tenants of other races, whether European, Indian or Coloured." The third grievance concerned the "ill-manners, lack of sympathetic understanding, general disinterest and lack of courtesy shown by the Council's officials in their dealings with natives." Hartley concluded his summary by indicating the need for Europeans to take more seriously the demands of the advisory board. He also left the meeting with the impression that "any action or decision made, which does not fully coincide with the wishes of the Native leaders, will certainly be interpreted as evidence of the lack of understanding by the Council."[37] This list of grievances and Hartley's perception of a changing political environment based on his interaction with the advisory board illustrates how the political climate had become radicalized after the General Strike and suggests the possibility of African politicians breaking through the impasse created by the state's insistence on granting only those Africans who agreed with state policy any semblance of real powers.

Mnyanda and Mzingeli were to team up as members of the advisory board to ask again for real powers in December 1949. At a native advisory board meeting, Mnyanda moved "that the City Council be requested to give this Board executive powers in regard to all matters affecting the Harari Township." Mzingeli supported the motion. Mnyanda argued that the "purely advisory" role of the board "could not give of its best and so engender the feeling of satisfaction in the minds of the residents of Harari." Mzingeli agreed with Mnyanda's reference to South Africa, "where Urban Native Administration was not a new thing," and "he supported Mnyanda's contention that there were certain posts in the Township which could be filled by Africans." Hartley, for his part as chair of the meeting, said that he "sympathized with the Board in this matter on the general question, but he could not support the proposal in its general form."[38] While the General Strike had shown the state the power of collective action, the state did not consider making concessions to African leaders in terms of political rights beyond their role as elite advisers. Mzingeli, once again faced with a door closed on his patient determination to obtain political recognition, did not give up. If anything, events in Harare township in the early 1950s would provide him with his best opportunity to organize and demand greater rights for residents.

The Fight against the Subversive Activities Act

Township advisory board elections offered a limited space for African politicians to expand their influence within the township—a process co-opted by Mzingeli's stubborn unwillingness to turn the advisory board leadership over to those handpicked yes-men Ibbotson and the municipality had originally hoped to put into office. At another level, however, the advisory boards remained a much less important challenge to white authorities than the real threat of further strike action after the 1948 General Strike. The government commission established to investigate the strike, led by Chief Justice Sir Robert Hudson, had advocated stronger legislation to handle future strikes and "disturbances." Mnyanda, who decided to leave Harare and return to East London, South Africa, and continue his political career there, later analyzed the implications of the legislation for Southern Rhodesian African politics in his 1954 book, *In Search of Truth*. According to Mnyanda, the Subversive Activities Act (1950) reflected the Hudson Commission's request that the act copy the "Union of South Africa's Riotous Assembly Act of 1914" and also include a new section to deal "with subversive activities as such." The minister of justice, when introducing the bill into Parliament, explained the need to fight subversive activity because of the new Cold War:

> We all know the methods which are employed by our opponents in this Cold War. They employ insidious methods of propaganda which has a certain appeal to ignorant minds, and it is unnecessary for me to stress what volatile material we have in this country which might fall a prey to propaganda of that sort. It is propaganda which is dangerous with ignorant, uneducated people.[39]

As Mnyanda described it, the minister of justice was careful to point out this new legislation was not going to interfere with the operation of white trade unions. It was clear from the outset just whom the Subversive Activities Act was directed against: "[there is] a type of literature disseminating in the

Colony now amongst our Native people stating that they should not do any-thing active to break the law but they must sit down and do nothing."[40] Mnyanda describes the objection at this point made by L. J. W. Keller, who asked why the government had not stated from the beginning that the Bill was directed only at Africans. Keller knew the real answer, that if the government had stated the truth of the matter, there would have been a chance of an imperial veto from Britain.

Mnyanda analyzed the true impact of the act: "so far from protecting his rights, it is aimed at the suppression of freedom of speech. For this reason (and, of course, there are others) it can only sow the seed of animosity between White and Black."[41] He noted the hypocrisy of the act's protection of white trade unions while "making it not only difficult, but also impossible, for Native workers to organize themselves into trade unions for their pro-tection." The act went much further, though, as it gave magistrates the right to ban any public meetings that would threaten "the public peace." It also gave the police the right to use "firearms in dispersing persons assembled at any prohibited gathering." Mnyanda asked, "Why should the police be empowered to use firearms in the suppression of public meetings attended, as they always were, by defenseless and unarmed Native people?" In addition, the act called for the creation of a new "Security Branch" within the Criminal Investigation Department (CID), which "has a list of what are styled 'dan-gerous and anti-white Native leaders.'" Mnyanda writes of the effect the Subversive Activities Act had on African leaders: "they are chary of criticizing Government. . . . They do not want to cause strife; but there can be no good life for a people who are so brutally suppressed." He concludes by quoting Edward Bellamy: "The primary principle of democracy is the worth of the individual. The raising up of the human being, without respect of persons, is the central and only rational motive of democratic polity." Mnyanda asks: "What has the Colony done to raise the dignity of the individual Native? If anything, it has only outraged it."[42]

Mnyanda's eloquent critique of the Subversive Activities Act was written in 1954, four years after it went into effect. Mzingeli, for his part, had tried his best to fight the bill before it became law, using his contacts with the Fabian Socialists in Britain and his allies within Southern Rhodesia. He also saw the act as a blow against interracial cooperation. It rejected recognition for African workers as "employees" under the Industrial Conciliation Act, recommending instead that Africans continue to be seen as a separate cate-gory of workers. To Mzingeli, this was further proof of the government's insincerity and once again the "result of political teaching of race arro-gance."[43] He states that although the RICU has "always fought relentlessly for co-operation of different races, it realize[s] that a practical co-operation can-not be reconciled with segregation policy. It is the opinion of the African people, rightly too, that the present so-called co-operation is designed so as to be carried at the expense of African people as a matter which makes genuine progress impossible in that direction."[44]

Mzingeli's campaign against the Subversive Activities Act brought him in contact with Hardwicke Holderness, a young white lawyer who would go on to advocate racial cooperation in the Federation period. Holderness recalls in his autobiography how Mzingeli brought him this memorandum against the bill, and how Holderness rewrote it to, in his opinion, give it "the best chance of carrying some weight" with members of Parliament.[45] But with hindsight, Holderness recounted that it seemed "pretty obvious now that Mzingeli's original was better and more effective than my redraft." More importantly, Holderness remembered his work with Mzingeli as making a "fundamental difference" in his approach to interracial politics. He characterized Mzingeli as "a touching and vulnerable man doing his best to help fellow human beings who were getting a pretty raw deal from white-dominated society, and doing it without any particular malice or racial antagonism towards whites."[46] This brief but failed attempt to fight the Subversive Activities Act as Mzingeli's legal representation gave Holderness a new urgency to reach out and work within the National Affairs Association to bridge the racial divide more directly.

In 1950 Mzingeli commented on the lack of support within the European population for Africans' causes. He suggested that nine out of ten whites shared the "pro-kkk" views of Charles Olley as expressed in Olley's *Rhodesia Monthly Review*, and praised the one-tenth of Europeans who fought for "fair justice." To Mzingeli, the latter group adhered "to the great charter of human rights. Not the charter that was made in the Atlantic Ocean under the pressure of that dreadful German leader. But one introduced by the Great Teacher . . . the great charter of all time."[47] Mzingeli recognized in the Subversive Activities Act the same motivations used by Olley in his attacks on Maasdorp for having met with Africans in the Location in 1944. After the Subversive Activities Act, a Cold War pretext was available to discredit those whites working with their African colleagues toward the goal of equal political rights for all Africans. Just as in South Africa and the United States, anti-communist intimidation in Southern Rhodesia had a chilling effect on social justice and civil rights activism, undermining the ability of Africans and progressive whites to work together for much of the 1950s.[48]

The general anticommunist fervor of the early 1950s spread to Salisbury, where anything remotely connected with improving the economic or social status of Africans was likely to be labeled subversive. Mzingeli produced a memorandum on the bill calling it "an infringement on the principle of human right[s]" that "definitely cannot be treated in any way as an accepted precept of Western Civilisation." Among the bill's recommendations Mzingeli criticized was one limiting access by Europeans to Africans. Specifically, it prohibited Europeans' contact with "African workers," as they were "capable of being misunderstood" by African workers, and therefore such Europeans could be kept from "contact with the African people."[49]

The late 1940s had been a difficult period for Mzingeli. In 1946 and 1947 Mzingeli and the RICU had failed to present any serious opposition to the implementation of the N(UA)ARA, deciding instead to fight the legislation through legal channels, and petitioning British authorities in hopes of organizing the use of the imperial veto. Mzingeli would later be criticized for collecting a strike fund in 1946 to use against the act. The idea had been to organize a general strike to oppose the N(UA)ARA, but this strike was never called, and the act was implemented without organized resistance.

Mzingeli was criticized at the Second Annual Congress of the RICU, in September 1948, for not having used the collected money for a strike. The issue came up during a discussion of the effectiveness of the new township advisory board. A Mr. Mhlanga questioned the motives of those on the advisory board. According to Mhlanga, "The majority of the Board were business people or people who were trying to build their prestige at the expense of those who elected them." A Mr. Chikodzi added to the criticism, claiming that although "he did not believe that members of the board were being blamed by people," he did hear complaints "that they raised money during the period and the leaders of this Union failed to lead [a] sit down strike." Mzingeli responded to these criticisms, stating that "the position was made quite clear to them when they were asked to contribute fighting funds, as they wanted the Union to do their request." He asked whether the members expected "us to make all representation we did and negotiations etc. etc. at our expenses."[50]

The success of the 1948 General Strike had shown African leaders the potential of channeling African labor as a political weapon, but the actual ability to harness that energy still evaded them. The 1950 Subversive Activities Act made the challenge all the more difficult. Then, beginning in the early 1950s, the Salisbury Native Administration Department began to implement the N(UA)ARA more strictly, carrying out sweeping raids of the Location to arrest women without marriage certificates and unregistered male visitors. This intrusive form of control caused a public outcry from many residents who, in turn, looked to Mzingeli for leadership.

At the same time, the increasingly radical rhetoric and results of African politics throughout sub-Saharan Africa in the early 1950s allowed Mzingeli to take advantage of this new mood. In South Africa this new radicalism was clear at the national level with the African National Congress's defiance campaigns against the new apartheid legislation.[51] In Ghana, postwar strikes had helped to usher Kwame Nkrumah into power in 1951 as a first step toward independence. In Southern Rhodesia, a similar groundswell of defiance would be mobilized around the demands of urban women, and Mzingeli's RICU represented and championed this protest movement. Mzingeli's success in organizing the RICU undoubtedly had to do with his "authenticity" as a township resident and as "a man of the people." This latter image was resented and privately criticized by more elite Africans. Terence Ranger has found evidence in the Samkange papers of the animosity and disdain prominent leaders of the Bantu Congress in Salisbury, in particular Aaron Jacha and B. J. Mnyanda, held for Mzingeli. Mnyanda wrote to Reverend Samkange in March 1947, "'Tommy, let us now fight to *crush* Mzingeli.'" Later in 1947, Jacha, wrote to Samkange to complain of Mzingeli's approach to the N(UA)ARA: "'He is instigating people to cease work as a protest against the Act, which means he is instigating people to revolt. The Act is a law of the state and cannot be protested against by ceasing work.'" As Ranger comments, "It was small wonder that Mzingeli regarded Congress with scorn."[52]

This elite criticism continued throughout his career, and Mzingeli responded to it by claiming that the source of his own authority and power came exactly out of his closeness to the common man and woman of the township. The *African Weekly* in November 1949 paraphrased and quoted him as follows:

> A rumour was circulating among the educated African that he, Mzingeli, owed his popularity to the fact that he associated himself with ignorant people. He was not sorry about this accusation. It was a compliment to him. If he neglected the illiterate and ignorant man, it was a waste of one's time to have a trade union because the duty of a trade union is to help the underdog. Education was good, but not if it meant despising those not so privileged. "Then it was a bad form of education. The educated man would only put himself down if he neglected the masses." "The Reformed ICU exists to help the underdog. Those who hinder and slander us in this cause will certainly not live to see the making of history. God refuses that a man should be a traitor to his race. A man must live to help his fellowman" he said.[53]

In order to move forward, Mzingeli combined a number of strategies—some international, others local—and concerned himself with assisting a small number of individuals in obtaining exemptions from the imposition of the N(UA)ARA. The culmination of these strategies was a respect and reciprocal nationalism that went beyond the written and verbal demands expressed in meetings and newspapers by the more elite nationalists. Mzingeli kept steadfastly to his longstanding tradition of weekly meetings in Harare township, using the opportunity to have township residents voice their demands to him and through him. During the week he worked with the municipal administration to try to reach compromises on specific cases. So great was his influence that people would come to him and say that the municipality would not let them do this or that because Mzingeli would complain if it was found out. By the early 1950s, Mzingeli had earned the unofficial title of the "mayor" of Harare township, and his politics represented a model of what could be achieved under African leadership that came to power based on direct service to the community.

Mzingeli's sincerity and commitment was even acknowledged by B. J. Mnyanda, the man who often competed with Mzingeli for positions of leadership in the township until Mnyanda returned to South Africa. Mnyanda gave the following praise of Mzingeli as part of his testimony to the commission investigating the 1948 General Strike: "He said Mr. Mzingeli had many African enemies, who sought his downfall, merely out of malice and ill-will. But Mr. Mzingeli had a cause; an ideal for his race, and therefore it was impossible to defeat a man like him in his appointed task. They, not him, would fail, because they had no cause."[54] The early 1950s would present a chance for Mzingeli to build a movement to fight for Africans' rights to the city and, by extension, to national citizenship.

3

Resistance to the Urban Areas Act
and Women's Political Influence

This chapter explores the role of Mzingeli's RICU in challenging the state's use of segregation legislation to reshape urban life for African residents. The potential impact of the N(UA)ARA in 1946 could have been dramatic given the ambitious goals contained within this legislation. It sought to engineer and plan urban residential segregation in ways that would maximize the availability of low-wage labor to urban-based industrialists while minimizing the continued growth of African residential areas in the "whites-only" suburbs and neighborhoods of the city. The costs were high for this plan to succeed, however, from the standpoint of the European bureaucracy that designed and implemented it. No contingency plans were made for African political opposition to the implementation phase, nor were the levels of passive and everyday resistance to the letter of the law by African residents as well as non-African landlords and employers realistically assessed. Six years after its inception, European bureaucrats were coming to realize the failure of the N(UA)ARA to regulate urban life, but from its beginning in 1946, the challenges to the status quo of township life were numerous.

Municipal administrators also tended to accept the N(UA)ARA as a necessary step to gain control over an increasingly "uncontrolled" African urban population. The director of Native Administration for the city, George Ballenden, recommended enthusiastically to the city council that it accept the provisions of the act because it would enable the city to salvage its Native Affairs finances through employer subsidies of rents while retaining control of "all housing of natives within its area" and increasing control over "the entry into, or the continued presence in, its area, of undesirable natives." Ballenden's optimism toward these advantages was tempered by the reality of the size of the area in question, and the need for the government to work diligently to control the areas outside the city's jurisdiction. If the government did not enforce the provision of the Land Apportionment Act that called for new African urban areas, according to Ballenden, then "the mere ordering of unwanted natives to leave the area and return whence they came is likely to lead to a congregation of natives on the outskirts of town."[1] The goal of the act was to tighten control over all areas, including such areas already under government control. This goal was eventually partially achieved, but the action against private compounds had to be done slowly, given the lack of alternative accommodations. The closing down of private compounds on European-owned land proved to be particularly difficult on working families. As one man who originally came from Nyasaland wrote in the *African Weekly*, the state's argument that women and children should return to their rural homes was not a possibility for many, nor was it possible to find adequate accommodations in Harare township. In a letter to the editor, Mr. A. N. Mtungie wrote, "I fail to understand the idea of raiding every African with a family out of where he is, when in the so-called Harare Township accommodation is not available."[2]

The municipality and the state hoped to use strict controls over who could legally reside in the "African areas" of the city to rationalize and stabilize the African residential areas. The N(UA)ARA tied housing to employment, allowing the municipality to evict men and women without proper proof of employment. The act also required women living in the township to prove their relationship to a legal male guardian in the city—either a father, a husband, or a guardian approved by rural male relatives. This last regulation made things very difficult for the independent women of the township, or those living in informal relationships with township men. An important segment of the latter group, women known as *mapoto* wives, had been a fixture of township life given the immense gender imbalance in the township. The term *mapoto* originated from the domestic services these women provided men—literally, wives "with pots." They, along with other informally employed women, most notably prostitutes and beer brewers, were ultimately the victims of the weekly raids organized by the municipality to enforce the N(UA)ARA in the township.[3]

As there were many more men than women living in the township before the 1950s, the *mapoto* relationship had developed as a way of having a "town wife" while working in the city and earning money to establish a rural homestead in the future. Since men were legally permitted to occupy housing, the women who entered into this form of cohabitation were not officially permitted rights to township housing, but many of them did manage to navigate and negotiate the township and evade the law prior to enactment of the N(UA)ARA. A letter written in ChiShona to the *African Weekly* in June 1945 expresses the "lament" of a man who claimed many men were losing their properties to such wives.

Why is it that some of us men, when we begin to take on a *mapoto* wife (*kana tatora vakadzi mapoto*), allow the women to bring their tables, chairs, and beds?

Initially, the man has all his, but when he proposes love to such women, his property is got rid of bit by bit, because some of these women have better furniture than the man's.

The man's furniture is sold, and thus the space created is used by the woman to place her furniture, and ultimately the house becomes occupied with the wife's property. If the man's bicycle breaks down, the wife offers hers. By and by, the man's bicycle is sold off, and if the wife's bicycle breaks down, it is repaired. At the end of the month, the man's wages are given to the woman, and she is told to buy whatever she wants—the man is left with nothing.

When they break up, the woman takes everything; including the bicycle and all that she bought using the man's wages. The house is left empty, the man has no money since he used to give it all to the woman. I am not discouraging taking *mapoto* wives, but let us refrain from getting rid of our property and working for the wife's bicycle.

I have come across many men who are experiencing problems with their wives in this regard.[4]

In the 1950s when the municipality began search raids in Harare township, they were attempting to remove a number of "unattached" women, especially prostitutes and *mapoto* wives, who had evaded detection by sleeping in the houses of relatives or boyfriends. One area of the Township that was rarely searched during such raids was the married cottages where people like Mzingeli, Patrick Pazarangu, Tobias Nhapi, and other members of the RICU executive lived. This section was not raided because of the respectable reputation of the residents and because the municipal officials did not want to stir up trouble with the RICU leaders; therefore, they purposely did not raid their houses. Women fearful of raids began to visit the houses of these men in order to ask for protection. As Tobias Nhapi remembers:

> Many such women gave us sleepless nights sometimes. We at times went to the police to ask whether there was an inspection on that particular night. If told no, we conveyed the message to these prostitutes and they would go away. . . . Whenever there was an inspection, the municipal police forewarned us, so that we would pass on the message to those women we knew.[5]

RICU membership grew more rapidly during the period of these raids against women and illegal tenants than at any other time in its history. In 1951 the membership was estimated at three thousand and by 1953 it had grown to nearly seven thousand. Mzingeli told the government that the majority of members in the RICU by 1953 were women.[6] It was the protection offered by the RICU against the raids in 1951 and 1952 that saw the real increase in active membership. Prior to these raids, Mzingeli had not been able to mobilize support from the uneducated and semieducated masses in concerted action against the N(UA)ARA; instead, his primary role was in maintaining a visible debate—his Sunday meetings of the RICU—and in serving as a constant source of verbal and written criticism of the hypocrisy inherent in a racist society that used the rhetoric of liberal democracy in its laws.

The RICU meetings were not just critical of white authority, as the following criticism against Africans in positions of authority shows a disdain for their abuses of power. At a Sunday RICU meeting held October 1, 1950, Freddy Chinhemba spoke to the theme—at least as Mzingeli recorded it in the minutes—of how "The African was irresponsible and did not have a feeling of brotherhood." Chinhemba reportedly stated: "If there was a train for Africans only and entirely staffed by Africans, accommodation would be for pals and he doubted if one would have a safe journey even as far as Que Que. 'When they put on a uniform or have some top-job they feel they are kings and their ambition is to persecute their fellowmen.'"[7] Mzingeli and others in the RICU were publicly debating the abuses of power by Africans in the service of the settler state. They did not, however, at this stage, refer to these men as "sellouts," as many of the unofficial supporters of the RICU worked in some capacity for the government and there was not a strong feeling that Africans should avoid working for the government altogether, except as pro-government yes-men whose opinions could influence British views of Southern Rhodesian African affairs.

The RICU would have likely remained a place for "letting off steam" by its mostly male membership had it not been for the state's decision to implement the provisions of the N(UA)ARA that prohibited "unmarried" women to live legally in the township. By offering an organized community defense against this harassment, Mzingeli's politics and his openness to treating women's issues as legitimate political demands made the RICU the most effective means of channeling the community's indignation into protests in the early 1950s.

Attendance at the monthly meeting of the RICU, held at the Recreation Hall on Sunday morning June 3, 1951, was beyond anything Mzingeli had seen in five previous years of holding monthly meetings. According to Mzingeli's and Pazarangu's minutes, there were 4,853 people in attendance. As was customary with large gatherings, the crowd was segregated by sex—men on one side and women on the other. But at this meeting the women far outnumbered the men, making it look more like a church meeting than a political one. The large number of women were in attendance, according to Solomon Maviyane, longtime chair of the RICU, because of a rumor that a big raid was about to take place in the Location; many women, previously charged a number of times for various petty offenses, were fearful that this time they would be arrested, including women living with their husbands in married quarters. The speaker's platform was then turned over to a group of women who described to the crowd their particular cases, accentuating the injustice of both the N(UA)ARA and the strict adherence to it by the municipality.

The first woman to speak, who went by the name "Justice," described how she had been a victim of the N(UA)ARA. She had lived for many years in the township, had children in school in the township, but when the man she was living with as a *mapoto* wife wanted a new house, he left her and "put another woman in the house." Her main complaint, as with many of the others, was that they were unable to go to the superintendent directly to make known their case for housing and remaining in the township because the African police and interpreters would not let them see the superintendent, sometimes asking for bribes and sexual favors, and that in either case these women risked being arrested on the spot or in future raids. Justice's testimony was met with some criticism, however, from certain married women in the audience, who asked her if she were not aware that married women were against the presence of unmarried women in the township. Another woman, Regina, called such criticism as "regrettable . . . since the majority of unmarried women were detribalised. Even in the native reserves, she said, men do commit adultery with another man's wife and such cases are dealt with according to the law." Another speaker, Emily Gahadzi, who had lived nineteen years in Harare township, recounted that

> many women were being kept by men before the coming into force of the Urban Areas' Act, and since its operation these men had to bring marriage certificates of their real wives from home thus throwing away the one who has been with him for years. As the result of this . . . many of us became displaced women, and subject to the persecution and prosecution of living in the Township.[8]

As with the other women, she complained of the unjust treatment she received at the hands of the police, especially when trying to go and see the superintendent. A woman in the audience accused Emily of being a prostitute, to which she replied that none of them wish to be prostitutes, but that even if other work was available, they could not take it because it was required that they had accommodations. This was the double bind such women faced, and the increased harassment by the police brought them to the RICU for assistance.

After the women had spoken, the RICU men began to make speeches. Moses Mwari, a Harare resident since 1919, told of how his sisters, born in the Township, were presently "wandering about in various farms . . . not because they wanted to, but because they could not obtain permits to remain in the Township." He replied to the married women who had been quick to criticize the single women that they should realize the important role such women played in the township. In earlier times, Mwari told the meeting, "when there were very few married men, there was always trouble of cases of people's wives found with other men."[9] Others spoke of the "disaster" created by the separation of young women from their families, in an interesting reversal of earlier arguments made about the disastrous effects of removing young women from the rural areas. Now, the families in the urban areas faced legislation that, in effect, could be seen to do the opposite—sending their daughters to the rural areas, where by now they often had neither relatives nor claims to land.

In the week following the RICU meeting, Mzingeli was successful at bringing in five of the eight women who had spoken at the meeting to talk with the township superintendent and the director of Native Affairs. These women were able to present their cases in person and were given special passes, which allowed them to remain living in the township. In addition, the testimony of these women and Mzingeli's personal appeal caused the firing of a notoriously abusive interpreter from the superintendent's office, to the relief of women who had previously dealt with the man. This immediate success for this small group of women brought even more women to the RICU, as testimonies to its intervention were given at the next meeting. But the success was not without difficulties, as Mzingeli was to find out in the following years. These women who were the saviors of Mzingeli's organization were also a threat to the respectability the RICU had always been careful to nurture. Mzingeli had never been as extreme in championing the causes of morality and temperance as B. J. Mnyanda and other elite leaders, but he had always tended to come out for restraint, inasmuch as he could argue it was for the good of everyone in the community. For Mzingeli, his own experiences brought him closer to those men and women victimized for their participation in illegal trades such as prostitution and beer brewing.

Respect for women was the theme of discussion at an April 1950 RICU meeting. According to an account from the *African Weekly*, "strong disapproval of the insult and lack of respect towards African women by their men folk was voiced at this meeting." In typical Mzingeli style the issue was linked to race pride: "a race that subjected its women folk to indignities such as the African woman suffers today, could not achieve a solid progress and the respect of other races."[10] Here Mzingeli had appropriated the Pan-African race-pride rhetoric and applied it to this specific situation where African women were being harassed by the police and authorities, as well as women who were not getting sufficient respect from certain African men. That he did not limit the Pan-African appeal to elites, or to women as defined by marriage, was a new outlook for an African politician, separating him from the Bantu Congress politicians who saw themselves as the "guardians" of African custom and therefore wanted to increase their control of women, with the state's help.[11]

The attendance at the March 1950 meeting had been 320 people. But now, for the first time, the women most threatened by raids were coming to Mzingeli and giving the RICU the sort of numbers he had never been able to muster from among the population of male wage laborers. Seeing the chance to develop a new sort of community politics out of the situation, he did not back down from the opportunity. He spent the next few years walking the fine line between this new constituency of "displaced women" and the growing number of elite men and women who continued to seek ways of protecting themselves from the marginal classes in the township. Both groups wanted representation of their interests to the European administration, and Mzingeli believed that he and the RICU could effectively serve both these communities.

At first, Mzingeli deftly incorporated the demands of those wanting his protection from eviction with the demands of those seeking to distance themselves from the poorer, "less respectable" residents. Using the raids and the women's demands to attack the nature of racial segregation and the inhuman treatment such women received during the raids, he challenged the image of a paternalistic settler state looking out for the interests of African subjects. Writing in the RICU newsletter, which he sent to Rita Hinden and the Fabian Socialists in London, Mzingeli told the following story:

> The other day a white gentleman was talking to our General Secretary [Mzingeli], "You Africans are now very happy under the Europeans. In the past you used to be hunted and hounded by the Matebele [*sic*] . . . You are happy now," said the white gentleman. The General Secretary had nothing to say to this optimistic remark, but the gods that control human destiny gave the answer which the white man needed, though he did not expect it. It was not three minutes when the General Secretary and the white gentleman stopped talking but looked in amazement at the sight of African women, some single, others with their children on their back, running and leaping over trenches, while the police were in hot pursuit. "What is that?" asked the white gentleman. "They are running away from the Matebele," said the General Secretary in dry humour. That closed the conversation.[12]

The battle in support of these women was not easily won within the Township. This was especially the case in the newly completed National Section, where the N(UA)ARA had created more tensions and ill feelings over recent divorces by men with their *mapoto* wives. The new wives, respectably married with a certificate, did not appreciate the continued presence of prostitutes and *mapoto* women in the Township, and as the RICU meeting described above shows, they were not allies with these women, and had not really been sad to see them go.

After the protests against the imposition of the N(UA)ARA by the RICU on behalf of poorer women, some among the respectable classes began to see the forced removal of women by the state as a positive contribution. For example, an article by "Our Reporter" in the *African Weekly* of August 1949 praised the work of the European authorities in implementing the Urban Areas Act and thereby forcing women to behave more responsibly.

> Before a little over a year ago, the freest section of the African community was the African woman. I am speaking of the unattached. She lived a completely free life, without the common obligations attached to the common decent person. . . . [Then] 1946 came, spelling doom to the lives of these women. . . . The enforcement of the N(UA)ARA after 1946 "haunted them like a ghost." They were arrested, as they still are, and finger-printed and fined, and threatened with a prison sentence if caught again.[13]

Such views show how far the elite class in the township had come to see the benefits of strict control of women's movement in the township.

Mzingeli's views on the raids on "displaced women" were carefully worded to portray concern both for the rights of these women and for the "rights" of their male guardians to control them. This worked to appease criticisms from men and women that the RICU was defending prostitution. Mzingeli defended his intervention on behalf of women who had come to the RICU, but this was combined with a more conservative view of women in town:

> Both men and women, of all tribes, in the Harari Township appreciate the measures intended to protect African daughters or to prevent any women who attempt to evade the control of the husband, guardian or parents by coming into the urban areas without any permit. But it is respectfully pointed out that in this respect, justice can only be done by tracing such offenders on request made by their guardian or as the case may be.[14]

This letter revealed Mzingeli's appeal to earlier debates and arguments over who should control the movement of women between the rural and urban areas and took as a premise that there was always a guardian who was responsible for a woman's actions and whereabouts. This was, of course, not always the case, and as Mzingeli's test case examples suggested, there were women in the urban areas without the link to a "traditional" guardian in the rural or urban areas.

By 1952 the continued sweeps of the township resulting in arrests of women now became a threat to the RICU itself, as two-thirds of its six thousand members were women. The "respectable" name of the RICU was threatened at times by association as some women, when refused entry into the township beer hall, showed their RICU membership card to the police as "the badge" of their right to do as they pleased.[15] Mzingeli at one point asked the membership at a public meeting to "come clean" and admit if anyone had been telling women that they did not have to seek permits to stay in the township if they were members of the RICU. At the same meeting, however, Mzingeli appears to have floated the idea of a civil disobedience campaign on the part of township women. Rather than running away from the police, Mzingeli advised women to "give themselves up" during township raids. He asked those who were not arrested to join the others at the police station. He also suggested that "husbands and relatives should stand and watch their wives or relatives off, but must not interfere with police work."[16]

Such advice demonstrates Mzingeli's awareness of international and regional events. He had only to look at the South African ANC's defiance campaigns for an example of passive resistance to segregation laws. It is also an interesting commentary on the gendering of politics. In this example, as Mahatma Gandhi had shown previously in his campaigns for Indian rights in South Africa, the ability of women and men to show discipline and solidarity by not interfering with police work called for a collective strength and a greater level of discipline than that of direct confrontation.

The director of the Salisbury Native Administration Department, Col. George Hartley, upset by Mzingeli's call for a campaign of defiance, countered with a smear campaign against Mzingeli in the press, charging him with encouraging prostitution.[17] The suggestion of such a protest campaign also illustrates the central role women played, as well as Mzingeli's understanding of the impact such a protest may have had on the international image of Rhodesia just prior to the founding of the Federation. Mzingeli did not back down against Hartley's insinuations that the RICU was supporting immorality in its defense of women against the police raids. Mzingeli's rebuttal to Hartley was printed in one of Salisbury's European papers, the *Sunday Mail.* He replied that "immorality and unhygienic standards are things we do not wish to see in Harare." He then took the opportunity, as was his style, to let European readers know that he and other African leaders were not threatened by Hartley's attempt to cover the real meaning of the raids with appeals to alleged immorality. Mzingeli stated:

> The African, like all men, claims the right to stay with his wife where he works. We strongly disapprove of the raids as such in the area which has been proclaimed for the exclusive use of the African people. We are indeed alarmed at the practice of conducting police raids against the African people at any pretext, particularly when these raids involve the arresting of mothers and pregnant women.[18]

Mzingeli addressed the contradiction of Rhodesian urban segregation, turning the idea of separate communities into an appeal for equal citizenship and equal respect for gendered rights in marriage. He was aware of the rhetorical strategy offered by a state that on the one hand blamed Africans for living "immoral lives" in the townships while on the other hand refusing to give Africans legitimate powers to govern their own communities. He therefore utilized a rhetoric that would be common in African nationalism, one that shifted the responsibility for poor living conditions and immorality back onto the European-controlled state.

Mzingeli had been careful to organize a defiance campaign, but the women who sought protection from the RICU were not always concerned with larger issues, nor did they have the necessary commitment to make such a campaign successful. For many women involved, civil disobedience was not a real option given the precarious nature of their existence in the township and the difficulties caused by arrests, fines, and most of all the threat of being evicted from the township. As in most cases involving physical abuse and intimidation, most of the women's grievances were directed toward those directly carrying out the state's policies—the African police and African court interpreters. A number of these women turned to Mzingeli to negotiate directly for them with the Native Administration Department in order to address the more blatant forms of abuse. As Mzingeli and the RICU went to new levels of strength on the support of women in need of collective protection and voice, the gap between elite women's participation in politics and that of the poorer, "displaced" women became more clearly articulated. Women such as Mrs. Mzingeli, aligned with the elites of the township— including Mai Musodzi, Mai Sondayi, Mrs. Daniels, and others—remained active on other fronts as the RICU took on issues they had been addressing on an individual basis in previous years. The elite members of the RICU attempted to forge a link with the poorer women by forming the RICU Women's Club. The club was modeled after the numerous successful women's clubs created by churches. In early 1952, at the height of women's participation in the RICU, Patrick Pazarangu, the longtime secretary of the RICU, made the following statement of the club's principles:

> to foster unity among the women folk in Harare, to instill a sense of responsibility and dignity in African women and to find means whereby the evils of town life to which many women have fallen prey can be combated. The present town woman has lost all her dignity and town life is leading her to destruction.[19]

Pazarangu's characterization is certainly directed toward a class of women who had little in common with the elite women associated with the RICU's women's section, or the Helping Hand Club, or other African women's groups. The RICU Women's Club hoped to rival the church and burial societies, but it was never able to compete successfully with these more established groups. The women's section of the RICU did, however, remain active behind the scenes stressing the social goals of education for family life and good morals. Beyond these clubs, elite women's involvement in politics remained primarily out of public view. Women would at times hold "birthday parties" where politics would be "quietly discussed." Such a strategy was often a result of the women or their husbands working for the government as teachers, clerks, and other key positions where political participation could lead to losing one's job.[20]

Women, Work, and Township Politics

The RICU had attempted to mobilize an alliance of poor and elite around the anger and frustration of the women who had rallied around Mzingeli and the RICU between the 1948 General Strike and the implementation of the N(UA)ARA in the early 1950s. Once the realities of the new restrictions had been accepted—and more importantly, new ways to circumvent them had been found—the most unrepresented section of the urban population, poor women, continued to survive in a community without recourse to group action or political protest.

At the same time, the urban African population grew far beyond the increases in the available housing stock promised in the 1950s. South African–style squatter settlements did not occur given the regulations of the Land Apportionment Act and the urban land-use controls of the N(UA)ARA. Instead, Salisbury's "squatters" were living inside existing housing as illegal lodgers and "registered guests." Dr. A. J. Wilkins, medical officer of health for Salisbury, who had worked in that position since 1935, commented on the overcrowding in Harare township: "The worst slums in Salisbury, particularly on the basis of overcrowding, are in Harari. And a large section of Harari is one big slum. The overcrowding is caused by illegal occupation."[21] Wilkins's evidence indicates how the N(UA)ARA had failed by the mid-1950s to adequately "control" the urban population and therefore failed to achieve the goal of limiting and stabilizing the urban labor force. By 1956 the estimated annual labor turnover rate in the industrial areas was still as high as 85 percent.[22] In the early 1950s the possible use of more women in formal employment became an unintended consequence of the employment-tied housing provisions of the N(UA)ARA, inadvertently making women's labor power more advantageous to local industrialists.[23] The European planners of the N(UA)ARA had assumed women would be housed primarily as wives, but the labor shortage in the early stages of the Federation period created opportunities for women to join the workforce in greater numbers as wage laborers and especially as "nurses" or "nannies" for the fast-growing European population.

Mzingeli's organizing of women against the N(UA)ARA had helped bring on a government investigation into the working conditions for African urban women. The board overseeing African employment observed in 1952 how that "African organisations are getting concerned over some of the existing conditions of employment of African women" and "that quite a number of women are members of African organizations in Bulawayo and Salisbury, and that trouble may be anticipated fairly soon, unless steps are taken to put their working conditions on a better footing."[24] This led to the Commission on Women in Employment, which heard testimony from witnesses in key cities and towns, including Mzingeli.

In Salisbury, it was the tobacco-processing firms that relied the most on female workers. George Hartley acknowledged to the commission that in the context of certificates of service for women, employers, instead of breaking the law, hired only married women, "whose husbands have got authorised accommodation in the townships."[25] Mr. S. E. Aitken-Cade of the Tobacco Warehouse, the largest tobacco-processing firm in Salisbury in the early 1950s, reported that 98 percent of its women employees were married. Asked if this was "not of some concern to him," he replied, "Yes, but it is the restriction on accommodation that makes employment of women so attractive to us. If accommodation were available then I think we would not be so keen on having them but as it is we know there is no more accommodation."[26] For many male migrants, the possibility of bringing their wives to live in houses in Harare township and later in New Highfield allowed them more readily to accept their wives' role as fellow wage earners. However, gaining married housing was not in itself sufficient motivation for some men who continued to oppose the idea of wives working outside of the home.[27]

As more women worked in industry, it became necessary to provide assistance to them in terms of child care and other services. Influential township women such as Mrs. Frank and Mrs. Sondayi organized self-help social services for women and children in the township. The African Women's Helping Hand Club, an organization established in 1953 in Harare with the idea of assisting mothers and children in need, was led by Mrs. Jasper S. Savanhu and Mrs. Emma Chigoma, among others, and they proposed to help needy families through cash payments.[28] These women were community leaders, even if they were not officially in the leadership of any African political organization. In later years both Mrs. Chigoma and Mrs. Sondayi served at times on the Harare township advisory board. These women maintained visible roles that helped to define the possibilities of female leadership in local politics.

By the early 1950s women were increasing their numbers within the formal economy, particularly among domestic workers who were given the task of raising the children of post–World War II white immigrants. The increase in this employment caused some degree of animosity between the sexes, particularly when women often commanded higher wages relative to male domestics. Male domestics, who had previously monopolized all aspects of domestic service employment, now relinquished the responsibility of raising European children, and in many cases also of cleaning houses. The increase in employment of female domestics not only caused friction over higher wages, but also brought out insinuations that such women were not working as hard as men. Many Europeans, especially those of the "older Rhodesian" generation, shared this view and saw the new postwar European immigrants as guilty of "ruining" the economic relationship between European house- holders and their domestics by paying too high a wage, or providing them with too many gifts, or even breaking social taboos by eating meals or drink- ing alcohol with their African employees at the same table.[29] In 1952 the labor officer for Salisbury wrote that "the employment of female native ser- vants in Salisbury has got away to a poor start and it is surprising to note the very substantial concessions which employers will allow to girls which they will seldom allow to male servants."[30] The resistance of the older Rhodesians to female domestics, and the resistance of male domestics to the loss of their employment, meant that women had a difficult time replacing male domes- tics outside of the woman's role as a nanny.[31]

Women's higher wages in domestic service also contributed to a biased view among working men toward women in other types of employment, although wages remained lower for women in industry. For example, women earned less than men in the tobacco industry, and even less if they were mar- ried women living with their husbands, as the employers were therefore not responsible for their rents. Testifying before the 1952 National Native Labour Board's Commission on Women in Employment, which was appointed in large part because of the influence women's demands gained through the RICU, Mzingeli was asked to present the RICU's position on women's wages. Mzingeli told the commission how women in the RICU had complained about unequal pay. Some of the women had told him how after working in the clothing industry for over one and a half years, they were still getting only £1 per week, which was less than what men were getting paid from the start. "They feel they should be paid equal pay for equal value," Mzingeli told the commission. Mr. Godlonton, the chair, asked how African men felt about this. Mzingeli explained how "the permanent residents in Harari would welcome reasonable wages being received by wives when they go to work. . . . The men from reserves who come and work for a few months and then go back do not think a woman should be paid equal pay."[32] Mzingeli's comments reflected the inherent tensions within the township between different groups of residents and their outlook on women's work, tensions that would contribute to violence against female workers in 1956.

Tobias Nhapi, as a member of the RICU executive, recalled accompanying Mzingeli to the industrial sites to try to keep the peace at times between groups of male and female workers. Rumors would sometimes surface that a certain firm—a bakery, for example—was about to hire women. Men, both those who worked there and the unemployed, would show up in order to physically keep the women from entering the gates of the bakery. Mzingeli and the RICU would do their best to sort out the conflict and convince both

sides to avoid violence, often resorting to tipping off the police that something might happen on a given morning. Nhapi also remembered a general
view held by men at the time that women were more popular with employers
because they worked harder and were generally more efficient: "Men were
slow because at times they took time off to smoke cigars."[33] In addition,
Mzingeli would announce new work he had heard about for women. At an
RICU public meeting on a Sunday afternoon in October 1952, Mzingeli
opened the meeting by announcing "that there would be a post for African
women in a new wheat factory to be opened about ten days time in the
Industrial sites, and that young women anxious to work should interview him
for details." Mzingeli was therefore not only representing women's interests
to the authorities but serving as a pseudo labor broker as well.[34]

Advisory Board Elections

While Mzingeli continued to address the demands of women residents and
workers, he found himself challenged by an elite group of young men who
wanted to take over control of the local township advisory board. Even with
a restricted electorate, the board elections soon became a big contest
between Mzingeli's RICU and other leaders in the township. Mzingeli and
the RICU had easily won a majority in the first three elections of 1947, 1948,
and 1949; but in 1950 the RICU's claim to be the voice of township politics
was shaken by a rival party known as the Harare Residents Party (HRP).
During the 1950 campaign, the HRP succeeded in defeating most of the
RICU candidates. As each voter could select eight members, the number of
candidates the RICU ran hurt its prospects: twenty compared with the HRP's
eight candidates. This strategy worked for the HRP as the final tally showed
Mzingeli and Pazarangu as the top vote getters, but the rest of the advisory
board consisted of HRP candidates, including Isaac Samuriwo, Jameson
Moyo, B. J. Mnyanda, J. P. Bassoppo-Moyo, Leopold Takawira, and P. G.
Phiri.[35] This list of HRP candidates contains many important future nationalists, indicating that the advisory board elections were more important as a
form of political representation than is often considered.[36] The RICU,
although upset over its lost majority in this new arena of electoral politics,
was at least able to celebrate Mzingeli's and Pazarangu's victories. The day
after the vote there was a "triumphant march of the supporters of the RICU
who on Sunday morning carried Charles Mzingeli round the Township for
all to see that he was still on the Advisory Board. He was borne aloft in a
chair, manned by four strong men, very much like his holiness the Pope,
while the Sena reed players blasted a tune behind."[37] Mzingeli, a devout
Catholic who had been excommunicated from the Church because of his
political activities, must have enjoyed this procession.[38]

In the 1951 election, J. G. S. Chingattie, a young educated man who had recently arrived in Harare township as a social worker with the Rhodesian Railways ran an election campaign complete with handbills and a lorry with loudspeakers attached to it. The lorry would move slowly around the township while supporters of the Residents Party would call out praises for their candidates. They also made a special effort to recruit voter support among the migrant population—the men Mzingeli and others in the RICU had experienced problems with in the past. The RICU complained that the Residents Party had made promises to the migrant workers that were impossible to keep, including offers of new uniforms, new work boots, better housing, and better beer in the municipal beer halls.[39] By taking a direct approach to hostel-dwelling workers, the HRP won the 1950 election and defeated the majority of RICU candidates, although Mzingeli and Pazarangu did remain on the board. According to *African Weekly* reports, turnout was higher than in 1949, despite heavy rains, as the HRP organized trucks to bring migrant workers back and forth from their rooms.

Mzingeli no doubt understood the serious challenge presented by Chingattie's platform and tactics, and he attacked the HRP in the African press two weeks before the 1951 election. "Mr. Chingattie's party stands for (a) Better beer and Better Beer-Halls; (b) Better and more Housing (*Dzimba Dzakanaka*) etc." But, according to Mzingeli, such a platform "corresponds well with the word in brackets behind his [Chingattie's] name." The word appearing on the HRP's handbills after Chingattie's name was "*Mapipi*," which Mzingeli translated as "magician."[40] Mzingeli continued this underhanded critique in the RICU's newsletter, questioning Chingattie's frequent movement from job to job—the railways, the hospital—and his scholarship to India. Mzingeli then compared the HRP to the joke about two brothers who come into a town, then one sets up a sweets factory and the other a dentist's office: "It will be seen that both businesses were there for their self gain rather than helping the unfortunate residents."[41]

Perhaps it was the inability of the HRP to deliver on all its promises that returned an RICU majority to power in the 1951 advisory board elections. Mzingeli was once more the top vote getter, and he responded to the news of the RICU's victory from London as the vote in December coincided with his visit there. In his victory speech, published in the *African Weekly*, he wrote:

> Our opponents must admit now that the Reformed ICU is an organisation of the people, for the people and by the people to paraphrase President Abraham Lincoln's definition of democracy. . . . It now rests with you [the residents of Harare] to see that your representatives to the Native Advisory Board make every effort that you wish them to. Harare Township is our home, a permanent home in the urban area where we must be able to help ourselves by creating happy surroundings for ourselves and our children.[42]

Figure 3.1. Charles Mzingeli at reception, Harare township, February 3, 1952. Mzingeli wrote on the back of the photo: "first from front Row: My Niece Miriam, Mrs. Mzingeli, my Grand Niece Sepiwo, my self, my little Grand Niece Janett, and the Vice President RICU, Mr. S. Maviyane." Photo by A. D. Ndindah, Salisbury. Source: Rhodes House Library, MSS. Brit. Emp. S. 365, box 99, file 3, fols. 63–50.

This period, 1948–52, represented Mzingeli's best years as a community leader. He had survived the backlash against him after the 1948 General Strike, and his organization had gained popularity through his role as mediator between the vulnerable residents and the state during the implementation of the N(UA)ARA.

A crowning moment affirming his leadership role in these years was his trip to England from October 1951 to January 1952. A farewell reception was held on a Saturday afternoon at the Harare Township Recreation Hall, where he thanked those who had supported him financially to make the trip, "'especially,' Mzingeli said, 'Europeans, Indians and Coloureds, who took great interest in the matter.'" He spoke briefly, providing a glimpse into his Pan-African vision, while also reiterating his belief in multiracial coalitions:

"I believe time has come now when the cream of the Colony, the intelligentsia should unite and join hands for the emancipation of the African people right

Figure 3.2. Crowd of supporters at Mzingeli's reception, Harare township, February 3, 1952. Mzingeli noted on the back: "The man in the uniform behind me in the right corner is a Union Messenger." Photo by A. D. Ndindah, Salisbury. Source: Rhodes House Library, MSS. Brit. Emp. S. 365, box 99, file 3, fols. 63–50.

through Africa. . . . What I would like to see is a united front for the working class irrespective of colour." When asked if he might stay in Europe for good, he replied, "Even if I were offered employment in America, England, or elsewhere I would not take it for I have great respect for my country and my people. I cannot even stay in Europe a little longer than necessary."[43]

Mzingeli's London visit was organized with the assistance of the Fabian Colonial Bureau and the British Trade Union Congress (TUC). During his stay he met and traveled around London with a "Walcott from the West Indies." This was likely Frank Walcott from Barbados, a trade unionist who, much like Mzingeli, did not begin his career as part of the elite but who, unlike Mzingeli, went on to have a successful career as a trade union leader and would become a nationalist hero. In 1951 it is likely that Mzingeli saw the same future trajectory for himself.[44]

The advisory board elections continued to grow in importance and in terms of participation during the early 1950s. By 1954 the polling "was

Figure 3.3. Charles Mzingeli (right) and RICU vice president Solomon Maviyane (left), on back of a lorry heading to a political ceremony in Harare township, February 3, 1952. Photo by A. D. Ndindah, Salisbury. Source: Rhodes House Library, MSS. Brit. Emp. S. 365, box 99, file 3, fols. 63–50.

the heaviest yet known," with residents casting their votes from early in the morning until eight in the evening when the police had to assist, as many people "returned home bitterly disappointed because they had not voted."[45] In that year Mzingeli again received the most votes, 608 compared to the next two candidates, Patrick Pazarangu with 271 votes and J. P. Bassoppo-Moyo with 208. This exercise in electoral politics within Harare township was soon to be eclipsed by new nationalist political organizations, but even when considering their limited powers, the advisory boards, particularly through the electoral process, give an indication that representative politics had a real following in the urban areas. In the next few years, as will be discussed in the next chapter, the creation of the Salisbury City Youth League and the Southern Rhodesian African National Congress would make demands on residents, particularly young people, for a new kind of politics that would discredit Mzingeli and his colleagues.

Women as Political Leaders

Mzingeli had taken on the issue of women's employment as an organizing tactic as more women joined the RICU, but there is also evidence that women were challenging him and others in the executive to be more aggressive in their approach. At an RICU meeting in October 1952, Tobias Nhapi spoke, as he often did, on the general condition of low wages for African workers. "Mr. Nhapi said the majority of African employees to his knowledge received 12/6 per week, and all the employer does is pay rent for one who has accommodation either in hostel or in the Harari township." A Mr. Chikwana spoke of a case where a man received 35/– per month and had to feed a wife and four children. He said the man's "reason for accepting this post was because of the house that he would lose if he did not find work by a specific time." Chikwana agreed with Nhapi that it was common for men to receive only 12/6 a week without food rations.[46]

While men of the RICU were lamenting low wages, one of the most outspoken women in the RICU, Eleanor (Elena) Solomon, went further in her oratory about the gender gap in wages, this time in reference to the higher wages female domestics were making compared to men in industry:

> Mrs. E. Solomon said in many respects women were better paid than men, but in spite of that a man is prepared to spend his meagre pay to make present for a woman even though he may have no shirt or spare trousers. She urged the workers not to depend on the way they were making the ends meet to-day. Even if you have land to supplement your income in the native reserve, time is coming when you shall have one home only, she said. She thought it was a good thing that women did not have to carry registration certificates because husbands would be in trouble as they would steal [their] wife's situpa [pass] and attempt to claim better salary. (Applause!)[47]

The combination of the increased competition for low-paying industrial work and the presence of higher-paid women in domestic work created a situation where a backlash against women workers was possible. This no doubt occurred at the individual level, but it was to surface publicly during the bus boycott of September 1956.

At a November 1952 RICU meeting, an older gentleman, a Mr. Guvira, kept up the theme of the "struggle for the breeches" (or trousers), noting that women were putting pressure on men to be more defiant. Mr. Guvira told the gathering how

> even his forefathers were able to unite, but people now-days were too gullible, it takes them a long time to realise what is good for them. Mr. Guvira, thought that there was a cause why there was "Mau Mau" problem down in East Africa. He said treatment of African people were getting from bad to worse both in the reserves

and in urban areas. He said time and again, our women have asked us to lend them our trousers so that they may try to lead us.[48]

This rhetorical appeal, expressed by both women and men in the township, for a stronger African political movement willing to stand up and fight against injustice and oppression was a familiar theme in the early 1950s, and Mzingeli, for all his efforts at organizing and fighting for residents' demands, would soon find himself unable, and perhaps more importantly unwilling, to take on a more radical position against the settler state.

A more traditional nationalist history would simply describe this transition as part of a natural "changing of the guard," relying on a teleology from a less cosmopolitan "protonationalism" represented by early movements such as Mzingeli's RICU to a more enlightened group of nationalist leaders who were to take up the reigns of the struggle. In doing so, such narratives fail to appreciate the nuances in the shift in outlook from Mzingeli to the new leaders. This transition also created a change in tactics toward the poor and working-class men and women who were the first to have given Mzingeli the support he sought for so many years. His support from poor women in particular was matched by his reciprocal notion of public service. Township residents supported him for as long as they did because he had proven his ability to address their demands, usually by means of personal interventions on their behalf with the municipal administration, or through the collective threat of strikes and protests that resulted in a less stringent enforcement of laws against women in the township. Mzingeli's politics therefore reflected a reciprocity of service that went beyond the stereotypical portrayal of his generation of township leaders in southern Africa. He was neither simply a "yesman" nor a self-serving politician. Given the environment in which Mzingeli operated and the long years of holding on to a vision of community politics that seemed very few others shared, his building up of the RICU to over five thousand supporters was quite an achievement. Much of this success was predicated on his understanding of the central role of women in township life and township women's willingness to stand up for their rights in ways the majority of men were incapable of doing in those years. As the next chapter shows, younger men who grew up in the townships were soon ready to challenge Mzingeli's leadership and rework the gender dynamics of community and national politics.

4

Changing Tactics

Youth League Politics and the End of Accommodation

In the early 1950s, at a time when the British were beginning to develop ways to accommodate nationalist leaders' demands to decolonize the Empire's African possessions, white politicians in Southern Rhodesia developed and advocated to Britain a plan to unite Southern Rhodesia with the two British colonies of Nyasaland and Northern Rhodesia. This Central African Federation would last for about ten years (1953–63) and proved to be very profitable for white interests, particular for those in Salisbury who made their city the capital of the Federation. Increased demands for copper from Northern Rhodesia benefited businesses in Southern Rhodesia as well. African politicians in all three territories, after many initially worked within the framework of the proposed "partnership" between the races, began by the late 1950s to organize a common strategy to end the Federation in order to move toward greater African political and economic advancement—and majority rule. During and after the battle over federation in the early 1950s, at the local level in Harare township, only the RICU had any sizable active mass support, and here Mzingeli's leadership had proven itself to be non-confrontational. The RICU continued to control the township's advisory board and membership of the Salisbury and District African Welfare Society, the two government sponsored bodies in which Africans had some representation.[1] From the vantage point of European authorities at the beginning of the Federation, the potential for organized opposition in Southern Rhodesia on the same scale and intensity that was developing in Northern Rhodesia, Nyasaland, and South Africa was viewed as slim. By the end of the 1950s, however, African nationalists in Southern Rhodesia would soon develop an organization capable of challenging white minority rule.

In the early 1950s the Federation had opened up possibilities for African political representation through six seats reserved for Africans in the thirty-five-member Federal Parliament (two from each of the three federal territories). In Southern Rhodesia, this meant that the African representatives were elected by a majority of white voters.[2] Mzingeli vehemently opposed the creation of the Federation and used what connections he had in Britain to try to stop it. As with so many political battles in Southern Rhodesia, however, no amount of written protests and appeals to British friends was strong enough to stop the creation of the Federation. Once created, as Michael West has shown, those African politicians who had worked with Mzingeli to oppose it, including Joshua Nkomo and Stanlake Samkange, quickly turned around and offered themselves as candidates for the federal parliament. Mzingeli contends that they did so after having agreed with him to boycott the federal elections. Huggins's party, the Federal Party, nominated two other Africans who had come out in favor of Federation, Jasper Savanhu and Mike Hove, both journalists—part of the African intelligentsia who had used the African press as a vehicle for social and political advancement. The predominantly white electorate passed over Nkomo and Samkange and elected Savanhu and Hove. Savanhu's ability to reemerge as an African member of Parliament after having started out much like Mzingeli shows the mobility Savanhu's education and social credentials offered.

But the anti-Federation campaign and the subsequent decision of the more educated elites to run for office marked the beginning of the end for Mzingeli's contribution to nationalist politics. Mzingeli would later reflect on how these Federal elections changed his view of his former allies in the anti-Federation campaign: "The boycott decision was to be treated as a secret weapon. But when it was announced that African Federal members of Parliament would be treated the same as European members regarding payment, allowances and other privileges, my friends broke the pledge and stood for election. It was then that I found difficulty in working with opportunists."[3]

Along with the failure of the anti-Federation campaign, Mzingeli was soon to suffer further setbacks in township politics. His hold over residential issues was first challenged by the Harare Civic Association (HCA), which developed an increasingly critical approach toward Mzingeli and the Harare township advisory board.[4] The HCA made demands similar to the RICU's in the 1940s: lower rents, further electrification of township homes, and better police protection for residents. Many of the prominent leaders in the association—including Shato Nyakauru, Reuben Jamela, and George Nyandoro, all of whom had previously been close to Mzingeli—were now beginning to part ways with him. Shato and Jamela had already established themselves as prominent and capable trade union leaders, and were beginning to enter Mzingeli's turf as executive members of the Harare Civic Association.[5]

Other public figures in the township had begun to challenge Mzingeli's popular base of support from working women. Mr. A. Mukarakate, "a prominent boxing promoter and well-known social figure of Highfields," formed the Harare Employed Women's League in July 1954.[6] Mukarakate told the African press that he had founded the League "because he had observed most men employed in towns did not respect those members of the fair sex who were in employment," and that the league's goal was "to afford its members the necessary protection."[7] Mukarakate's league was successful in attracting many women working as domestics away from the RICU.[8] One aspect of the "protection" offered by the Employed Women's League involved eliciting subscriptions not only from working women but also from rural parents who allowed young women to come and work in the city: "When parents in the reserves allow their daughters to come to the urban areas for employment they do not know what difficulties the girls face. We as an organisation are interested to see that these girls are well treated. A girl who comes to Salisbury in the name of the league will be assisted by the league."[9] The speeches given at the Employed Women's League's social gathering on July 10, 1954, expressed the paternalistic attitudes of elite township men toward young women. A pressing issue at that moment was whether single women should move into the newly completed women's hostel in Harare township. One of the many township VIPs in attendance, Isaac Samuriwo, told the girls how he had noticed that they were "confused" over this issue. "He reminded them that the English people wanted a person to obey first then complain afterwards." He then told the women not to be confused by calls to "refuse to occupy the hostel" because such a tactic would only harm the women.[10]

As an example of the paternalism of the times, Reverend Chieza of the American Methodist Church lectured the girls on restraint: "I am advising you to hasten slowly in your actions and to watch your company and other things carefully. . . . Keep your ways clean. I believe some of the young men here want to marry and are watching your league, if your league is good they will come to your leaders and get girls with good characters."[11] In contrast, Mzingeli advised women in a much more active and straightforward manner. A few months later in November 1954, when township women were upset over the decision by the municipality to stop their access to market gardens near the eastern side of the Makabusi River adjacent to the township, Mzingeli "urged the women and their husbands to join trade unions," but added that "women must form small vigilant committees that can put their claims clearly and strongly before the Board and the Authorities."[12]

As in other situations where his leadership had been challenged, Mzingeli did not accept Mukarakate's Employed Women's League without writing to criticize him in the African press. After hearing that Mukarakate had gone directly to the European authorities to discuss women's complaints over the proposed rents in the new Carter House women's hostel, Mzingeli became suspicious. As if this were not enough, Mukarakate had allegedly stated publicly that Mzingeli and the RICU were opposed to the building of the women's hostel. In his response, Mzingeli's refuted Mukarakate's claim and then entered into a characteristic personal attack:

> To this end, I am in sympathy with Mr. Mukarakate, whose so-called Women's Union came into existence only a few months ago. He will no doubt be interested to learn that the question of a girl's hostel was brought to the notice of the public by the "Christian Citizen Committee of the Methodist Church" long before he was born and I supported the idea all along amidst the opposition of the local Africans, the so called *vana vevu* [sons of the soil]. . . . Mr. Mukarakate would be doing the community some service if he organised an organisation to accomplish some genuine good rather than seeking to be a rival of the innocent Reformed ICU."[13]

Mukarakate resigned his position in 1955, but the emergence of his group pointed out the weakening hold of the RICU over labor issues in the township. The growing size and complexity of the urban working population had begun to overshadow the RICU's community-based structure. Brian Raftopoulos has cited data on the African population in Salisbury showing an increase from 22,126 in 1936, to 28,119 in 1941, 45,993 in 1946, and 75,249 in 1951.[14] According to Raftopoulos, these demographic changes, along with a growing class of urban-based intellectuals and the construction of more housing in New Highfield and Mabvuku, contributed to Mzingeli's diminished control of township politics.[15]

If Mukarakate represented the RICU's loss of influence among working women, the biggest threat to Mzingeli's hold over township politics came from the Southern Rhodesian Trade Union Congress (SRTUC). Salisbury and Bulawayo trade unionists, notably the railway workers union led by Joshua Nkomo and Reuben Jamela's African Artisans Union, agreed upon a national Trade Union Congress constitution during a national unity conference in Gwelo in 1953. In 1954 the SRTUC was established with Nkomo elected president and Jamela elected vice president.[16] The SRTUC was more focused on workers' grievances than was the RICU, and more importantly it dealt directly with employers and the state on wage issues. Mzingeli had never developed a real workplace presence or even a negotiating role with employers, relying instead on direct appeals to the government and testimony before the National Native Labour Board and numerous commissions looking into African wages and living conditions.

Once the SRTUC was officially launched, Mzingeli was openly antagonistic to its presence in Harare, especially as large crowds came to hear the dynamic young president, Joshua Nkomo, who traveled from Bulawayo to help mobilize support among Salisbury workers. Following the recruitment of thousands of members based on the RICU's campaign against the implementation of the N(UA)ARA, Mzingeli by 1954–55 watched his support move away to new and more dynamic organizations.[17] Male workers, especially those in semiskilled and skilled occupations, were now joining the SRTUC and its affiliate unions. Jamela remembered how even in the late 1940s, he and other trade union leaders had decided it would be necessary to part ways with Mzingeli:

> We were running away from him [Mzingeli]. He thought we were against him, but we did not want to continue to mix everything. We wanted to organize genuine trade unions. He had no time for that, but just wanted everybody together, and still call it a trade union. We advised him to call it something else. We also informed him that we were not against him fighting for electricity in Harare, or for tarred roads and that we were together in this.[18]

Jamela's skill as a negotiator was proven in 1954 when he gained an agreement for African builders and artisans with the Salisbury City Council allowing them to obtain contracts from the city, but only for those artisans in Jamela's organization. Thus Jamela succeeded in gaining access to contracts previously denied to Africans by racial segregation laws in the Land Apportionment Act, which had codified the white builders' color bar and had limited African artisans to work outside of the city limits.[19]

The familiarity of many of the SRTUC leaders with Mzingeli's tactics and organization intensified the competition between the SRTUC and the RICU. Both groups held their meetings in Harare township on Sundays—Mzingeli's RICU meetings had been moved to Luna Park because his previous gatherings had become too large to fit in the Recreation Hall, so the SRTUC began to hold its meetings in the Recreation Hall. When the SRTUC asked Mzingeli to affiliate his union with them, he refused, countering with a public attack on the questionable legitimacy of the SRTUC Gwelo Convention constitution. He threatened to resign as leader of the RICU if the decision was made by RICU members to affiliate with the SRTUC. In the weeks that followed, the SRTUC hired a full-time organizing secretary, Mr. P. Kadzutu, who went to work immediately bringing in new unions while creating others. The next week, some RICU members requested that the RICU should also hire such a full-time organizer. Mzingeli rejected the proposal, saying that such work should be done by members on a volunteer basis, reflecting his trademark style for the previous twenty years.

After it became known that the RICU would not affiliate with the SRTUC, Kadzutu wrote a letter to the *African Weekly* defending the legitimacy of the SRTUC's constitution and the Gwelo Convention's decision to form a national trade union congress. Kadzutu explained how the RICU delegates at Gwelo had even agreed to allow its members to join the various unions represented by the SRTUC. He then went on to praise Mzingeli's leadership and his role as a prominent leader for so many years, setting up a critique of his intransigence: "If, on the other hand he should be uncooperative, he should know that he is abusing his talent and consequently disappointing the many people who repose great confidence in him."[20] Mzingeli countered two weeks later on the *African Weekly*'s letters to the editor page, chastising Kadzutu as a newcomer who did not have his facts right about the "Gwelo fiasco" and ending with a typically sardonic comment: "Who told him that my work as a Trade Unionist is well known to all and that I am highly respected for my integrity?" Mzingeli concluded that Kadzutu's "flattering remarks do not help him in his efforts to smash the Reformed ICU."[21]

For Mzingeli, the growth of a more focused labor union movement may have appeared to him as simply yet another "upstart" group threatening his control of the RICU, but in reality the situation was now fundamentally different. The loss of support came primarily in the form of alternative trade union and workers' associations that were more effective in addressing workplace issues than Mzingeli's RICU had been. Brian Raftopoulos has noted Mzingeli's disappointment in 1952 after learning that the International Confederation of Free Trade Unions (ICFTU), based in Brussels, had selected the SRTUC rather than the RICU as a recipient for its financial support.[22] This left Mzingeli with residential issues, which to a certain extent were about to be partially ameliorated by the building of improved housing and facilities in Mabvuku township and the New Highfield homeownership scheme in the coming years. Mzingeli was therefore losing his mass support, and what was left of his legitimacy was soon to be challenged and derided by the Salisbury City Youth League with its more confrontational tactics.

Elite Opportunities during the Federation Period

From the more educated elite African standpoint, the period of Federation offered room to maneuver in ways that would never have seemed possible only a few years previously. Federation had brought about some recognition, or at least the promise, of the "Imperial citizenship" that Mzingeli had so strongly advocated in previous years. As the door was opening a bit for the elite, those who had seen Mzingeli as a less educated local hero were passing him by as they put forward their claims to government positions and international trade union affiliations.

Among this new generation, however, was a group of educated young men employed in skilled occupations who quite clearly experienced the limits to the increased opportunities opening up in the labor market. Although they were now permitted to work as a junior clerk or accountant, for example, the laws and a prevailing racial discrimination—the color bar—meant they would not be allowed to run their own businesses in the city center; they would instead remain perpetual "junior" employees. Many of these men became the leadership nucleus of the Salisbury City Youth League in 1956.[23] After Jasper Savanhu and Michael Hove, the two editors of the African newspapers the *African Weekly* and *Bantu Mirror*, respectively, became the first African MPs in the newly established Federal Parliament in 1953, it was the young, often college-educated men at the rival newspaper, the *Daily News*, who would work to form a new political organization.[24] Modeled after the Youth Leagues in other African colonies and in particular South Africa, the Salisbury City Youth League (SCYL) became the springboard for a new style of local and national politics.

The *Daily News*, in keeping with the regulations of the N(UA)ARA, was responsible for housing its employees, so the newspaper rented a house for Fidelis Nhapi, Edson Sithole, Herbert Munagatire, and Nathan Shamuyarira.[25] Of this group, Nhapi and Sithole, along with Thompson Gonese and Enos Nkala, spent much of 1954 and 1955 discussing and arguing about how to form a more effective political organization in Southern Rhodesia. They were in close touch with the Nyasaland African National Congress and attended its meetings in Salisbury. One Nyasaland ANC member in particular, Dunduza Chisiza, who was employed by the Indian High Commissioner in Salisbury, provided support and ideas to the core organizing group from the *Daily News*. Perhaps the greatest influence of the Nyasaland ANC was its leaders' vocal disdain for Southern Rhodesian African elites and intellectuals during this period, through characterizations of them as puppets of whites who were more interested in joining multiracial organizations than African nationalist political organizations.[26] The support for the Federation by Hove, Savanhu, and Nkomo had shown to these young men that their most capable leaders were not going to challenge the system without some pressure.

Another influential figure in the core group was James Chikerema, who had been politically active in South Africa and was being closely watched by authorities due to his involvement in the African National Congress Youth League there, as well as in the South African Communist Party. Chikerema, according to Lawrence Vambe's account, was brought up under the Catholic discipline of his father, one of the founders of Kutama Mission in the Zwimba Reserve. Chikerema went to South Africa and eventually ended up in Cape Town where "he was irresistibly drawn to the Communist Party"—an act of rebellion, according to Vambe, against his parent's strict Catholic upbringing. After the election of the National Party in South Africa, and the campaign against the Communist Party there, Chikerema was tipped off that his name was on a list of foreign CP members who were to face arrest and deportation. He then returned to Southern Rhodesia. Vambe notes the importance of these years in Cape Town in forming Chikerema's political vision: "He had come into contact with some of the most eminent non-white intellectuals in South Africa, men and women with experience in resisting oppression. Now he was to begin to use his knowledge among his own people who were sorely in need of sophisticated leaders."[27] Fidelis Nhapi recalls Chikerema's role before SCYL took form:

> Chikerema was employed by Central African Airways in Belvedere. We used to go there during our lunch hour, or after work to meet him, asking him for information about the Youth League in South Africa. We used to ask him for advice as well. He was, however, not enthusiastic about taking part in the formation of the organisation, since he had been warned not to involve himself in politics.[28]

George Houser, the American civil rights activist and pacifist who became influential in Africa through his work for the American Committee on Africa, recalled that Chikerema had been in the ANC Youth League at Cape Town University before having to return to Southern Rhodesia. "He brought with him the South African Youth League constitution, which became the guideline for the Youth League that he helped set up in Salisbury."[29] The SCYL held its first public meeting in September 1956, at which only a handful of people turned up, including men such as Paul Mushonga, James Bassoppo-Moyo, and Rodrick Mangwiro.[30]

New Highfield became the natural base for the SCYL as many of the educated bachelors and married men relocated there. As Brian Raftopoulos notes, New and Old Highfield also began to represent a growing presence of individuals and families born in Southern Rhodesia, with "59.27% of families and 74.99% of lodgers" in 1957 being from Southern Rhodesia.[31] In this way, the demographics of the African townships created the possibility for a new generational politics. In 1956, after a meeting in which Chikerema was elected president, the decision was taken to create SCYL branches in Highfield as well as in Harare. Edson Sithole became chair of the Harare branch, while Herbert Munagatire was selected chair of the Highfield branch, as he had moved out of the *Daily News* quarters and had bought into the homeownership scheme. As each new section of New Highfield was completed and people moved in, a new branch was established.[32] The building of New Highfield accommodated nationalist leaders from other areas as well. For example, Maurice Nyagumbo attended political meetings as a delegate from Rusape, but later in 1957 he purchased a house in the Egypt Section of New Highfield. After 1958 Highfield had become the virtual headquarters of the nationalist movement, as the SCYL was transformed into the Southern Rhodesian African National Congress (SRANC). There was also, however, a very active political nucleus located in Mabvuku township. As the *Daily News* reported in November 1958, "For reasons that are difficult to explain, Mabvuku Township is gradually becoming the most active centre and the heart of the Congress movement in and around Salisbury."[33]

Prior to the creation of the SRANC, the SCYL's initial strategy involved taking control of the civic associations and the advisory board, and this meant direct confrontation with Mzingeli. George Nyandoro had learned how to use populist rhetoric from Mzingeli, having been himself a political student of Mzingeli's since 1949. Tobias Nhapi recalled Mzingeli's influence on Nyandoro's political awakening:

> He had learnt that [politics] from Mzingeli, since he had most of the books on politics. Mzingeli knew what to do politically. . . . He even referred Nyandoro to the library at Parliament to read books whose titles he had written down. This is also where Nyandoro learnt all the oppressive laws of the colonial government. After learning this, he concluded that the trade union movement had no direction, nor direct assistance to the people.[34]

According to Vambe's account, Nyandoro had received his formal education at the Anglican St. Mary's mission school in the Seke Reserve near Salisbury. He was employed in 1949 as a clerk for the African stores owned by the Farmers' Co-op and then worked as an accountant for other stores, eventually being promoted to an assistant accountant, which was "for him a real break-through, for generally such openings were reserved for white people only."[35] In 1956 he left to start his own business as an accountant for African businesses in the townships. In the process, he was constantly harassed by the police for allegedly circumventing segregation laws.

Nyandoro served as treasurer of the RICU in 1951, but he told Vambe that it was a position held "only in name," no doubt because Mzingeli was unwilling to relinquish his control of RICU finances. Nyandoro and Mzingeli worked together on the All-African Convention in 1952, but as Vambe tells it, "the time was to come when he [Nyandoro] felt that Mzingeli was an incorrigible obstacle to unity and that he must break with the lion-hearted patriot, who had suffered so much for his country."[36] Nyandoro had learned a great deal from Mzingeli, and his personal challenges to the new, more educated elite clearly echo Mzingeli's earlier campaigns against the elitist Congress in the 1940s. Michael West has described a rather theatrical moment in 1956 at a function in honor of the recently returned medical doctor Samuel Parirenyatwa. Nyandoro told the crowd of elites how "he 'opposed the creation of class barriers' among Africans. The Youth League, he continued, believed 'all Africans are the same. Chitepo, Parirenyatwa, [Stanlake] Samkange . . . should be the same; they should get equal treatment.' "[37] As West suggests, this speech took the wind out the elitist gathering of professionals who were invested in the partnership offered by the Federation and in their own prestige as the most respectable group in

Harare township. The power of such rhetoric was reminiscent of Mzingeli, and Nyandoro understood that this was necessary in order to guarantee the success of the SCYL with those township residents who were not invited to the reception—some of whom were watching the elite spectacle through the open windows from outside.[38]

By 1956 Mzingeli had become marginalized as the new generation of radical politicians stepped up to the podium, or at times literally took over the podium. In any case, Mzingeli did not give up without resorting to his caustic pen; he would spend the next phase of his career criticizing the younger leaders for their inability to control township violence during strikes and protests. He also chose to criticize them for what he saw as their personal concerns with gaining power rather than a genuine commitment to uplifting the entire township community. As Nyandoro and others were taking over RICU meetings, Mzingeli had grown to fear them, as they would address the gatherings without allowing others to speak. "Mzingeli found himself a mere listener, as they propounded, politically, on the problems people faced at work."[39] But in the press he criticized the new leaders and especially "Nyandoro, the George," as he sarcastically named him. The Youth League had been launched by educated young men cognizant of the worsening living conditions created by the N(UA)ARA in Harare township, and envious of the small number of elites who experienced economic advancement while they themselves saw only a future as "African clerks and teachers."[40] One month after the first inaugural meeting, and at a time when important bus boycotts were occurring in South Africa and the southern United States, the Salisbury bus boycott was the first real test of this new leadership style.

The Harare Bus Boycott and the Raiding of the Women's Hostel, September 17, 1956

In the archive files of the Salisbury Native Administration Department (NAD), there is a file labeled "Crimes: violence: Press Cuttings, 1952–1958." What is most interesting about the file is the way it documents the fear of the NAD officials over the eventual arrival of violent urban protest in Salisbury. The file starts with clippings from the *Sunday Mail* and *Rhodesia Herald* covering the 1952 East London and Kimberley riots in South Africa, as well as the Copperbelt riots of 1954, where the stoning of vehicles became a common tactic. In 1954 the *African Weekly*'s editors commented on the Copperbelt "Stone throwing Incidents" with an elitist tone: "We know that those who indulge in this sort of thing are the uneducated Africans but the harm they do to race relations has far reaching consequences."[41] The European press in Salisbury commented on the relative "peace" then being experienced, similar to the calm before the 1948 General Strike, and took it as a sign of the "benevolence" of whites toward "their" African populations. For example, the *Rhodesia Herald* highlighted the lack of stone throwing at the scenes of traffic accidents, in contrast to what had occurred in Northern Rhodesia and South Africa, and praised the exemplary "behaviour of Natives in townships and village settlements."[42] Four months later, however, such optimistic views of a contented "native" population were shattered by incidents in February 1956, as "a crowd of natives stoned a police truck in the Harari Location" following a liquor raid and arrests.[43] Stone throwing during liquor raids was not particularly out of the ordinary. It was the violence associated with the bus boycott in September 1956 that would make it clear how similar Salisbury's situation was to that of South Africa and the Copperbelt.

The violence associated with the September 1956 bus boycott shattered the illusion held by Salisbury's Native Administration and most of its white population that Southern Rhodesia was immune from violent rioting, but the events of the boycott also challenged the African leaders of the SCYL, Nyandoro and Chikerema in particular. Their attempt to use nonviolence was soon overshadowed by the spontaneous responses of the urban crowd. How they responded to criticisms after the riots suggests a different approach to political leadership and responsibility among this new generation than had been the case with Mzingeli and his colleagues after the major strikes and disturbances of the 1940s.

Although the bus boycott was planned as a peaceful protest against high bus fares and rising prices for other consumer items, by the evening of the first day things got out of hand and young men began throwing stones at cars and buses, tearing down shacks, and eventually smashing the windows in the girls' hostel, breaking in, stealing money and personal belongings, and raping sixteen residents. The established African leadership denounced the rapes and "hooliganism" as vehemently as did European officials. However, as time passed, the raping of the women from the hostel became incorporated into a nationalist argument about the need for discipline. The women in the hostel later were portrayed as having brought on the rapes as a form of punishment for disobeying the call to boycott buses. The rapes have been dealt with in ways that have maligned the victims either as secondary to the real "struggle" the boycott represents or even as sellouts who deserved to be raped. Nathan Shamuyarira, in his book *Crisis in Rhodesia* (1965), blamed the "girls" for the rapes:

> Girls in the Carter House, the only modern girl's hostel in Harare, were raped—and immediately there was an outcry from Europeans that this was utter barbarism and the wanton desire of strikers and rioters to victimize these girls. It was in fact calculated revenge by strikers for the way the girls had defied the strike orders and

boarded buses. One girl was heard saying she had enough money to pay the extra threepence; she would not obey the strike orders from poor men.[44]

Shamuyarira plays on the racist interpretation of such incidents as the over-riding factor, while at the same time basing his statement on the assumption that retribution against sellouts is acceptable, even in the form of raping women.

Another nationalist writing about the bus boycott made similar claims to rationalize the rapes as part of the larger nationalist struggle. Maurice Nyagumbo, in his book *With the People* (1980), blamed the police for causing the men to enter the Carter House, and then blamed the "girls" for having disobeyed:

> The police had provoked the African masses on their way to the townships [walk-ing home from work] and the reaction to that provocation was spontaneous. Of course, the leaders of the Youth League were terribly embarrassed by the unruly youths who had attacked the girls at the Carter House for ignoring the call for a boycott. Personally, I had no reason to feel regret for the incident. I actually believed that the girls deserved their punishment.[45]

These writers, in their attempt to place the boycott in a progressive line of achievements and victories toward the ultimate goal of independence, gloss over the actual contradictions—both in terms of class and gender—expressed in the event of the boycott, as well as displaying the sexist treat-ment of rape as the victim's fault.

The primary catalysts for the bus boycott had been the city council's pre-vious decision to give the African townships' bus routes to one company: the United Transport Company. Prior to the decision, three independent bus companies, two of which were owned by Africans, competed for passengers between the city and the townships. The opening of New Highfield further aggravated the situation, as fares to the city center were higher than the per-mile cost to Harare. Perhaps the most important catalyst for the boycott was the intervention of a group of leaders who wanted to challenge the city council on a number of issues, but who had yet to find a rallying point from which they could gain sustained support. The bus fare complaint became such an issue by September 1956. Led by members of the newly formed SCYL, the bus boycott Action Committee was successful in arousing the interest and support of African commuters. The Action Committee submit-ted a memorandum to the United Transport Bus Company and the minister of Roads, Local Government, and Housing, protesting the high fares and stating that "it is no exaggeration to say that over a third of the Africans in the urban areas, earn less than it costs to live." The Boycott Action Committee also made a quid pro quo demand for bus-fare subsidies: "If it pleases the Europeans and the Government to put African residential areas out of the sight of Europeans, they should pay for this pleasure by subsidising the cost to the Africans of traveling as far as they have to."[46] After calling off a boycott in August in the hopes of coordinating a series of protests in each of the three townships, the leadership decided to begin the boycott on September 17 in Harare. According to one participant, on the morning of the seventeenth, workers in Harare refused not only to board the buses but also to go to work.[47] Another boycott participant remembers how, in Harare, "some people boarded buses innocently, but we thought they were acting under instruction, so we had to beat them up. Beating people always sent a message quicker among them."[48]

The morning of the boycott went relatively smoothly. The African press reported that it was "very orderly," and that "a big mob of good-natured Africans" was congregated at the Harare bus stop.[49] The *Daily News* covered the morning's activities with an eyewitness report: "One of the men seen to be walking to his place of work was Mr. George Nyandoro, one of the leaders of the boycott. He was coatless and sweating, but obviously in very good spirits."[50] When evening came, the crowd "made up mostly of teenagers" was now being described as "restive and growing."[51] The troubles relating to the women's hostel started at this time, according to the account given by Nyandoro:

> Violence was provoked by the conduct of two women from a . . . Hostel near the bus terminal in Harare. [They] boarded the bus to town in the morning and returned in the evening in the empty busess. . . . The two women who were under police escort retorted to the cheers of the people—who were amused at seeing empty buses . . . that men had no money and they had the money sufficient to pay.[52]

The crowd left the bus stop and made their way to the Ardbennie Road, throwing stones at passing cars and at cars parked at Harare homes. The United Transport Company's waiting room was destroyed, which was specifically for passengers to Nyasaland, Kwenda, and Mtoro, and people waiting for long-distance buses were stoned. Then, near eight o'clock in the evening the crowd left the market area and "started a township-wide looting." They raided the Carter House women's hostel, stabbing one woman and raping sixteen others. A young girl was also raped at the No. 8 Football Field, and a man who tried to assist her was attacked. The police "only got the situation under control as late as 10 pm."[53]

More details were published in the *Rhodesia Herald* based on testimony at the court case against twenty-one men charged with the violence and rapes during the boycott. The testimony of Moses Mphala, a social welfare worker at the hostel, showed that the police had actually arrived at the women's hostel in time to protect the women but then decided to leave the women there to defend themselves. "The girls were told by the police: 'There is not time to look after you now, go to your rooms, lock your doors and turn out the lights.'" The police then left, "rescuing" the European warden. Immediately after the police trucks had left, according to Mphala, "he heard shouts of 'Get hold of them!' The crowd went to the hostel singing a Shona tribal song used in war. The words were, 'It is meat, it is meat; kill it kill it.'"[54] Sadly, then, the police had made the decision not to stay and protect the hostel when it would have been possible to do so. The police did not return until after 10 p.m., and reports indicate it took until after 11 p.m. to regain control of the hostel. In the meantime, a number of women, including two under the age of nineteen, were raped and beaten by the attacking mob.[55]

The following day blame was ascribed in the press to the leadership of the Boycott Action Committee for not being capable of controlling the crowd. In the week following the rapes, a reporter from the *African Weekly* observed a "turn of phrase" being used by the young men in the township. He saw these "scores of hooligans" as being "over-intoxicated by their supposed victory," in having escaped arrest. The Shona phrase, he wrote, was "coined to 'commemorate' the attack on the girls' hostel. . . . It is mainly used against any girl who assumes an indifferent attitude to anything the brutes do to attract attention. The literal translation of the phrase is 'Be THANKFUL that you were not in the hostel when I went there.'"[56] An *African Weekly* columnist, responding to letters printed in the European papers about the riots and the raid on the hostel, suggested that "they are shedding crocodiles tears," as it was originally European opposition to a women's hostel being built nearer to the European homes where these women were employed that had led to it being built in what he labels "a danger zone." He urged concerned Europeans to go to the city council and ask that such hostels be relocated nearer to the European neighborhoods.[57]

A week after the boycott and riots, James Chikerema told the African press that the action committee was against the hooliganism displayed on that night:

> It is a great pity that a hooligan element took the bus boycott for riots, and started engaging in acts that are a disgrace to our race. I as an individual, and the Action Committee which I represent, sympathizes very deeply with all the residents who were unfortunate victims of the riot. We have instructed local branches of our committee to discourage looting and rioting in any form.[58]

The events of the Bus boycott showed to the CYL that the forces they could "command" were, in fact, capable of considerable violence, but not necessarily always controllable. This was a point Mzingeli had already understood, as his life was in danger more than once by gangs of irate workers when rumors circulated that he had sold them out. In a 1971 interview, Mzingeli expressed his fears of the potential violence of the urban population he had defended over the years—in this case Shona men from the eastern regions bordering Mozambique:

> The Manyika were worthy—they were very strong chaps . . . a very strong people. They are easily organised and they are very emotional, and one had to be careful in working with them. . . . So one had to control them—they are really destructive from these other tribes, in braveness and I must say, give them that credit. And if you are not a good leader, they stone you.[59]

The relative failure of the bus boycott in Highfield also showed the extent to which intimidation was used to launch the boycott. The combination of physical intimidation, and the power it gave to those who used it, may have contributed to the "mob psychology" that eventually led to the violence against women in the Carter House women's hostel. The African press did its best to separate out the goals of the bus boycott from the mob violence that transpired, but the European press was quick to blame the SCYL leaders for the violence and so were some African leaders, particularly Mzingeli, who saw the "failure" of the boycott as a vindication of his own leadership style versus that of Chikerema and Nyandoro. In a letter to the *African Weekly*, Mzingeli chastised Chikerema for the way the committee dealt with criticism after the boycott:

> The so-called Action Committee (Mr. J. R. D. Chikerema) which has come into being as a result of the bus boycott has gone too far. He and only he and his henchmen (the George Nyandoro group) have the monopoly to criticize, castigate and condemn efforts of others.
> . . . Finally, I must point out that the Chikerema Action Committee has been a complete failure whether they want to know that or not, and the more noise they make from the legs of Nyandoro, the George, the more will the public want to know what sort of leaders they are.[60]

Mzingeli's caustic criticisms came in the midst of his own battle with the SCYL over control of community politics. As Shamuyarira describes it, "The CYL's first object was to break Mzingeli's power." They were able to do so because Nyandoro and Chikerema had the trust of Highfield and Harare residents, particularly the younger generation.[61] The younger group managed to defeat Mzingeli in 1957, his first defeat since the inception of the advisory boards in 1947. An American observer of these events, Consul General Lloyd Steele, described the campaigning of the City Youth League against the older generation. Steele described how "Nyandoro attacked Mzingeli and the other officers of the Civic Association as representatives of a group grown old in power which is composed of 'sellouts' and 'yes men.'"[62] Steele, who acknowledged Mzingeli's "extreme stubbornness," did not think Mzingeli deserved to be called a yes-man. Steele's characterization of Mzingeli's acerbic pen in the African press captures the latter's character well: "His letters to the press often have a strong overtone of omniscience and reflect their author's surprise that his opinions could be questioned."[63] Nyandoro and his associates in the SCYL were ready, however, to respond to Mzingeli's public attacks. Both generations were displaying the uncompromising characteristics that would become the standard political style in Zimbabwean politics. This style was characterized by an unwillingness to accept compromise with potential rivals, and the use of strong-arm "character assassination" in order to convince followers (and voters) of the "sellout" nature of those who had control of a contested area of political patronage.

When Nyandoro began to edit the SCYL's publication, *Chapupu* (witness), in 1957, Mzingeli became a favorite target. In the June edition, a letter from "Pedzi, New Highfields" boldly states how Mzingeli

> continuously refers to the "Harari riots" which took place during the "bus boycott." Who caused these riots? To the best of my knowledge police threw tear gas to a peaceful gathering at the bus terminus, and the trouble started that led the mob to the Carter Hostel because some girls had insulted and geared [*sic*] at the Africans who were opposed to boarding the buses. But Mr. Mzingeli always sees fit to blame the leaders of the bus boycott as irresponsible.[64]

Pedzi goes on to suggest "Mr. Mzingeli is approaching the last stages of sanity for calling the Youth League extremists." In the August edition of *Chapupu*, in the "*Murombo Munhu*" column, Mzingeli is criticized for having been elected chair of the Inter-Racial Association. The column suggests that since this association was in the process of "dissolution," "it therefore could not have chosen a better silent method to dissolve, than electing a man [Mzingeli] who is unpopular both with the African intelligentsia and the masses, as its chairman."[65] This rhetoric would have been all too familiar to Mzingeli, had he taken the time to dwell on it, as it was similar to his own form of condemnation of rivals over the years in the African press. Most likely, however, he would have continued to counterattack the SCYL leaders as "irresponsible." This style of verbal dueling had become a major hallmark of African political expression.

The bus boycott in Salisbury had started out as a positive example of collective action but ended in tragedy as the leadership failed to exert sufficient control over the gangs of township men who then took advantage of the situation to attack and rape women in the Carter House women's hostel. The subsequent justification of the rapes as a form of discipline against women who failed to honor the boycott showed that the new political environment was not going to be about local demands and defense of community as Mzingeli's politics had stressed. Instead, it was the need to defend the movement's leadership that mattered. Such language began to invoke a sort of privilege for leaders and a sacrifice among followers beyond existing norms.

Six years later, Angelina Mhlanga wrote a perceptive editorial in the *Central African Examiner* in which she referred back to the rapes at the Carter House as a turning point in both nationalist politics and also in the role of women in politics. Mhlanga wrote:

> One morning in 1956 working girls in Salisbury's Carter House in Harare township found themselves hitting the country's headlines. Many had been raped by a riotous mob. The country soon forgot all about it, but not so the working women. They suddenly found themselves forced in a most impalatable manner to realise that their position henceforth was with the men. Up to then, they had considered themselves unimportant in public affairs—minors for all time.
>
> The main point leading to the insults on the working girls was that they had not helped the men to strike and fight the proposed increased bus fare. "No workers are to use the buses," was the order from the men, counting women as their equals in this respect. "We are only women and cannot be expected to walk to town, and why should women join the strike?" was the women's attitude.
>
> This was a serious break with tradition and customary laws. For the first time, men recognized that women were part of the "voice of the people"; that alone they stood as a flower with only part of its petals in bloom.[66]

Mhlanga's ability to turn the "blame the victim" mentality around to make greater demands for equality was a creative one, and it represents one aspect of a long trajectory of women's challenges to the notions of male superiority. The reality, however, was that the predominance of men in the leadership of African nationalism would continue to produce a rhetoric reflecting notions of male defense of women's honor, rather than greater equality.[67]

Nationalist Politics and the Restructuring of Women's Roles

A year after the bus boycott the City Youth League had transformed into the Southern Rhodesian African National Congress (SRANC). In 1957 Joshua Nkomo agreed to take the post of president of the new SRANC. This organization became the foundation for the National Democratic Party (NDP) and then ZAPU, until its division into ZANU and ZAPU in 1963. The role of women in these nationalist organizations was defined early on in terms of dominant respectable-class ideology, extrapolating the ideology of the family to the struggle: men as the protectors of women as wives and mothers. Earlier political movements, such as Mzingeli's RICU, had considerable difficulties using a paternalistic bent, particularly as the rhetoric of domesticity had little to do with much of township life. By the mid-1950s, however, with the building of new married housing in Harare and Highfield, this rhetoric was becoming entrenched and more effective. The social distinctions between working and migrant urban dwellers and the more educated youth league leaders made the new leadership all the more conscious of the political need to make populist appeals to such groups. Nyandoro's message combined elements of Mzingeli's urban populism with more confrontational language of Africans standing up against the state and white settlers. The common denominator in this approach was an appeal to a new masculinity that would emphasize the protection of African women and the domestic sphere from police raids and pass laws.

The official paper of the SRANC, *Chapupu*, edited by George Nyandoro, related this populist tone in the editorial in its first issue of June 1957. Arguing against a new proposed version of the N(UA)ARA that would permit more elite Africans new rights to urban housing and services, Nyandoro suggested there was no longer any interest among nationalists to cooperate with the government's attempt to divide the African population by giving greater privileges to certain classes:

> The assumption that the emerging African requires different treatment from the rest of the African people is very incorrect. At no time have the African people requested to be subdivided into classes according to their educational or economic achievements. What the Africans have said now and again in reference to the Pass Law and other discriminatory laws is that they must all be *abolished.*[68]

This new interpretation of an old problem reveals how the new generation of nationalists was to widen the rhetorical scope of those who could benefit from political protest, eclipsing the privileged position of the educated respectable elite whom they now attacked as elitist collaborators. In the state's attempt to appease elite mistrust of the Federation and partnership, certain privileges were conceded to elites, but Nyandoro and many others were, at least rhetorically speaking, taking a page from Mzingeli's strategy and identifying their own lot with less educated populace living in the township.

The same editorial reveals how the more confident respectable class residing in Highfield, spatially independent from the migrants and poor in Harare, were no longer confronted with the very real need to defend women against the arbitrary application of the N(UA)ARA, as Mzingeli had done. For Nyandoro and his peers the beer brewers and the *mapoto* wives no longer had to be addressed as possible allies, nor as groups requiring specific issues to be resolved. Women were now primarily portrayed as wives by the nationalists. For example, when Nyandoro argued against the application of new laws requiring women to carry passes, he appealed to men as protective husbands, in a masculine tone indicative of nationalist rhetoric in this period:

> It is one thing to subject the African men to the Pass Law system. It is another to place the African women under the same system. It is rather going too far. This may create an embarrassing situation for the government.

No reasonable African will tolerate the sight of Police Officers interrogating our mothers and sisters. And no man who is worthy of his salt will ever condone the humiliation and frustration of having his dear wife picked up by the police for having failed to prove her identity. . . . But as for the extension of the Pass Laws system to cover our mothers sisters, and wives we will say No "NO" in unmistakable terms. We will refuse our women to carry passes, identity Books or Cards. On this issue we refuse to co-operate.[69]

Such humiliations were not unique to the generation of the 1950s, but the reworking of a rhetoric of manliness—to stand up against the system and to protect one's mother, one's sister, and one's wife—included threats to those Africans who took part in carrying out laws that humiliated or exploited women. In October 1957 Nyandoro's journal strongly criticized the rural Native Council in the Chinamora Reserve for "forcing women to work with picks and shovels on the roads":

There is a very strong feeling against this practice. The African resents any authority that interferes with his wife. If I may advise the Native Council—hands off from the African women for road construction, and for other work the Council would like to see done. If the Chinamora Council continues this type of forced labour I am afraid it is walking over very dangerous swamps, which will soon put an end to the existence of the Council in Chinamora Reserve.[70]

The new language of Nyandoro and the SCYL implied a physical threat to collaborators, something that had never been a part of Mzingeli's rhetoric.

While the rhetoric of nationalism took on a more masculine tone, the image of the woman as wife slowly changed as the movement became increasingly militant after 1960. In the 1950s, however, the idea of a woman's proper social role remained couched in the images of respectable elite women and of the responsible mother and wife. An example of this is the *African Weekly*'s "Women's Page" article highlighting Mrs. Ruth Chinamano, who in September 1955 was just about to set sail for London to join her husband, Josiah Chinamano, who was studying in England at the time. Ruth Chinamano would later become one of the most outspoken advocates of women's rights and political participation in Zimbabwe, but in the 1950s the portrayal of her in the male-dominated African press remained within the boundaries of proper elite behavior for a woman as wife: "She is a great inspiration to her husband, and continues giving him wise counsel in the responsible jobs he has held. She is reserved, but resolute in public affairs; loving and lovable at home."[71] The politics of women's rights and access to political power had a long way to go at this point, and although it found occasional expression in the African press, such rights were far removed from the struggles of poorer women who had briefly asserted their collective political power with the RICU in the early 1950s.

The End of Accommodation

The year 1958 was a turning point in Southern Rhodesian politics as the remote possibility of a workable political solution involving both African and white politicians in a common future was all but ending. Hardwicke Holderness, in his book *Lost Chance*, describes the cabinet "coup" against the liberal prime minister Garfield Todd in January 1958, and how Todd's former supporters turned against him, thinking he had drifted too far in favor of advancing African interests. Many white politicians accused Todd of being too close to the African National Congress leaders and to one key white supporter and member, Guy Clutton-Brock, in particular. The governing cabinet, in their decision to disassociate themselves from Todd, thought that he should not have met with Clutton-Brock or African politicians associated with the ANC. This would have been difficult for Todd and Holderness, as both men were involved with the interracial associations that had attracted a large section of the African intelligentsia, including men like Herbert Chitepo, Samuel Parirenyatwa, and Leopold Takawira. Ruth Weiss, in her biography of Garfield Todd, locates the origins of the crisis a bit earlier in 1957 when Todd responded to increased pressure for his support of a widened African franchise. Noting Todd's personal close relationship with African National Congress leader Stanlake Samkange and others, Weiss describes how Todd attempted to defend his position at the Scottish Caledonian Society's celebration in Bulawayo on November 30, 1957. He started out his comments by characterizing the ANC's constitution—written in part by his friend Guy Clutton-Brock—as a

> "reasonable document" to which he had adopted a wait-and-see attitude. He then claimed that "George Nyandoro has in effect supplanted Mr. Nkomo in effective leadership" adding that "those Africans who wish to take their place amongst the civilized and reasonable community" were being intimidated. He warned that restrictions may have to be imposed and asked Clutton-Brock and Nyandoro to "throw in their weight with the forces of law and order."[72]

Todd's defense of the political tradition he hoped to keep alive also contained a threat to Nyandoro and others to remain within the boundaries of the political space afforded them. Todd and his associates were watching the concept of partnership spinning out of control as a more radical urban-based element began to champion the grievances of urban and rural Africans alike. The possibility of such a mobilization galvanized white politicians and voters against a more gradualist attempt at compromise, opening the way for a more intransigent politics first in Todd's own United Federal Party (UFP), and later in the Rhodesian Front (RF). As Doris Lessing observed after her visit to Salisbury in the mid-1950s, "The architects of Partnership, which in essence is a last-ditch attempt to stave off an explosion of African bitterness, which is a policy of intelligent self-interest, lie awake at nights not because of the Africans, but because the white voters might suddenly put the brakes on."[73] The brakes were engaged when Todd's own party decided he was too compromised by his previous connections to African interests for the UFP to survive as the ruling party.

The resignation of Todd's cabinet in early 1958 opened the way for a realignment of white politicians behind a more conservative candidate, Sir Edgar Whitehead. Whitehead had served in the Huggins administration as the minister of finance from 1946 to 1953.[74] After that, however, he had been sent to Washington, D.C., to serve as the High Commissioner for the Federation. When the UFP nominated Whitehead as candidate for prime minister in the 1958 election, he only learned of his selection by a phone call to Washington. Whitehead became prime minister after the UFP victory in the June 1958 elections. As Holderness suggests, Whitehead's long absence from the country during those years left him out of touch with conditions in the country, and in particular the immediacy of Africans' political demands.[75] The white electorate gave him a sweeping victory, and according to Holderness, "whatever hope there might have been of white Rhodesians finding common political ground with Rhodesian blacks ceased to exist on 5 June 1958."[76]

For the African nationalists in the SRANC, the prospects of future cooperation were also dimming, although most nationalists held on to the real possibility of a peaceful takeover of power from the white minority, particularly with the help of Britain. But as the Whitehead government used the state to harass and ban SRANC leaders and followers and tightened the state's legal ability to put down protests and dissent, the likelihood of a peaceful transition of power was fading.[77] As prime minister, Whitehead was willing to negotiate on African political participation within a narrowly defined political space, one that would keep Britain engaged without too much interference, but a political space that made use of repressive laws such as the Subversive Activities Act Mzingeli had fought against in 1950 and a whole new arsenal of legislation aimed at making sure African nationalist leaders and organizations would have a difficult time organizing for majority rule.

The Plewman Commission and Another Lost Chance for Accommodation

In July 1958 the Southern Rhodesian Parliament discussed the Plewman Commission's *Report on Urban Affairs*, which had been set up to give recommendations for the future of urban planning and in particular the status of Africans as residents in segregated towns and cities. The Plewman Commission's findings went against the regulations of the Land Apportionment Act and the N(UA)ARA; it recommended that Africans be allowed to purchase homes in the cities and that more areas in the currently Europeans-only sections of the major towns be opened up of for African workers and their families. The growing white political resistance to African rights made for a conflicting reception in the Southern Rhodesian Parliament of the Plewman Commission's recommendations. Much like the Fagan Commission Report in South Africa, issued ten years previously as the Nationalist Party came to power, the Plewman Commission's recommendations remain as evidence of a different road that could have been taken away from settler intransigence on the issue of African rights to the city.[78]

Prime Minister Whitehead agreed in principle with the Plewman Commission Report's recommendations to invest more money to help ease the overcrowded townships and, most importantly, to reduce the city's reliance on male migrants. Citing rural population data, he suggested that even with the "finest efforts of the Land Husbandry Act in coping with our existing population, there is no possibility of providing for the population twenty years hence"; "[therefore,] our objective of building up a settled urbanized population in our towns will be of the utmost benefit to the African population of this country, and in the long run to all of us."[79] Whitehead also acknowledged the end of the migrant labor system evidenced by the appearance of urban unemployment in the late 1950s. "After many, many years in which every agency we possess has been trying to secure sufficient African labour, we have at least reached the stage in the urban areas where there is some sort of surplus."[80] He hoped, therefore, that the offering of homeownership in the towns would make possible the settling of more indigenous Africans in towns and the phasing out of recruitment of workers from the northern territories and Mozambique.

Whitehead's supporters in manufacturing were behind him on this commitment, and a year later, in February 1959, it was announced that some £4,000,000 were to be made available over the next four years for African homeownership schemes. The building societies, important sources of finance capital in Southern Rhodesia, had promised £1,340,000 for the African Housing Fund, "in the spirit of providing homeownership for all races who are increasingly supporting them through their monthly savings."[81] Whitehead's acceptance of the Plewman Commission's recommendations was not, however, shared by the more racist MPs, and it would be these politicians who would ultimately succeed in taking over the government when the Rhodesian Front claimed the leadership role in 1962.

Typical of this intransigent "white settler" view were the remarks of MP S. E. Aitken-Cade, who characterized the Plewman Commission "as a tremendously fine piece of work, but very, very, suspect." During parliamentary debate over the Plewman Report's recommendations, Aitken-Cade suggested they were a call for the Land Apportionment Act to be "whittled away with as little delay as possible." He then asked Parliament:

Why should the European area be continually under attack, continually whittled down and the Land Apportionment Act at the same time be continually emasculated? . . . This Act has been looked on as a charter, almost as a bill of rights in this country. I cannot agree with the Commissioners where they feel this has never been looked upon as something which should continue for ever. In the time it has been in operation—and this is I think since 1931 and there was another amended Bill in 1941—it has served to preserve harmony in Southern Rhodesia. There can be no question of that. We have known our place. The African has had his place and his rights entrenched in that.[82]

The rhetoric of settler nationalism that was by this time heating up around the preservation of white privileges enshrined in the Land Apportionment Act would become the cornerstone of the Rhodesian Front. Given the prevalence of these views among many white politicians, it was little wonder that the SRANC viewed with suspicion the state's offer and promises of new housing schemes and homeownership. Whatever gains might be made through new home ownership schemes for urban families, these were compared at the time with real and lasting movements toward independence in Ghana in 1957 and negotiations toward political independence in the near future throughout British colonial Africa.

The SRANC as a Radical Organization

It was in this context of increased white intransigence that the rhetoric of the SRANC became increasingly radical. Since much of the remainder of this book shifts to American diplomatic sources, it is worth introducing this shift in tone based on observations made by an American diplomat, Richard Murphy, the American vice consul in Salisbury at the time. Murphy provides a detailed report of dinner conversation at Lawrence Vambe's home on March 2, 1958. Vambe had invited Murphy and his wife to dinner along with "Miss" Marjorie Perham, a British academic expert on African politics, who wrote extensively on African responses to colonialism during this period. Also in attendance was Miss Glynn-Jones, an Oxford graduate who was teaching at the Chisipite Girls School.

The dinner was organized so that Perham could be introduced to the SRANC leadership, and after about an hour of waiting, the leaders arrived: James Chikerema, George Nyandoro, and Paul Mushonga. These three men had spent the entire day in congress meetings, including a large rally in the morning at the Harare Township Recreation Hall, which Glynn-Jones had attended. Before the SRANC leaders arrived at the dinner, Glynn-Jones had been telling the others how she had been "disturbed to hear so little constructive talk both from the Congress leaders and from speakers from the floor." Chikerema's closing of the meeting by launching "a curse upon Sir Patrick Fletcher" had particularly bothered her. Fletcher was the leading opponent of Garfield Todd within the United Federal Party, the party that had been formed by Prime Minister Godfrey Huggins when Huggins became prime minister of the Federation. According to Glynn-Jones, Chikerema's curse invoked "ancestral spirits and Christian saints against Sir Patrick, whom Chikerema likened to Judas Iscariot," ending the curse "with the fervent prayer that Fletcher would meet the same fate as Judas." After Glynn-Jones had told Vambe and others of this, Chikerema and the other leaders arrived at the house.

During the dinner conversation, Perham interviewed the men about their views on intimidation and the future of the Congress. She asked whether members of the Congress would be allowed to belong to other political parties. According to Murphy, Chikerema replied:

> There are two kinds of intimidation. The one is physical; the other moral pressure. I certainly feel we must exert all possible moral pressure to persuade Africans from joining any of the established political parties. Those Africans who join the UFP will be used by Welensky as stooges when he makes his case for Dominion Status in London in 1960. These Africans do their race great harm by joining the European parties. There are, unfortunately, some Africans who will do anything to get political power.[83]

Perham suggested that it was impossible to know exactly "what was going on in another man's mind when he took a political decision." Mushonga and Nyandoro replied that they had heard that Africans were joining the European parties for money. Nyandoro denied knowing whether any money had indeed "changed hands" but acknowledged that certain Africans had said so, adding, "There is no money in Congress."

The leaders explained to Perham why they could no longer remain tolerant. Nyandoro said that "The 30's and 40's were the time for cooperation with Africans in this country; not 1958. . . . Aside from Mr. Todd, all, no matter who the parties put into power, Whitehead included, are against African aspirations." Perham told the men, "I know that sooner or later their weight of numbers means that the Africans will control this country" then asked the leaders what Congress's plans were for the future. Nyandoro explained that Congress was just beginning an "active stage" that revolved around "ending discrimination in such areas as post-offices, shops and cinemas."

Perham then asked how she should read accounts of the meeting in the morning, whether it "could be interpreted as a call for hatred of the European and for violence against them." Murphy explains the leaders' responses:

> Chikerema then stated flatly, "Bloodshed is unavoidable in this country." Nyandoro attempted to soften Chikerema's statement claiming, "But we can control

our followers. We know that when we threaten the very livelihood of the European through attempting to change the present economic organization, they will try to shoot us." "And," said Chikerema, "then our people will rise."[84]

At the end of the dinner, Perham agreed with the leaders over the injustices of the Federation and the Southern Rhodesian government, but she told them "Do not press too fast." After the dinner guests had left, Murphy chatted with Vambe on how "Chikerema seemed far more troubled and aggressive than he had in the past." Noting that the conversation between the leaders and Professor Melville J. Herskovits in June 1957 had been much less antagonistic, Murphy said:

> These three were far more anxious to listen and learn than they were last evening with Miss Perham whose understanding and sympathy with African nationalist movements is, I believe, well known. They were irritated by her arguments based on historical development of movements in other countries. They obviously could not have been less interested in the historical view.[85]

When Perham had told the nationalists she was disturbed by Chikerema's curse on Fletcher at the end of the meeting, the others said it had been spontaneous and not part of Congress's plan. Chikerema replied, "Fletcher deserved it."[86]

5

The Early Sixties

Violent Protests and "Sellout" Politics

1960 was proclaimed "The Year of Africa" with independence celebrations planned for seventeen new African nations, including all the remaining colonies of French West Africa, the Belgian Congo, and Nigeria, but the political climate was still hardly festive in southern and central Africa. Nationalists in Nyasaland and Northern Rhodesia were jockeying to be the next leaders, while events in South-West Africa, South Africa, and Southern Rhodesia were to show just how serious the settler states were about denying Africans any significant political power. Protesters had been shot in South-West Africa in September 1959; in South Africa police had shown their willingness to open fire on peaceful protesters in March 1960 during the Sharpeville massacre; and in October 1960, police shot unarmed men in Harare township.[1] With hindsight, it is very difficult to think that a peaceful transition to majority rule in Southern Rhodesia could have occurred, especially given the human and psychological toll caused by the violence in the years following 1960. It is important, however, to try to reassess these crucial years of the early 1960s as they were experienced by those involved, and not to assume that the factional violence that dominated the period between 1962 and 1964 was the only possible outcome. If the following material is considered from the historical actors' perspective, it is possible to consider the gradual realization among nationalists that violence was the only alternative available to them. If this sort of careful historical reconstruction is followed carefully, the reader still must consider the extent to which violence against the settler state can be separated from violence used as part of the factionalism and "sellout" politics during this period. It is important to try to think of the dilemmas these leaders faced in the early 1960s, rather than assume they could have possibly known just how costly and detrimental this factionalism was to become.

State Violence and Rethinking Nonviolent Protest

Approaching the events of 1960 and after requires careful attention to the mood in Salisbury and the townships toward the future. Individuals, political parties, and states are not capable of changing tactics immediately to fit new situations, and it is almost always the case that some groups move more quickly than others to respond to changing circumstances. Often the most tragic aspect of a political showdown is that the crisis may have been averted had the radical elements on both sides not been able to mobilize their followers to extreme positions before a middle ground or compromise could be reached. Once violence becomes the dominant form of political discipline, it is extremely difficult for moderate voices to prevail. Events after 1960 in Southern Rhodesia took such a course—although some may argue there was never a sufficiently strong political moderating force in the country capable of averting the oncoming disaster.

The Federation period had, to a certain extent, opened up possibilities for forging a middle ground politically between African politicians and intellectuals and sympathetic white politicians and intellectuals. Two aspects of the Federation period (1953–63) are important to note. First, as was intended, the economy of Salisbury benefited remarkably from federation. The Federation provided markets for industries based in Salisbury, and the administration of the Federation, by its access to the profits from the Northern Rhodesian Copperbelt, created an economic boom in the Federation's capital city. African employment in the city increased for factory workers and also for a growing number of educated clerks and professionals employed in the bureaucracy and in service industries in the city. But by 1959 African nationalist mobilization in the two northern territories, Nyasaland and Northern Rhodesia, and the increasingly active SRANC brought on a crisis for Southern Rhodesia's continued political hold over the Federation.

The European response from Salisbury was to arrest large numbers of nationalists in all three territories on February 25, 1959, including Nyandoro and Chikerema, and to ban the SRANC on the pretext that its leadership was conspiring with nationalists in Northern Rhodesia and Nyasaland to carry out the violent overthrow of the Federation government. Eshmael Mlambo's account of this period in *Rhodesia: The Struggle for a Birthright* argues that these arrests and the banning of the SRANC helped to galvanize support for the nationalists and made heroes out of the key SRANC leaders who were detained, including Nyandoro, Chikerema, Maurice Nyagumbo, and Edson Sithole. Mlambo also points out how the UFP miscalculated the response from Highfield residents following the detention of the SRANC leaders. When the UFP attempted to hold a rally on March 14, 1959, in Highfield, ostensibly to discuss the fate of the detained leaders, as Mlambo explains it, the rally did not turn out as planned:

> When they [UFP African leaders] avoided mentioning their names [of the detained SRANC leaders], the speakers were shouted down, and within thirty minutes the meeting was a near riot. . . . P. J. Chanetsa, one of the leading U.F.P. supporters, was stoned, his mother was knocked unconscious; and the houses of African U.F.P. supporters were stoned. This was the first time Africans had attacked their political opponents, and a new era had been introduced into African politics.[2]

According to Mlambo, the arrests of the SRANC leaders appeared to fit in with previous events in Ghana and Kenya, and many felt it would only be a matter of months before their leaders went from prison to the statehouse. They would not, however, be released until February 1963, and while these "prison graduates" became the central nucleus of Nkomo's support, none of them could have anticipated how long the journey to majority rule was going to take or how violent township politics was to become by 1963.[3]

Perhaps the key event in the transformation to a more confrontational politics was the standoff and eventual violence between nationalists and the police in Salisbury, just outside Harare township, in July 1960. The Whitehead government had decided to use force to meet the nonviolence of the National Democratic Party (NDP), the organization created after the banning of the SRANC. Acting first by arresting many of its leaders in the early morning of July 19, the Southern Rhodesian government was not prepared for a protest march organized that evening with over thirty thousand people marching from Highfield toward Harare township with plans to march into Salisbury's city center. Terence Ranger was a firsthand observer of the march, and he subsequently wrote an account of that evening. Herbert Chitepo, Southern Rhodesia's first African lawyer and soon to become a prominent nationalist leader, told the original crowd of four thousand in Highfield "to be disciplined, courageous and non-racist." George Silundika, another important African elite pushed into a leadership role with the arrest of the NDP leaders, told the crowd that since the NDP was now unlawful, "they should all go and give themselves up to the police." After marching from Highfield to Harare and gaining numbers along the way, the leaders were informed that Whitehead "would 'under no circumstances address an illegal gathering nor will he meet a delegation from such an illegal gathering.'" The crowd decided at this point to leave Harare township and head for the city center and the prime minister's office. "On the outskirts of Harare," as Ranger describes the scene, "they were stopped by lines of police with armed soldiers standing by."[4]

Stanlake Samkange, a well-respected NDP leader, was one of the leaders arrested that night. Samkange would later share his personal account of that event with Ranger, praising the leaders for their ability to control the crowd right up until the point when "the police charged on the crowd firing tear gas. From then onwards the crowds had no leaders. The police and the people were at each other with truncheons and tear gas bombs being met with stones." Samkange concludes that the events of that evening had shown the people "that peaceful demonstrations will not achieve anything."[5] Fortunately, on July 19, the police did not open fire on the protesters, but the Southern Rhodesian police did not show the same restraint during riots just a few months later, in October 1960.

The October 8, 1960, shootings and violence in Harare township began when a European motorist hit an African pedestrian, which in turn led to rioting and the subsequent shooting and killing of ten African men by the police. The shootings and the wounding of many others occurred in Harare's main beer hall and near the Matapi Hostels. Ranger, writing as a coeditor of the protest publication *Dissent,* responded soon after the killings in an editorial, entitled "The Terrible Mistake Policy," critical of Sir Edgar Whitehead's "decision to adopt a policy of rigid repression." Ranger questioned the police claims to have instructed officers to fire only as a warning:

Seven people were shot dead and scores wounded by gun-shot. Yet it is far from clear that there was need for the police to open fire at all. There are disturbing stories, which seem well authenticated in many cases, of innocent by-standers being shot; of men shot in the back while running away; of police rudeness or worse to people clearly not connected with the rioting. Law abiding Africans in the townships, whom Sir Edgar claims to be protecting by sending in troops, talk bitterly about these things and about the folly of the police in breaking up beer hall gatherings without warning by the use of tear gas. They wonder whether the presence of troops ("rifle ready for action but still eager to show . . . (they're men) . . . of goodwill," as the Sunday Mail puts it) will not mean that more people will be shot next time.[6]

The shootings changed the mood in Harare and Salisbury. The deadly political violence in the Congo, in South-West Africa, and in South Africa had finally reached Harare. The battle lines were unfortunately being drawn. Michael West has called these clashes in Bulawayo and Salisbury in 1960 where the police shot and killed unarmed Africans a "political and psychological turning point, marking as they did the first time since the uprisings of the 1890s that blood had been shed in open confrontations between the security forces and the colonized people."[7] Certain whites in southern Africa had decided to make 1960 a showdown year, attempting to contain Africans organizing for majority rule; as a result, the "winds of change" were not going to be felt as strongly in southern Africa as the nationalists and their followers had originally believed.[8]

The arrests of the SRANC leadership in 1959 and NDP leaders in July 1960 had also caused a crisis for the nationalists, and it would take some time

Figure 5.1. Joshua Nkomo, president of the National Democratic Party, 1960. Photograph from the National Archives of Zimbabwe.

before a new group would take over the leadership while George Nyandoro and James Chikerema remained in detention. A crisis of leadership followed, but the combination of increased use of state violence and the prospects of a negotiated settlement for African majority rule helped push men like Robert Mugabe, Ndabaningi Sithole, and Nathan Shamuyarira to join the nationalists. Joshua Nkomo had avoided arrest both at the banning of the SRANC and later at the banning of the NDP in December 1961, and he would remain as the leader of the nationalist movement until his leadership was publicly contested by the August 1963 split between ZAPU and ZANU.

The realization after the events of July and October 1960 that the Rhodesian state was not willing to work with the nationalists put Nkomo and other leaders in a tough predicament. On the one hand they were able to use evidence of state violence to prove to their international supporters the repressiveness and intransigence of the Rhodesian government, while on the other, it left them strategically in an ambivalent position. Like the ANC in South Africa after the Sharpeville massacre and the subsequent state of emergency, which also had left the ANC virtually leaderless, the NDP had to regroup and decide on the best tactics moving forward. As early as the late 1950s, the nationalists were aware of the risk that their protests would likely provoke a violent response by the state. But Chikerema's bold formula for a mass uprising—he had told Margery Perham, "First they will shoot us, and then our people will arise"—was, in part, not as simple to achieve and channel once the violence had begun.

Disciplining "Sellouts"

If the response to state repression would take time to organize, the strategy of creating a more disciplined loyalty to the nationalists began almost immediately. The first targets were Africans still openly supporting European political parties. In December 1960 a new form of intimidation appeared in Harare and Highfield in the form of petrol bombs. In a dramatic story written for the *Daily News* two years after the incident, A. Z. Murwira describes how on the fateful day of December 16, 1960, four houses—two in Highfield and two in Harare—had petrol bombs thrown into their windows simultaneously at two o'clock in the morning. The victims seemed to have been carefully chosen as each house represented African members of the four different European parties in 1960, and the timing of the attacks appeared to have been in protest to the expulsion of Nkomo from constitutional talks in London. By July 1962, when Murwira wrote his article, the fear caused by petrol bombs had changed the political mood in the townships:

> The bombs' appearance on the Rhodesian political scene—at least as far as the African is concerned—has meant the complete curtailment of the use of his free will. In addition, the petrol bombs have now a direct bearing on almost everything that is done in this country—by Africans, that is.
>
> To mention but a few examples, support of the new constitution is failing because of the fear of the petrol bomb, multi-racial bodies are less favoured now because of fear of the petrol bomb, African Advisory Boards no longer evoke as much enthusiasm as they did before because of the fear of the petrol bomb. Even

the present mass unemployment is directly or indirectly attributable to the appearance of the Petrol Bombs.[9]

A more "patriotic history" of the early 1960s would, at this point in the narrative, emphasize the outpouring of support for the nationalists in the urban areas, noting the large crowds attending rallies in Harare and Highfield, as well as in the rural areas and other towns and cities. This was a time of cultural nationalism, when the nationalist spectacle first surfaced in ways reminiscent of Nkrumah's display of Ghanaian nationalism in the 1950s. But the outward appearances of mass rallies and cultural nationalism could not erase the difficulties the African nationalists faced confronting a state determined to use any means necessary to defeat them.[10] As the new leaders confronted the extreme levels of state surveillance and intimidation, splits within the leadership over tactics and the emphasis on a new forced discipline among urban residents created a new style of politics in Harare and Highfield.

Americans in Salisbury

It was in this highly volatile situation that two very different groups of Americans were trying to exert their influence. The official representatives in Southern Rhodesia were led by the American consul general, who was based in Salisbury and had a relatively large staff in 1961 to administer U.S. Agency for International Development (USAID) programs and State Department programs such as scholarships for Africans, and the U.S. Information Agency, which ran a large library and cultural exchanges. The consul general also had foreign minister status in the Federation, and according to Edward Mulcahy, who served as consul general from 1960 to 1962, the diplomatic post had a large staff of sixty Americans and twice as many Southern Rhodesians employed at the consulate.[11] The State Department in the early 1960s was eager to support African nationalists and hopefully to nurture relations with these new leaders in order to keep them pro-American in the Cold War competition with the Soviet Union and Communist China. The Kennedy administration had made great strides in gaining the initial support of many Pan-Africanist leaders, including from Kwame Nkrumah in Ghana.

The other American interest present in Southern Rhodesia was the AFL-CIO, which, after a visit from Maida Springer in 1960, began a program to assist African trade unions and especially to support their legal funds to help fight the detention of trade union leaders by the Southern Rhodesian government.[12] Once Springer had established the initial ties, the real development of relations between the AFL-CIO and African trade unions was left to Irving Brown, an American based in Paris who had a long history of supporting pro-Western anticommunist trade unions in Europe after World War II. Brown, who had many contacts in North Africa after the war, sought to spread his campaign to sub-Saharan Africa. He worked closely with Tom Mboya in Kenya and hoped to find a similar connection in Southern Rhodesia. It is important to point out from the outset that Irving Brown's anticommunist trade union strategy was often at odds with the State Department's new approach of supporting African nationalists, and therefore Brown and the American consul general's office found themselves at times in disagreement. Their differences led to misunderstandings among African nationalists who wanted and needed American financial aid, monies they initially saw go more to the trade union movement than to their own accounts. This disparity led them to question the motives of the Americans and of the Southern Rhodesian Trade Union Congress (SRTUC) president, Rueben Jamela. The following section covers this crisis and conflict in detail, as it would have lasting repercussions on subsequent forms of political violence, particularly as it relates to "sellout" politics.

Throughout Africa, nationalist politicians had incorporated the trade union movement, a potentially powerful mass movement that could successfully orchestrate national strikes and other labor actions, into the nationalist movement. In the early 1960s a faction within the NDP/ZAPU leadership lead by Robert Mugabe, Jason Moyo, and George Silundika attempted to bring the Southern Rhodesian Trade Union Congress, an organization with a membership of more than thirty thousand workers led by the outspoken Jamela, into their camp.

Reuben Jamela, Sellout Politics, and the Fight for Independent Trade Unions

Reuben Jamela, who had been a longtime member of Mzingeli's RICU and later branched out on his own as a leader of the Builders and Artisans Trade Union, was by the 1960s leading a trade union movement against the backdrop of this battle between the state and the nationalists. The timing could not have been worse for Jamela, in that he had been working for many years to gain recognition for African workers under the existing Industrial Conciliation Act (ICA), legislation that white politicians had jealously guarded against inclusion of African workers and their trade unions. The growing strength of the SRTUC combined with the government's need to make concessions to take the wind out of the nationalists' sails had created an apparent window of opportunity for Jamela to make substantial gains for his members, including recognition as workers under the ICA.

In Jamela's case, therefore, the state was not as dangerous as those within the nationalist movement willing to turn the public violence in the township against him and his trade union supporters. By the early 1960s, the term "sellout" no longer simply applied to those who were seen as working for the settler government, or those such as Mzingeli who were branded as such by

Nyandoro and others, but also to other intellectuals and politicians who tried to forge ahead independently of the leadership clique around the NDP and later the Zimbabwe African People's Union (ZAPU), which was formed in December 1961, one week after the banning of the NDP.

Although Jamela had been an active trade unionist for many years, he came to lead the SRTUC only after many of the other prominent leaders of the movement had joined the NDP executive. Jamela had been elected president of the SRTUC in part because both Joshua Nkomo and Michael Mawema had been elected president and vice president of the NDP, respectively, and also because Jamela by this point had been promised financial support from European, British, and American trade unions. He brought with his leadership a new centralized organizational structure similar to one he had observed in Austria, in which each member union would pay 75 percent of its union dues directly to the SRTUC central office. Jamela also set into motion negotiations with the minister of labor for a new minimum wage for African workers that was to be set somewhere between £7 and £25 per month. The deadline for reaching an agreement with the government was September 1, 1961.[13] For a brief period between 1961 and 1962, Jamela also had access to international funding through the AFL-CIO and the ICFTU, and he used these funds to expand the SRTUC into a national trade union congress with the ability to negotiate with the state and employers. The presence of foreign money and the strategies he used to keep the SRTUC separate from the NDP and ZAPU placed Jamela in a very tenuous political position, one that would ultimately have a bearing on nationalist political violence in the townships and help to bring a style of violent political factionalism to the forefront.

Using the financial resources of American and European trade unions, Jamela successfully shaped the thirty thousand members of the Southern Rhodesian Trade Union Congress into a force capable of exerting economic and political influence in the early 1960s. Jamela's rise in status, popularity, and political clout did not go unnoticed by Nkomo and the rest of the NDP leadership. Jamela was also a member of the NDP, and although not a part of the executive, he had become a leader within the Highfield branch, arguably the most important branch of the nationalist party. Jamela's rise to popular leadership in Harare and Highfield townships also had to do with his long time political work as a member of the Highfield Civic Association and his leadership of the African Artisans Union.

Before March 1961 Jamela had successfully combined his trade union work and his work as a branch leader of the NDP. For example, in February 1961 Jamela led an NDP delegation to present a "Christmastime petition" in support of the release of the fourteen nationalists who were still detained after their arrest two years before. Jamela and the delegation met with H. J. Quinton, the Minister of Native Affairs. According to an account of the meeting printed in the *Manchester Guardian,* none of the arguments of the

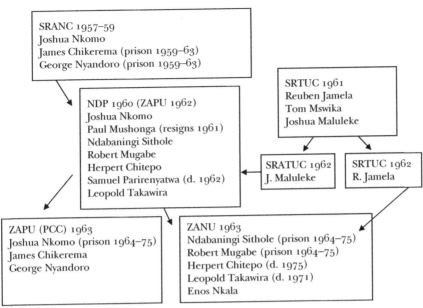

Figure 5.2. Diagram of political and trade union splits, 1957–64.

delegation of former detainees were accepted, and Quinton told them that "as long as there were petrol bomb attacks or acts of intimidation in African townships the detainees and restrictees could not be released. He added that in Ireland some political prisoners had recently been released after 17 years in prison without trial."[14] Attitudes such as these among government officials only served to convince a number of nationalists that a negotiated sharing of power was unlikely. Jamela's leadership of the delegation showed that he was both a respected trade union leader and a member of the NDP. His ability to wear both hats was to be challenged beginning in March 1961, when he would join a number of NDP leaders in opposing Joshua Nkomo's initial decision to support a compromise constitutional proposal.

The strategies used during the negotiations over a proposed 1961 Southern Rhodesian constitution became a major issue in the realignment of African nationalism away from possible cooperation with the minority-rule government and toward greater confrontation. The British government had hoped to convince the Whitehead administration to negotiate a new constitution that would allow a larger African electorate (characterized by a complex two-tiered system of voting qualifications and different "A" and "B" rolls, which sought to allow more Africans to vote while also guaranteeing European electoral control), a Bill of Rights for Africans (to finally recognize Africans as full citizens with the same legal rights as whites), and a provision of fifteen African seats in the Southern Rhodesian Parliament.[15] The negotiations for this new constitution were held in London, and Joshua Nkomo, along with Reverend Ndabaningi Sithole, represented the NDP, while Herbert Chitepo and George Silundika went along as their advisers.[16] After the negotiations got under way, Nkomo announced his initial support for a draft constitution based on the inclusion of a nonracial Bill of Rights and the fifteen African parliamentary representatives. Robert Mugabe, who was then the NDP's publicity secretary, told a press conference on February 7, 1961, how "several major features proposed in the Constitution have fallen into line with the demands that have been made by the N.D.P. since its inception. These have been the enshrinement of a declaration of rights, the outlawing of discrimination and the protection of the rights by the Courts."[17] Nkomo had returned from the December 1960 constitutional conference confident that he had achieved a milestone for Africans with the attainment of fifteen seats in Southern Rhodesia's Parliament.

Jamela recalled how Nkomo came back "boasting that he had moved a mountain."[18] Jamela, disagreeing with the decision, led a delegation of the Harare branch of the NDP to the March 1961 party congress held in Bulawayo. The congress had been called in order to rubber-stamp approval for Nkomo's position on the constitution, but in the weeks leading up to the meeting there had been growing opposition on this issue. Edson Sithole, a friend of Jamela's and one of the NDP's founders, was still in detention at the time of the congress. Writing in 1962, he explains how the detained leaders heard about Nkomo's agreement to the constitutional provisions, and how he and others in detention were the first to protest the decision. The next protest came from Leopold Takawira and Paul Mushonga, both serving in London as NDP representatives, and the third protest came from Jamela. According to Sithole's analysis of the situation, Jamela's position as the leader of an "organised body" that had passed a resolution against the proconstitution position made him Nkomo's enemy.[19] Sithole writes, "When at the March 1961 NDP Congress Jamela was reported to have kept the NDP Executive on its toes on the constitution of Southern Rhodesia, he was building one thing for himself—more disfavour and distrust by NDP leadership." After the conference, Sithole claims that he "noticed efforts being taken to remove Jamela from the leadership of the T.U.C."[20]

Just how seriously Nkomo had taken the opposition to his decision on the constitution can be seen in his suspension of the NDP vice president, Michael Mawema, for openly criticizing the decision. Hastings Banda in Nyasaland had also made a public statement claiming that the NDP executive had been "spineless" in accepting the draft constitution.[21] According to Jamela, the trade unions had remained quiet on the issue until the March NDP congress held at Bulawayo. The following week after the NDP congress, according to Jamela, "the TUC held its own congress—an emergency congress—and completely rejected the constitution, without conditions. It was an unconditional rejection. That was when we were targeted. . . . I was a hated man from there. I was a man to be watched."[22] Mlambo also suggests that Robert Mugabe did not agree with Nkomo over the constitution negotiations, and that Mugabe, working with A. Mukahlera from the Makokoba branch of the NDP, along with D. K. Naik, an Indian NDP member from Bulawayo, began to campaign within the NDP to overturn the decision to accept the bill of rights and the fifteen seats.[23] Terence Ranger also recalls Robert Mugabe working behind the scenes to repair the damage caused by the initial support of the draft constitution in London. Mugabe approached Ranger and John Reed to organize quickly a meeting of the NDP's Salisbury City Branch—of which Reed was the leader—to vote against the acceptance of the 1961 proposed constitution. The Salisbury City Branch overwhelmingly rejected the constitution. Ranger remembered how "the African members revealed a tremendous disgust with the educated leadership. The members would tell us how they didn't trust these educated people because they were looking for a bargain."[24]

This theme of "selling out" the people by negotiating seats for Africans in the Southern Rhodesian Parliament was turned into a strongly worded populist message by Michael Mawema, who, after leaving the NDP over the constitution issue, formed the Zimbabwe National Party (ZNP). Mawema's rhetoric sounds very much like Mzingeli's language—how educated leaders cannot be trusted. He writes of the NDP:

> Our God and great-grandfathers will not forgive anyone of us who shall betray this land or fear to suffer for it because of wanting pleasures and money. . . . What moral right have they in the name of Zimbabwe to continue to sell us for luxury and money which they have already? Of recent times many people are going about without food and jobs after being misled to go on strike; many lay in prisons, some died, but the people who asked them to violate the laws are free, enjoying themselves without worry or giving help to the people who are suffering.[25]

The ZNP would not achieve the level of support as the NDP and ZAPU, but Mawema's criticisms of the NDP leadership reflected older class-based differences between the majority of township residents and the more educated elite. As a new generation of elite, mission-educated leadership came to fill the positions of the nationalist leadership, they were met with a greater suspicion than the hagiography around their early careers might suggest.

In May 1961 the NDP was growing in confidence. After Nkomo addressed a gathering of seven thousand supporters in Salisbury, Takawira told the audience that Nkomo "would take over the Government within 12 months." He also told the crowd, "Nkomo was going to unite the African people, but he would demand complete obedience. Africans must lie with their faces on the ground and tell Mr. Nkomo 'Here we are, your people. Tell us what to do.' "[26]

Dr. Samuel Parirenyatwa, who became the vice president of ZAPU after the banning of the NDP, was calling for similar discipline among the ZAPU cadre: "when your leaders say stop doing one thing you must stop—otherwise you spoil the cause. It is the leaders who tell you to go or to stop."[27] Given that the growing public displays of obedience were translating into acts of violence against collaborators, it became increasingly likely that NDP supporters and Jamela's supporters would eventually enter into some sort of battle. After Nkomo and his executive realized it had been a mistake to enter into constitutional talks, the decision to end negotiations with the Whitehead government and the British unless full universal suffrage was on the table helped to gain support for the NDP internationally. The sudden addition of new African nations to the United Nations also helped to give Nkomo and the NDP confidence that they could use international pressure to isolate the settlers and force the British to pressure the Southern Rhodesian government to accept universal suffrage in any new constitution.[28]

Years later, in interviews with the author, Jamela maintained that Nkomo had set him up to fail in a rather backhanded way. At stake had been the ability to use organized labor for strike actions that could help the nationalist cause. According to Jamela, Nkomo had agreed with him on the importance of keeping the trade union movement out of politics, although workers could participate as party members. He suggested that Nkomo understood the dangers of incorporating the trade union movement into the nationalist movement given the precarious nature of Southern Rhodesian law, the risks of banning, and the high cost to the political organization in leadership and assets after such bannings. Jamela's close ties with the ICFTU also meant that he and the SRTUC would be protected from banning, as the Southern Rhodesian government did not want the bad publicity from the British TUCs should they ban the SRTUC. A similar international solidarity protection had been originally given to Tom Mboya and his Kenyan Federation of Labour.[29] Jamela would be responsible for industrial strike action; Nkomo, for political strike action.

In July 1961 the NDP organized and called for a general strike to protest the new constitution and to make it clear that Africans were not about to accept anything short of universal suffrage in a new constitution. The Whitehead government was not about to allow a successful strike, and it was prepared with troops to force workers to remain on the job at key economic points such as the Wankie coal mines. Jamela claims Nkomo approached him after the failure of this NDP call for a general strike and advised him to call off a planned SRTUC general strike scheduled for September 1, 1961.[30] Jamela recalled his conversation with Nkomo:

> He said if I went ahead with my call for the strike and met with the same reaction from the authorities, then labour would be no better than them and African

nationalism would suffer irreparable damages. He advised me to suspend my call for the strike and pave way for negotiations. I agreed and had a dialogue with the minister, Mr. Abrahamson. I got the concession that each industry would have a [wage] board appointed, which would look into the complaints of the employees.[31]

Jamela, however, avoided the difficult task of personally calling off the strike. He left the task to his vice president, Tom Mswaka. This may not have been the best time to delegate such an important task, as it came back to haunt him. The calling off of the strike also coincided with Jamela's trip to the United States arranged by Irving Brown of the AFL-CIO.

The timing of this trip, let alone the trip itself, was used by his rivals to question his motives in calling off the strike and gave his rivals ammunition for the conflict that awaited him upon his return. Ignatius Chigwendere recalled how, "the Union leadership was very angry at this failure and accused Jamela of collaborating with the government."[32] Jamela recalls what happened next: "All my counterparts, both in the party and the trade unions, who had advised me to call off the strike as it was likely to damage both the struggle (under the party) and the trade union, went behind my back and told the people that I had called off the strike and gone to the U.S., so I was a coward."[33] In fact, Mswaka wrote a very tactful letter to Jamela in New York informing him of the difficulties Jamela's wife, Joyce, and his family faced back in Highfield. First Mswaka told him how a group of two hundred workers at a meeting of the Salisbury branch of the Commercial and Allied Workers Union, upon hearing the news of the postponement of the strike, began to call for Jamela's resignation. Mswaka then held a press conference on Monday morning to officially call off the strike, and his message was played on the radio. Mswaka called the Sunday night meeting "one of the rowdiest meetings of the Trade Union I have ever experienced." He then told Jamela about threats against Jamela's wife and their house in Highfield:

Since you left, there are people who are said to be going to your house during the night to intimidate your wife[. T]hey are said to have been there twice, and she has since moved away from the house. She is now staying with her brother in Highfields but she is safe anyway, and we have reported to the police so that they keep the house proparty [*sic*] and then watch whether there is nobody staying in it. You should not worry very much about this, it is not as serious as you may imagine it to be, but we thought your wife should stay away while you should come back.[34]

This must have been nerve-racking news for Jamela to receive. The threat of violence against his wife and family was not something he would likely have anticipated. It was only the beginning, however, of a period of harassment and physical intimidation awaiting him upon his return home.

The coming clash between Jamela and Nkomo was not predicted by the Americans, particularly Irving Brown, the American representative of the ICFTU, who had sensed Jamela's unwillingness to use the SRTUC for political purposes and had been eager to support Jamela as a noncommunist nationalist voice.[35] Brown did, however, also hope to gain influence with Nkomo as well. The American consul general, John K. Emmerson, reported a conversation between Brown and himself in which Brown reported to have "presented Mr. Nkomo with money for the party's 'legal defense fund.' " He said Nkomo, who had been displeased in an earlier conversation with Brown over the question of a contribution of funds, had been pleased by the generous gift which amounted to about [U.S.] $2,000. Brown believed it has put the AFL-CIO in a very good light at this time with both African political, as well as, African trade union officials."[36] Brown continued, however, to believe Jamela was the most stalwart anticommunist in Southern Rhodesia.

After starting with some successes, 1961 turned out to be a difficult year for the NDP. As Terence Ranger wrote in August 1961, Sir Edgar Whitehead was quite pleased with the turn of events that had led to the weakening of the NDP both in international circles and within Southern Rhodesia. Ranger, who had joined the NDP that month, describes how Sir Edgar had managed to turn British opinion around through the constitutional talks with Duncan Sandys, the British Secretary of State for Commonwealth Relations, as the NDP leadership "made not one but a whole series of mistakes" in these talks.[37] According to Ranger, the first mistake the NDP had made was to have signed on to the process in the first place and then to have accepted parts of the negotiations. Their subsequent reversals and rejections of the fifteen-seat African representation did them little good as Sir Edgar had succeeded in showing the British that the African nationalists were willing to work together with whites to create a new government and allow the predominantly white electorate to pass the referendum in support of the new constitution. The other major factor in the NDP's losing strength was the failure of the general strike in July 1961. Ranger quotes Whitehead's comments after the defeat of the strike: "We have killed the NDP."[38] Doubting the accuracy of this last comment, Ranger was nonetheless openly critical of the way the NDP had lost ground in 1961. It was from this vulnerable position that the NDP's leadership decided to confront Jamela's power base in the SRTUC.

In October 1961 Jamela told the Americans how "his opponents were exploiting the situation because the wage boards had yet to announce their wage increases," therefore leaving him "vulnerable" to attack. Consul General Emmerson took this information to Abrahamson, who responded that he was "aware of Jamela's difficulties" and understood "the need for a 'quick decision from the wage boards' "; however, Abrahamson pointed out the NNLBs claimed they did "not have the personnel available for processing the matter more expeditiously." According to Emmerson, Abrahamson, the minister of labor, had promised Jamela a formal announcement in January if not sooner.[39] As it turned out, January 1962 would be too late as the NDP and NDP-supported leaders within the SRTUC organized a coup against Jamela while he and the SRTUC vice president, Tom Mswaka, were attending to Pan-African trade union business in Dakar. The meeting in Dakar was the inaugural congress of the African Trade Union Confederation (ATUC), a direct response to John Tettegah's All-African Trade Union Federation (AATUF). At the ATUC congress, Jamela was elected a vice president along with Tom Mboya.[40] Irving Brown received a telegram urging Jamela to return home immediately from Dakar because Josiah Maluleke was making accusations in the press that Jamela had stolen TUC funds and was publicly demanding Jamela's dismissal.[41] Jamela's relationship with anticommunist Pan-African organizations was not turning out to be as profitable as he had hoped.

Intimidation in the Townships

As a political climate of intolerance surrounded Jamela's defense of an independent TUC, an environment of intimidation enveloped Harare, New and Old Highfield, and Mabvuku. In January 1962, for example, the frequency of petrol bombings in New Highfield began to increase. Houses of people known to support the European-dominated UFP, which had recruited African voters to join its ranks and form branches in Highfield and Harare, were the initial targets. In one such case, a petrol bomb was thrown into the kitchen of a house in the Engineering section of New Highfield at 12:30 a.m. No one was hurt, as the two young men who usually slept in the kitchen had moved that night to sleep in the front room of the house. The men had recently joined the UFP.[42] It was during this new campaign against Africans in the township who publicly supported the UFP that Charles Mzingeli resurfaced as a supporter of the UFP. He had even spoken publicly at the UFP convention in support of the 1961 constitution and the proposed new voter qualifications for African voters. It was this unwillingness to accept the nationalist position in the 1960s that tarnished Mzingeli's role in nationalist history. His animosity toward the younger generation who had challenged him and shouted him down never seemed to falter, and he expressed as much in a debate in the pages of the *Central African Examiner*.

Although a pro-NDP journal, the *Central African Examiner* would often publish pro and con positions on pressing issues. In December 1961 its editors asked for alternative views on the question of universal suffrage. Mzingeli wrote the con position arguing against universal suffrage. His argument was more about the irresponsibility of leaders than against the concept of universal suffrage per se. A product of his generation and the earlier political defeats he experienced, Mzingeli was now very suspicious of how politicians would act once universal suffrage arrived. He described the potential results with his trademark dramatic flair:

> Indeed, under adult suffrage immature African politicians or voters would have a good ride, taken for sundowners in one of the municipal beer gardens for free drinks. It would be the day of great freedom—Freedom now!
>
> But the bitterness that would follow would be so great that no one would be able to allay it. For as soon as an unscrupulous politician gained power he would see to it that at the next general election there would be no more "one-man-one-vote" but "one-vote-for-one-man." We have already seen from those who shout at the top of their voices about freedom what freedom they mean.[43]

Mzingeli's commentary was prophetic given the political history that would follow. At the time, however, such views only furthered the notion that Mzingeli was out of touch with the political situation. His criticisms of African leaders had crossed over the divide of what was rhetorically acceptable. He had, in effect, come to represent for the younger generation the very type of African politician he himself had loathed throughout his earlier career—the yes-man used by European politicians to support their compromised policies. Alternatively, however, from the vantage point of historical hindsight (if it were possible to remove our judgment from the Manichean world of settler-versus-African politics), he can be seen to have been still defending township residents from the "unscrupulous politician" he felt he saw in the new nationalists ever since he had parted with them in the mid-1950s. Mzingeli, often seen as a conservative in his approach, may have represented a more radical notion of rights and freedoms than that of the new nationalists. Cold War rhetoric in the early 1960s would make this contradiction between the intentions of leaders and their rhetoric all the more pronounced.

In the summer of 1961 the NDP had organized its own referendum on the draft constitution for a direct vote by Africans. As Mlambo explains, "A total of 372,546 people voted 'No,' while 471 voted 'Yes'. The figures were impressive in comparison with the official referendum which recorded 41,949 voting 'Yes' and 21,846 voting 'No.'"[44] Part of the success of the NDP's referendum, according to Mlambo, was in showing the world, and whites in Southern Rhodesia, that Africans in Southern Rhodesia were entitled to a constitution more similar to the 1961 constitution introduced by the British for Nyasaland. The response by the Whitehead government, however, was to continue to repress African nationalism, and it showed this by banning the NDP on December 9, 1961. Nkomo, who had been in Tanganyika for independence celebrations when the arrests occurred, returned and established the Zimbabwe African People's Union (ZAPU) on December 17, 1961.[45]

Jamela had managed to avoid capitulating to Nkomo in 1961, but the year had not gone well for the NDP. Instead of taking control of the government and moving into the statehouse, the nationalists were forced to strategize new tactics to confront the settler state. Nathan Shamuyarira, writing in the *Central African Examiner* in December 1961, reflected on the difficulties Jamela's control of the SRTUC had caused for Nkomo's political strikes and the NDP's plans to "cripple industry" during 1961. Jamela had told the press, "I cannot destroy industry when at the same time I want the industries to flourish so that my followers may get better and higher wages."[46] Shamuyarira noted that the combination of Jamela's popularity and his unwillingness to give up control of the SRTUC to the NDP stood in the way of Nkomo's plans. In addition, Shamuyarira questioned the popularity of political strikes given workers insecurity as "increasing unemployment" meant "workers both in and out of jobs feel more insecure." Shamuyarira went on to quote Robert Mugabe, the NDP's publicity secretary, who "admits there will be suffering, but makes the point that 'our people should suffer once and get what they want, rather than suffer perpetually.'" Shamuyarira remarked, "This is a sacrifice many workers will find it hard to make."[47]

Jamela's Clash with ZAPU

Three months following the banning of the NDP, Jamela continued to make statements about the necessity of trade union autonomy. Attending an African trade union conference in Tananarive (Antananarivo), Madagascar, in April 1962, he took the opportunity to criticize the continued dominance of European economic interests in the newly independent African countries:

> To the workers, political independence is incomplete in a country if it does not bring about economic independence. For it is true today to say that political independence has come to many countries in Africa but that even in many of these countries, the replicas of colonialism are still found in the economic field. We still have our economies controlled by former colonialists who in many cases are foreigners. This has resulted in the continuance of a small highly paid section of the community surrounded by masses of Africans earning starvation wages. As long as wages remain as low as they are today, Africa will remain a source of raw material for colonial powers, and will remain economically controlled by them.[48]

Jamela's speech was likely a continuation of his debate with John Tettegah and the insistence of the Convention People's Party's of Ghana on the primacy of politics over trade union and wage issues. As Richard Jeffries has described, the realities of the new elite in Ghana were already becoming clear during the 1961 strike action in the key shipping and railway center of

Sekondi-Takoradi. The Ghanaian strikers expressed their frustrations over the growing "elite-mass gap" in independent Ghana, as "the Nkrumah government did nothing to reduce the gross inequalities in the wage and salary structure inherited from the colonial civil service."[49] In response to the strike, Nkrumah required the resignation of six ministers, including Krobo Edusei, whose wife had bought a £2,000 bed on a London shopping spree.

After returning from Madagascar, Jamela found himself again under verbal attack from sections of the NDP leadership. These public attacks against Jamela had led the American consul general, Mulcahy, to question Jamela's political future. Mulcahy had a good relationship with the nationalists. He would later describe in an interview how Nkomo and Mugabe would come to his residence for parties: "They were often at my house, drinking my beer. Robert preferred my Scotch."[50] He turned to Robert Mugabe for his opinions of Jamela, and Mugabe told Mulcahy that he did not think Jamela was going to be around much longer politically. According to Mulcahy,

> Mugabe admitted that African political or labor movements in this country cannot stand on their own without financial backing from some external source. However, Mugabe felt that Jamela's activities have proved beyond doubt that he is acting under ICFTU direction. Although Mugabe admitted that Jamela was one of the most able African trade unionists, the former did not think that he [Jamela] was capable of "riding the tiger" without "ending inside." . . . He said ZAPU, unlike the SRTUC, owes no allegiance to either the East or West. He warned that as long as Jamela follows instructions from Brussels, ZAPU will not only withhold its support of him but will brand him an "enemy of the African cause."[51]

Mugabe and Silundika kept up the campaign against Jamela in April, but American diplomat Paul Geren notes that the campaign suddenly quieted down when Nkomo returned to Southern Rhodesia.[52] The public campaign against a trade union leader known in Britain and the United States was bad for ZAPU's image, as well as revealing of a split inside the ZAPU executive.

Jamela did not back down, however, when faced with both the Maluleke coup and breakaway union and ZAPU's public attacks. Instead, he began to use the Cold War rhetoric of anticommunism against ZAPU and Maluleke's SRATUC.[53] The SRTUC's *Zimbabwe Labour News* of June 2, 1962, included a brief article entitled "Mugabe the Communist Puppet Must Go!" The article claimed, "It is obvious that some leaders in the ZAPU like Mugabe today are taking a line that is ANTI-DEMOCRACY."[54] Citing an article from ZAPU's *The People's Voice* (which is said to deserve "no other name than 'Mugabe's Voice'") that allegedly stated: "We do not hate Jamela nor Maluleke, but we have a grave concern over the present situation confronting the Trades Union Movement in this country. We must remember that our struggle is not for wages but mainly for Independence." The *Zimbabwe Labour News* article replied,

> We regard such statements if conveyed to a TU movement as subversive, for if a TU movement adheres permanently to a political party control it would result in oppressing workers of this country. . . . A Trade Union Movement can only back a political party but it would be betrayal to the workers if their movement would pass into the control of RELIGEOUS [*sic*], TRIBAL and POLITICAL groups. . . . It is high time leaders like Mugabe remember they are not Trade Unionist."[55]

This escalating imperialist-versus-communist rhetoric helped Mugabe and others in their campaign against Jamela; and among the rank and file in ZAPU, Jamela became even more the "sellout" and therefore deserving of suspicion and punishment. The Americans were still cautiously optimistic about Jamela in June, although Mulcahy noted that Jamela was under severe pressure from "some of the most powerful guns in SR African nationalist circles." Although Mulcahy believed the jury was still out as to who would come out on top, he believed it would lead to some "interesting fireworks in the not too distant future."[56]

6

The "Imperialist Stooge" and New Levels of "Sellout" Political Violence

Reuben Jamela managed to gain a brief boost in popularity following a disastrous strike call by rival union leader Josiah Maluleke in May 1962. The Southern Rhodesian government arrested most of the key SRATUC leaders including Maluleke, and many striking workers were fired from their jobs. Jamela was able to negotiate the rehiring of some fired strikers, given his close ties to the Department of Labour and employers' preference for his union over the new one. Even though the May strike had failed, workers complained of intimidation in the morning and of having been beaten or threatened by groups of youth as they left for work. One man claimed to have been chased by "a gang of some 30 youths soon after leaving the bus stop." The man recounted how that evening, the youth returned to his house and shouted "that since I had gone to work that morning I should come out and face the youths. When I refused, stones and bricks were rained on my house, breaking all the windows."[1] Now that the trade union movement was out of Jamela's leadership, employers and the state decided to use Maluleke's pro-ZAPU position to punish workers. The director of African Administration for Salisbury described this new strategy:

> There is no doubt that the expression of political opinion is the cause of the most violent and frequent lawlessness in the township. This particular method of expression is now also undertaken by trade union organisations and is the result of appeasement of past African demands and we have reached the stage whereby the African is confident that whatever demands he wishes to make will be met providing he displays sufficient force. A rude shock it is hoped, a change to this line of thought was evident after a strike held in May of this year, when a number of Africans who took part in the strike, found themselves unemployed on their return to work.[2]

The shift in leadership to Maluleke and the confusion caused within the trade union movement had also taken its toll on the effective use of strikes by the African trade unionists. In addition, greater levels of unemployment in the early 1960s allowed employers to take a harder line against strikers. The ambiguity over whether a called strike was economic or political in nature, combined with the increasing job insecurity in the 1960s, left workers and trade union leaders in a difficult position.

Jamela was not able to regain complete control of the labor movement, and in June 1962 the public attacks on Jamela intensified, especially as rumors began to surface that he was planning to form a new political party to participate in the upcoming 1962 elections—elections the nationalists were demanding African voters should boycott. In late July 1962, in response to these rumors that Jamela was involved in forming a new party, a letter arrived at the SRTUC head office located on the second floor in an Indian-owned building at 60 Moffat Street. The letter was addressed to Jamela and was signed by Mugabe, as ZAPU's "Acting National General Secretary" and included the following justifications for Jamela's recent expulsion from ZAPU:

You [Jamela] were warned persistently by the National President Mr. Joshua Nkomo and other national leaders from at least 1961 that we Africans are firm on and jealous of our principles of non-alignment and positive Pan-Africanism and that we would not tolerate any compromise of any aspect of these principles by affiliation to any of the world blocs or their agents.

You have ignored all this patient advice and advocated continued affiliation to the ICFTU on the grounds that it supplies you with money. The principles we uphold are not exchangeable with money, they have no economic value, they have values of their own.

The National Executive has, therefore, arrived at the conclusion that your continued indulgence in these anti-liberation adventures is incompatible with your continued membership to the ZIMBABWE AFRICAN PEOPLE'S UNION. It, therefore, confirms the decision of the Harare Branch.

As your activities are inseparable from those of the SRTUC and as the SRTUC continues to be an affiliate of the ICFTU, and as your General Secretary admitted having maliciously made an official statement which then read that ZAPU and the National President had communist leanings and was never subsequently made good, and finally as the SRTUC is daily conducting a campaign of filthy slogans in condemnation of the National President to pave way for your new Party and leadership, the National Executive now wishes you to know that it regards the SRTUC as part and parcel of imperialistic agents which must disappear from ZIMBABWE.
I remain,
True to the Struggle,
R. G. MUGABE
ACTING NATIONAL GENERAL SECRETARY[3]

Edson Sithole, who had written openly in the *Daily News* about the opposition to Nkomo on the constitutional talks in 1961, once again felt it necessary to address the contradictions in the ZAPU criticisms of Jamela in
1962. Sithole wrote a lengthy article entitled "Real Reason Why ZAPU
Expelled Jamela," in which he attributed the ZAPU executive's jealousy of
Jamela's powerful SRTUC support as the real reason for ZAPU's support of
Maluleke's breakaway SRATUC. Sithole pointed out the difficulties caused
by the trade union split for international trade union affiliations and finan-
cial support, as the SRATUC could not get support from the ICFTU because
Jamela had it and also because ZAPU had used his affiliation with the ICFTU
as a reason for denouncing him as an "imperialist agent." Additionally,
Sithole argued that it was hypocritical for the ZAPU leadership to put a limit
on trade union support from America when ZAPU itself was getting
American support: "ZAPU has representatives in America who live on
American money. It is therefore insincere to say he who receives money from
the ICFTU is an imperialist agent and he who buys a Rambler car and main-
tains his representatives by American money is a Pan-Africanist."[4] Sithole was
by now in open opposition to Nkomo and ZAPU. He detailed in his usual
straightforward journalistic style the main contradiction underlying the
whole logic of "sellout" politics: those who would shout the loudest about
another's imperialist connections would themselves be turning to the same
sources for funding. It was not possible to fund a resistance movement from
internal sources, and access to international support became the lifeblood of
the nationalists by 1962.

Dr. Parirenyatwa's Death and Violence against Jamela

Jamela, in his interviews with the author, explained his special relationship
with Dr. Samuel Parirenyatwa, who had worked to patch up relations
between Jamela and the ZAPU leaders. Evidence from the American diplomats indicated this to be the case. Parirenyatwa was, according to U.S.
diplomat Paul Geren, equally critical about the relationship between
Jamela and the ICFTU, but he had hoped to bring Jamela back into ZAPU
without a confrontation.[5] In March 1962, for example, Jamela described to
consul general Mulcahy a six-hour meeting with Parirenyatwa to try to
work out a compromise. Parirenyatwa had asked Jamela to disaffiliate from
the ICFTU and in return take an executive position in ZAPU. Mulcahy
would tell the State Department that the "Ghana oriented extremists wants
open party assault on Jamela" while Parirenyatwa wanted to limit the
attacks in case it "might build up Jamela's prestige." Interestingly, in March
1962 Mulcahy cabled that "another important factor in ZAPU is [the] pro-
Jamela voice of Nathan Shamuyarira, editor of [the] influential *African
Daily News.*"[6]

Figure 6.1. Dr. Samuel Tichafa Parirenyatwa, first vice president of ZAPU. Photograph from the National Archives of Zimbabwe.

Many years later, Jamela believed that he was finally ousted from the party only after Parirenyatwa's death because Mugabe and Silundika had respected Parirenyatwa's friendship with Jamela. What followed was a violent attack against Jamela at Parirenyatwa's funeral. Parirenyatwa, as the vice president of ZAPU when he died in mid-July in a car accident, was the leader many believed to be best poised to take over as president of ZAPU from Nkomo. The attacks on Jamela reached a crescendo at Parirenyatwa's funeral in Murewa, where "Jamela was brutally beaten and his car burned by ZAPU youth."[7] Jamela, as a *sahwira* with Parirenyatwa, was determined to attend his funeral. The *sahwira* relationship in Shona culture designates a very close relation between individuals who were not blood relatives. The *sahwira* traditionally plays a key role in important family events, such as funerals where it was often expected that the *sahwira*, in the old days, would act out the death of their friend. Jamela summed up the situation: "There was no way I could not attend the funeral, but I nearly died for it." It was a dramatic scene.

Jamela had parked his car at the side of the road a few hundred yards from the farm where the funeral was to take place, and he walked alone to Parirenyatwa's father's home where everyone had gathered. Most everyone in ZAPU's executive was there, including Nkomo, Mugabe, Chinamano, and Sithole. On one side of the yard was a singing group to console the mourners, while on the other side sat the ZAPU leaders. Nkomo watched as Jamela entered the house to speak with Parirenyatwa's father. While Jamela was inside the house, disbelief turned to anger because he had dared to make a public appearance at his friend's funeral. ZAPU youth began to gather weapons, *badzas* (hoes), and sticks; a group went out and set Jamela's car on fire. Jamela described what happened from that point:

> I was in the house with old Parirenyatwa. Somebody came and told me there was going to be trouble there. This was Robert Marere, a personal friend, who asked me to leave since there was a plot to do me harm. He also offered me protection. The executive of Sithole, Mugabe, Chinamano and all of the big ones came. . . . They came up and started escorting me to my car. They were not enough. People, the youth started calling for my blood. They [the defenders] were all around me; Mugabe here, Sithole here, Takawira there and so on. When they [the attackers] were so many now, others got through and started hitting me. Some protected me. At that time, Mugabe called out for order with a megaphone. I nearly died on that day. There was blood all over. . . . From there it was open war now, between Nkomo and me.[8]

Lawrence Vambe, who was present at the funeral, later wrote of the significance of the scene for those in attendance: "Joshua Nkomo who made the funeral oration was deeply angry and could scarcely contain his emotion. As we eventually dispersed, some of us had the premonition, I know, that our immediate future was to be even darker than the present."[9]

The following day, factional fighting erupted between the SRTUC and ZAPU in the townships of Salisbury and Bulawayo. The *Daily News* ran a large headline on Monday, August 20: "TUC Will Meet Force with Force—Jamela." Jamela, his head in bandages with six cuts to his head and several on his hands, told a *Daily News* reporter, "I must say I was very lucky to come out alive. I know that I owe a debt of gratitude to the Rev. Ndabaningi Sithole, the ZAPU Chairman, and to Mr. Joshua Chinamano, who together with a few others helped to pull me away from my attackers."[10] An editorial on the front page of the *Daily News* asked just what the beating of Jamela meant for ZAPU, and suggested it showed "members of ZAPU's Youth Council are running out of the control of the Central Executive." The editorial also mentioned previous warnings and intimidation against Jamela such as the July 23 meeting of the SRATUC in Bulawayo's Stanley Square, where Mr. F. Nehwati, a Bulawayo trade union leader, heavily criticized Jamela to a crowd of five thousand: "The meeting ended with a mock burial of Mr. Jamela, including an imitation coffin."[11]

The *Daily News* editorial called for disciplinary action against the ZAPU youth involved in beating Jamela. The editorial gave a list of assumptions that could be drawn should ZAPU fail to control its youth wing: "It would be assumed that the party approved of the sad incident," or, that "the democracy the ZAPU is fighting for in fact means freedom for party members only" or, that "the party leadership (which was represented at the scene of the incident) in fact has lost control of its restless, impatient youth section."[12] The *Daily News* editors, still at this point acting independently, voiced their apprehension over the use of violence against rival politicians. From this point on Jamela had his TUC youth and Nkomo had his ZAPU youth. Jamela turned to organizing his supporters for protection to fight against the ZAPU youth in the townships. Geren's description of this shift in Jamela's image, from the former darling of American trade union interests into the organizer of "thugs" to fight for the SRTUC, showed his frustrations (although this phase of organizing was perhaps more in line with the American trade union tradition than Geren was willing to concede): "Following the Murewa incident, Jamela devoted most of his resources to the formation of a SRTUC Youth League to attempt to counter the ZAPU Youth Front. Classical trade union organization went by the boards. During the last two weeks in August there were numerous open fights between the two groups."[13] The fighting was not sustainable, as more and more trade unionists made the decision to leave the SRTUC in order to protect themselves.

If the factional violence between the SRTUC and ZAPU was not enough, the buildup to the 1962 general elections witnessed growing violence against any "sellout" African politicians who tried campaigning for the existing predominantly European parties or those who attempted to create new African political parties to run in the election. ZAPU youth threatened township residents to stay away from the elections and any other political party besides the now banned ZAPU. There were also threats of violence against township residents who did not honor calls for strikes. In one case, a fourteen-year-old boy was arrested under the Law and Order (Maintenance) Act

(LOMA) for distributing "subversive leaflets . . . which stopped men and women from going to work"; the *Daily News* reprinted part of the leaflet:

> From Monday onwards no man, women or girls shall go for work—he or she who goes to work shall be killed—no hitting—but killing. We want everyone to play Chachacha. Edgar shall play this tune, sell-out shall play this tune till the day we shall take over. Prepare your arrows, bows, picks, mattocks, shovels and the panga men should be on the field for the game to kill every enemy, sell-out and everything white.[14]

According to Andrew Sardanis, in his memoirs of politics in Northern Rhodesia at that time, dancing the Chachacha had been a popular phrase used by the United National Independence Party (UNIP) in Northern Rhodesia and was based on "the Congolese Afro-Cuban rumba music song, 'Cha Cha Cha Independence,' which in 1960 celebrated the end of Belgian rule in the Congo."[15] It was in this climate that Jamela, already unpopular with ZAPU youth, announced that he was going to form his own party, the Pan-African Socialist Union (PASU). Perhaps part of a last-ditch effort to regain political clout, Jamela's decision to form the party was, according to Geren, "apparently based on talks he had held with liberal elements of the UFP who wanted a sizeable African participation in the SR elections." Geren states that several sources had told him Jamela had been "strongly influenced in his decision to form a party by South African journalist, A. J. Levin, who acted as a go-between for Jamela and Abrahamson and who filled the vacuum the ICFTU left when it did not name an adviser for Southern Rhodesia." Geren reported that PASU "was a flop and actually never had a chance to get off the ground before the UFP announcement of early elections made planned PASU participation impossible."[16]

In addition to SRTUC's struggles, the experience of any competing vision of an African national party attempting to survive in the context of the early 1960s is shown in the failure of the Zimbabwe National Party (ZNP), which Geren would refer to as a "tragicomedy" in September 1962. Patrick Matimba, who was later expelled, had formed the ZNP. Jamela's friend Edson Sithole was also involved with PASU, and—along with Paul Mushonga; former SRTUC leader Phineas Sithole; and former leader of the NDP's Women's League, Lizzie Ngole—worked to form the party in September. Geren reported this information based on a press conference held by Edson Sithole on September 17, 1962, in which Sithole "said that the country needed a non-capitalist organization to establish equality between the worker and the employer." Geren was not optimistic about PASU's future, primarily given its small base of support and the inability of the leadership to work together. The big question on everyone's mind was whether the rumors were true that PASU had been in part instigated and encouraged by Minister of Labour

Abrahamson and Salisbury journalist A. J. Levin. Geren reported that "Jamela has not yet publicly disclosed his affiliation with PASU, but it is commonly believed that he has had a key role in its formation."[17] According to Geren, Jamela had described his plans to form a new party once the Southern Rhodesian government had announced the expansion of a wider electorate and the creation of four African government ministers. This never happened, but the link of Jamela to the discussion of such a plan with Abrahamson and Levin was an open secret among ZAPU leaders. Nathan Shamuyarira managed to obtain a letter connecting the three men and plans for a new party, leading to headlines in the *Daily News*. According to Shamuyarira, during September 1962 "Joshua Nkomo had handed me a letter written by a legal firm for someone unnamed, which offered Jamela and his Trade Union Congress £120 a month and a truck for the purpose of enrolling Africans as voters."[18] Shamuyarira was charged in court for refusing to reveal the source of this letter, and although ZAPU officials later admitted they were the source, Shamuyarira resigned as editor of the *Daily News* over the lack of support he received from the paper's white management.

But if the new PASU was to replace the ZNP, one might consider the rhetorical position of ZNP before its demise. The ZNP platform confirms the rhetorical value of a more radical anti-imperialist rhetoric in order to criticize other competing parties for their negotiations with outside interests. The ZNP's rhetoric was therefore dedicated to exposing ZAPU as an imperialist party. In June 1962 ZNP member Mr. Chimombe told the *Daily News* that Mushonga and the ZNP would "never work with ZAPU" and lashed out at the negotiations between ZAPU and the Rhodesians on the constitution: "ZAPU is an imperialist sponsored party. We are not going to co-operate with any political party which does not agree with our policy of transference of power from the white man to the black man."[19] To further distance themselves from ZAPU, the ZNP's leaders criticized ZAPU's multiracialism. Chimombe used the example of ZAPU's Terence Ranger to make his point: "The ZNP is fighting a battle in which our guns are directed at the white man. Our guns will soon be fired. We do not expect men like Dr. Ranger to turn round his gun and direct it to his fellow white man or to his cousin, just because he wants to maintain the rightful status of the African in his fatherland."[20] At one level, the ZNP rhetoric echoed the language used back in 1958 when Mushonga, along with Nyandoro and Chikerema, had told Marjorie Perham and the American consul general in no uncertain terms that violence was inevitable. For Mushonga, Nkomo and the ZAPU executive had subsequently become overly involved with the international dimension of the struggle, spending too much time at the United Nations. Chimombe told the *Daily News* that the ZNP did not expect the UN "to fight our battles for us" as the "UN has never liquidated colonialism in any country. It is just an 'International Cooling Chamber.'"[21] The leadership split in 1963 would once again bring these themes out into the open, particularly the claims by each faction that it alone embodied the "true" Zimbabwean people against those African politicians aligned with "outsiders."

The violence did, however, increase the level of intimidation in the townships and therefore helped to justify the Southern Rhodesian government's banning of ZAPU on September 20, 1962. After the banning, Nkomo put Ndabaningi Sithole in charge of ZAPU international affairs from Sithole's base in Dar es Salaam, while making Josiah Chinamano and Nathan Shamuyarira ZAPU spokesmen in Southern Rhodesia. According to Geren's readings of the situation at the time of ZAPU's banning, the Whitehead government was determined to try to keep the possibility open for working with ZAPU, but sought "to separate Nkomo from Robert Mugabe and the ZAPU left." More significantly, there were no serious African political parties to replace ZAPU, something that the attacks on Jamela had helped to ensure.

During the violence before the elections, Jamela remained a target for ZAPU's mobilization of violence in the township. A photo in the *Daily News* for September 22, 1962, for example, ran the following caption:

> The picture shows police who guarded the huge crowd which gathered last Sunday at Chaminuka Square Harare. This was a Zimbabwean African People's Union meeting. Soon after the meeting about seven hundred people marched to Mr. Reuben Jamela's house and smashed every window pane of the house. A man was also beaten to death by the crowd. Another regained consciousness at the hospital.[22]

The violence in the townships between the supporters of Jamela's SRTUC and ZAPU was now deadly. The ZAPU newsletter *Zimbabwe News* for September 1962 ran a story claiming victory over Jamela and warned "anybody who will continue supporting Jamela either in the ICFTU or any where else will be considered a sworn enemy of the African people of Southern Rhodesia."[23] At the same time, Nkomo and others in ZAPU had larger issues than Jamela with which to contend, as the decision had been made in September 1962 to obtain weapons from Egypt and to start training soldiers to fight the RF government. Nkomo would write in his autobiography of the decision: "We had not wanted the armed struggle—but we were under attack, and we had to defend our people."[24] Whitehead's public claim that his government's strategy to widen the electorate for the 1962 elections was working was therefore made a nonevent by ZAPU and the strong intimidation it used against those willing to present an alternative African political party.

Assessing Jamela's International Support

When Geren visited Jamela on October 16, 1962, he found "Jamela very depressed during a conversation at SRTUC headquarters."[25] Jamela had realized, according to Geren, "that at least for the time being the association of his name with the SRTUC meant no SRTUC progress." Perhaps as an indication of Jamela's commitment to trade union unity and of his political savvy, Jamela suggested to Geren that his supporters might join the SRATUC in order to "prepare the way for a future unification of the TUC's."

Throughout all of this turmoil, Jamela continued to lobby his Western contacts at the ICFTU and AFL-CIO. He wrote to Stefan Nedzynski, the assistant general secretary of the ICFTU, in November 1962 to explain that the split had been orchestrated by ZAPU in order to alienate him, and that he and his supporters were "wrongly accused of standing in the way of African Nationalism. This we categorically deny because we are not." Jamela defended his role and that of the SRTUC "in the struggle for African majority Rule," arguing that the desire to remain an independent trade union had "invited the wrath of some of our fellow country-men and outsiders, the latter being the chief culprits."[26] Jamela most likely had the Ghanaian John Tettegah in mind here, believing that Tettegah had helped Mugabe and Silundika understand the power of an anti-western rhetoric as a means of weakening independent trade union leaders. Jamela assured Nedzynski that he was not concerned with accusations that the ICFTU is a "British, American or Western Imperialist weapon," nor did Jamela see the ICFTU standing "in the way of African aspirations. We do believe that it does not encourage communism and fascism and here we agree." And, in a insinuated attack on those in ZAPU who were attempting to gain financial support from both sides in the Cold War, Jamela concludes: "That is the reason we disagree with people who give some sweet language to some visitors and they have other things to say to other visitors." This was to be the end point of Jamela's support from the ICFTU. As Brian Raftopoulos has shown, ICFTU representative Howard Robinson's arrival in September 1962 made it clear to Brussels that Jamela was on the outs with the nationalists.[27]

Consul General Geren reported back to the U.S. State Department the information Robinson had gathered while meeting with ZAPU, SRTUC, SRATUC, and other groups in Salisbury. Robinson's debriefing with Geren related a meeting with Robert Mugabe and J. Z. Moyo in which the two ZAPU leaders maintained the need to keep the labor movement "part and parcel of ZAPU during the African fight for political supremacy." Because they viewed Jamela as compromised by his having worked closely with Abrahamson, they "insisted there was no possibility of reaching an agreement" with Jamela. Already convinced of Jamela's "demise" from the point of view of the ICFTU, Robinson was mostly concerned with gauging Mugabe's and Moyo's sentiments toward future cooperation between the ICFTU and ZAPU. Robinson told Geren he was optimistic about further cooperation, and that he "was encouraged by a Mugabe question, 'Can the ICFTU support two organizations in one country?' "[28]

Geren would later explain, in December 1962, how tough it had been for the ICFTU to abandon Jamela, as "the switch in the ICFTU policy in Southern Rhodesia, which has seen that organization drop support of one [of] its best friends in Africa, Reuben Jamela, has undoubtedly been distasteful to the ICFTU."[29] As "distasteful" as the decision was, it also indicated the transition of Cold War strategies away from Irving Brown's idea of building strong personal links with anticommunist trade unionists such as Jamela and Mboya, and toward a more direct approach to obtain influence among the nationalist leadership. Robinson's personal conversations with Geren revealed Robinson's own assessment of why the ICFTU had continued to support Jamela even as reports of opposition to him were being received from many African trade unionists. Robinson had been shown letters from Nedzynski to Jamela, letters dated even as late as October 1962, stating, "Jamela could be assured the ICFTU was not going to desert him." According to Robinson, then, it was not only Brown's support but also a concerted effort between Nedzynski and his British allies who supported Jamela without the ICFTU's full support. Geren wrote: "Tying together the apparent Jamela-Abrahamson cooperation, the British TUC correspondence with SRTUC, and Nedzynski's actions, Robinson said it appeared to him the British were cleverly using the ICFTU to the advantage of the Southern Rhodesian Government and at the expense of the reputation of the ICFTU."[30] The repercussions of this external intervention—whether from the British or from the American Irving Brown—shows just how vulnerable Jamela had become, with or without his promised international financial support. Robinson told Thomas Byrne, an American diplomat in Dar es Salaam, "that since Mr. Jamela's political and union futures seem indeed dark, he decided to withhold an ICFTU £1500 subsidy which has been periodically granted to Jamela."[31]

Having abandoned Jamela, both the ICFTU and the Americans were quick to seek more direct influence with ZAPU. Geren described the special efforts of the ICFTU's Robinson to meet with Reverend Ndabaningi Sithole, who was in Dar es Salaam, in order to "obtain, if possible[,] ZAPU's blessings for ICFTU support of the SR trade union movement." According to Geren, Sithole requested funds for ZAPU and "the ICFTU gave ZAPU £600 to assist the party in operating its office in Dar. Robinson also met Sithole in Ethiopia and assisted him in obtaining [a] £5,000 grant from Haile Selaisse [*sic*]."[32]

In addition, members of ZAPU were now approaching the ICFTU and the AFL-CIO directly for support.[33] On the same day that Jamela wrote to Nedzynski of the ICFTU, Enoch Dumbutshena, serving as ZAPU's London representative, wrote to Maida Springer of the AFL-CIO asking for financial assistance. After first stating he was sorry he had missed meeting her while he was in New York, Dumbutshena wrote, "I would like you to help me in getting people to whom I could talk to and who can help us financially because we need a great deal of money."[34] At around the same time, the AFL-CIO had reassigned Irving Brown to New York City after years in Paris. His campaign to support Jamela had failed to produce the hoped-for anti-communist political movement. Geren notes Jamela's "standing among Africans as having fallen to a level only slightly higher than that of Tshombe" by early 1963.[35] Geren, who characterized Jamela as "the only trade union leader with courage to defend the position of the unions against ZAPU," urged the U.S. State Department to avoid giving Jamela any open assistance from either the ICFTU or the AFL-CIO in early 1963. He did, however, confirm that the "Consulate General has recommended consideration of some form of clandestine assistance to Jamela." But Geren must have had second thoughts about this, as he crossed out that line in the original.[36]

Given Geren's hesitation, it was unlikely that Jamela would have continued to receive any substantial U.S. funding, particularly as the leaders of ZAPU were to receive direct American assistance. If Jamela did continue to receive funds, he would have used it later in the year in organizing his urban supporters to defend Ndabaningi Sithole and others in ZANU during the ZAPU-ZANU split in August. As an intelligent and realistic politician, Jamela would reemerge as a ZANU supporter, and he offered protection for ZANU leaders during the early phase of organizing in the townships. As the next section shows, Sithole, Mugabe, and the others who broke away from Nkomo and ZAPU in 1963 would find themselves on the receiving end of a campaign similar to the one used to discredit Jamela's leadership.

How, then, had this divisive battle between ZAPU and the SRTUC affected the nationalists' campaign against the settler state? In August 1962 Herbert Munagatire, who had helped launch the SCYL and was now a reporter for the *Daily News*, had a conversation with Geren in which he detailed the shift in ZAPU strategy. He explained how "the ZAPU executive has almost completely given up any hope of the settlers' agreeing to hold new constitutional talks." He reported that Dr. Parirenyatwa's death had set back ZAPU's new strategy of strategic mass demonstrations, such as the one scheduled for August 17 at the Southern Rhodesian Assembly to be "led by Mrs. Parirenyatwa and Mrs. Josiah Chinamano." It was called off because of Dr. Parirenyatwa's death. Most importantly, Munagatire told Geren that the decision had been made by ZAPU to "concentrate its efforts in the rural areas. This strategy is based on ZAPU's judgment that the settlers can easily crush any large scale demonstration in Salisbury or Bulawayo." The plan was to use "acts of sabotage and violence . . . organized on an individual basis thus making effective police counter-measures extremely difficult."[37] It is significant that the strategy to limit strikes and demonstrations in the cities should come after the failure of strikes organized by ZAPU and SRATUC in the summer of 1962. The weakening of Jamela's position as leader of what was once a powerful trade union congress must also have factored into the decision. The main impact on ZAPU strategy was that factional infighting—first between Jamela's SRTUC and ZAPU in the summer of 1962 and then the much more dramatic violence during the summer of 1963 around the ZAPU-ZANU split—would bring political violence to Harare and Highfield, making what should have been, with hindsight, a more strategically sound plan to abandon urban protests much less effective.

The Impact of Political Violence in the Townships

Intimidation in Highfield and Harare were on the increase as well. The Southern Rhodesian government published a collection of accounts of harassment in 1962 obviously written and embellished for distribution in Britain and in the United States. The publication, "Our Fight against Hooliganism and Thuggery: Victims' Stories of Intimidation, Fear, and Arson and Their Struggle against Racialist Extremism," elicited a strong rebuttal by Reverend Ndabaningi Sithole, who entitled his criticism of this government document "Our Fight against Sir Edgar Whitehead's Hooliganism and Thuggery" and distributed it to the United Nations and to the AFL-CIO. Sithole claimed the accounts in the government pamphlet had to have been written by a European. For example, Sithole writes, "The African author is artificially made to say—'Our Government advocates freedom of poverty, superstition, witchcraft and other inherent beliefs of primitive peoples.' Only a white author could have written that."[38] Sithole did not, however, refute the claims made in these accounts of township harassment, intimidation, and violence but emphasized the Whitehead government's responsibility for township violence. For Sithole, it was Sir Edgar who, after the arrest of "more than 300 experienced African political leaders and more than 2,000 African supporters of ZAPU, cannot escape the charge that he is the promoter of hooliganism and thuggery which will go on until massive African oppression ceases."[39] Nevertheless, the government pamphlet gives an indication of the way politics was being carried out in the township, as the stories were corroborated by similar accounts published in the *Daily News*. An example from September 1962 describes how ZAPU youths entered a township resident's house on a Sunday morning. They wanted to know why he wasn't on his way to the ZAPU rally. They demanded that he "come along or else!"

> When we neared the rally I was ordered to take off my jacket, tie and shoes as a mark of respect. Naturally, I did not want to do any of these absurdities but I had to obey or be badly assaulted. At this meeting everyone was ordered to remove

these items of clothing. I was disgusted to see some youths molest girls who were wearing stiff petticoat skirts. They were accused of being dressed in an un-African fashion, and their stiff petticoats were torn off from them.[40]

Other accounts included in the government's publication described ZAPU youth entering houses and demanding to see ZAPU membership cards. The occupants were told that a "register" was being kept of all the houses in the suburb, and also that any owner of a house who was not a member of their party " 'would be remembered' when the appropriate time came."[41] The Salisbury director of African Administration noted in 1962 how township residents were "relieved" when the nationalist parties were banned: "One reason for such relief is the knowledge that for a time at least there will be no intimidation to attend political meetings or house to house inspections to discover whether or not the occupants are paid up members of 'the Party.' "[42] Although it would be expected for the authorities to claim the banning of meetings as universally popular, comments such as these provide evidence of the battle under way in the townships. The failures of ZAPU to produce the promised quick goals of majority rule and "independence" meant party discipline was all the more crucial to sustain pressure and to prove to the world the party's "mass support." By the end of 1962, the ZAPU youth had managed to develop a level of surveillance and intimidation that was arguably more effective than the township police. The party youth had become a force with which township residents had to contend, and as the battles with Jamela's supporters had shown, the party youth were willing to fight, intimidate, and harass those still attempting to represent something other than ZAPU.

African members of the Federation Parliament were also targets for public humiliation and violence. Lawrence Vambe, who returned to Salisbury from London in August 1962, noted that now many prominent African politicians had to travel around with bodyguards: "Some of my friends bore scars from the attacks they had suffered at the hands of black youths who regarded them as *imbgwa dze vasungate*—'running dogs of the imperialists.' "[43] The emphasis on discipline among party members meant that those who left the party to start a new organization were to be victims of violence and intimidation. The police were now competing with the Youth League of ZAPU, and all sides turned increasingly violent. By 1963 a divisive factionalism among ZAPU leaders would make life even more difficult for those who tried either to stay clear of politics or to criticize this style of urban politics. There was, of course, a catch-22 sort of logic to this ever-heightening "sellout" politics, as no African nationalist party could possibly succeed in financing a political party or an armed resistance movement without some relations with outside interests, as Mugabe had told Mulcahy, the American consul general, in April 1962. As the next section argues, the gap between rhetoric and reality was to become even greater in 1963, with devastating consequences for a more democratic nationalism. All the efforts made by the leadership to consolidate power within ZAPU during 1961 and 1962 were about to come unraveled as a bitter leadership struggle drew attention away from establishing a strong position against the RF government.

By the early 1960s the legal powers of the Southern Rhodesian state were formidable. The 1959 Preventive Detention (Temporary Provisions) Act and Unlawful Organization Act made it possible to ban African political parties and to detain leaders and anyone viewed as a member of such movements. In addition, 1960 saw the enactment of the LOMA and the Emergency Powers Act. As Larry Bowman saw it at the time, "Taken together, these acts all but eliminated the notion of the rule of law within Rhodesia. They gave the government broad powers to curb freedom of speech, movement, privacy, expression, assembly, and association."[44] Before exploring the implications of township violence in 1963 and 1964 in chapter 7, it is worth noting how the ZAPU executive, both those ready to remove Nkomo from the leadership role and those defending Nkomo, replicated the "sellout" rhetoric used against Jamela just one year previously. John Day and other contemporary observers became highly critical of the "international nationalism" of these years. Based on American archives, it is possible to see just how close the ZAPU executive had become to the Americans in Salisbury and even in Washington as information of the split circulated through the U.S. State Department and the White House. The ability of the ZAPU leaders to invest so much of their rhetorical fire into the issue of American support was ultimately costly, but it would be the residents in the townships—and the older structures of community politics and democracy—that would pay the highest price for the leaders' intrigue with the Americans and others during the Cold War.

On July 16, 1963, two weeks after the news of an impending split and just three weeks before the official launch of ZANU, Herbert Chitepo was in Washington meeting with State Department officials to provide his view on the ZAPU split. Chitepo explained that he was "very much a party to the split and that his sympathies were entirely with the anti-Nkomo element." He told the meeting that what the nationalists wanted most from the United States "was meaningful help and 'not just words.'" Although Chitepo understood that the Americans were not in a position to give money outright to the nationalists, he thought they could direct private citizens or organizations that could help the cause. The deputy assistant secretary for Africa, J. Wayne Fredericks, explained to Chitepo that American officials had recently arranged this for the Reverend Sithole, having "personally steered him successfully to private American sources of funds." But Fredricks worried if whether now that Nkomo was labeling Sithole "an American stooge," it may work against Chitepo and others to be associated with American financial support. Chitepo replied that the State Department "should have no worry about such 'stooge' charges, particularly coming from the insignificant personalities they did. He laughed and said he would very happily accept '500 million dollars' from the United States and still defy anyone to call him 'an American stooge.'"[45] Chitepo's jovial comeback may have been an astute diplomatic maneuver, but it clearly downplayed the violence associated with the "sellout" label back in Salisbury.

As word of the split grew and details of the plans to form a new party led by the suspended ZAPU executive in Dar es Salaam reached Harare and Highfield, Nkomo and Chikerema began to lash out at the United States as having orchestrated the leadership split precisely to facilitate the creation of a competing nationalist organization. On July 24 George Silundika and Josiah Chinamano had a discussion with Aristone Chambate, an employee of the American consulate general in Salisbury. According to an account Chambate wrote of the conversation for Geren, Silundika was quite upset over news given to him by Edson Zvobgo concerning American support for the Sithole group. Zvobgo had told Silundika "that while in the United States the Reverend N. Sithole had private meetings with Governor G. Mennen Williams. Silundika claimed that it was at these private meetings that the plan to depose Nkomo was 'hatched.'"[46] What is most interesting about Silundika's claims is his characterization of the difference between "the intellectuals" and those leaders who still had the support of "the masses." According to Chimbate, Silundika "admitted that the new group had the support of the majority of the intellectuals, but he felt that the group had not the slightest chance of winning the support of the masses. He noted that the power is with the masses."[47] Silundika then gave the examples of Balewa in Nigeria and Nkrumah in Ghana, both of whom "did not have the support of the intellectuals in their countries."

Chimbate then asked Silundika why he thought the Americans would want to replace Nkomo with Reverend Sithole. Silundika replied that since Nkomo had shown himself to be independent and because the Americans thought Nkomo to be "pro-East," they "would like to see 'their stooges in power.'" Chambate described Silundika as being "in an angry mood" and Chinamano as "all the time nodding his head to indicate his agreement with Silundika." After Silundika had left, Chambate asked Chinamano "whether he thought these accusations against the U.S. were true." Chinamano, according to Chambate, did not put a lot of trust in the source of this accusation—"presumably a reference to Eddson [*sic*] Zvobgo"—but he did think "Sithole had made an indelible impression upon many people at the UN last year. Chinamano said he himself had heard many people ask why Sithole or Shamuyarira were not in Nkomo's position." Chinamano also explained how "a good number of African leaders in the Pan African movement think that Nkomo is not equal to the task before him." In defense of Nkomo,

Chinamano concluded that although "these leaders feel that way, we cannot afford to have leaders imposed on us from outside our borders."[48]

Zvobgo's information about a meeting between Sithole and Governor Williams, the U.S. assistant secretary of state for Africa, was not so unreliable. Reverend Sithole had met with Williams on April 16, 1963, as part of his diplomatic visit on behalf of ZAPU. The transcript of the meeting, however, does not indicate any negotiations between Williams and Sithole toward the formation of a new party, or to remove Nkomo; on the contrary, Williams and Sithole were at odds over future strategy, and Sithole seemed to be tactfully threatening the United States that if more tangible help on behalf of the nationalists was not forthcoming, they would be forced to look elsewhere. Sithole told Williams of the "heavy pressure on the ZAPU leaders" from younger Rhodesian Africans, including the two university students who attended the meeting—a Mr. Zvinoyira, who was studying at American University, and Mr. Razemba, who was studying at the Hampton Institute. Zvinoyira told Williams that the ZAPU leadership had "been patient too long" and that "the people were now serving notice on their leaders that the time had come to take the initiative themselves and, since all other methods had already failed, begin a campaign of violent demonstrations to convince the British that it was necessary for them to intervene."[49]

Reverend Sithole told Williams that such views among university students were common, and he explained how he received letters "from students in the US, in England, in India, 'and in the East' saying that they were willing to interrupt their educations and come home and fight." Sithole then added a veiled threat: "Help was being sought from all quarters, he said; a drowning man does not question the character of the man who extends a hand to help him."[50] In the Cold War context of 1963, such a statement was a challenge to the Americans to make their position more clear. Governor Williams gave a diplomatic answer, stating that the United States "was trying to be as helpful as possible in ways that would not always be apparent to ZAPU and subject to many practical limitations upon our scope for activity." Williams assured Sithole and the students that they "should rest assured" the motives of the United States "were always clear."[51] The account of this meeting shows Reverend Sithole's adept diplomatic skills at playing on the Cold War fears of the Americans. The meeting does not provide direct evidence that Americans were "orchestrating the split," but Reverend Sithole was able to raise funds for ZAPU during this visit to Washington, although these funds did not come directly from the U.S. government.

Nkomo's supporters in Dar es Salaam were correct in reporting meetings between American Ambassador William K. Leonhart and Reverend Sithole in July. Correspondence from the U.S. Embassy in Dar es Salaam records a series of meetings between Leonhart and Sithole. On July 8, 1963, Leonhart sent a "secret" telegram to the secretary of state's office and asked that the "following information . . . should be strictly held." In the telegram, Leonhart describes a "long talk with ZAPU's Sithole at his request this morning." Leopold Takawira had already telegrammed Leonhart to explain the need for the split in the ZAPU leadership and the need for Sithole to meet with Leonhart to, in the ambassador's words, "acquaint me with succeeding developments in their plan to revitalize ZAPU leadership." Sithole described the decision made after Nkomo had refused, in a letter dated July 6, to attend a special meeting organized by Takawira and Kenneth Kuanda of Zambia. The executive members in Dar es Salaam then proposed giving Nkomo one more chance to agree to meet, and "if he [Nkomo] again refuses [, a] meeting will be held in Dar-es-Salaam July 10 and Nkomo deposed." Sithole described how the executive had voted to depose Nkomo, "five favoring (Mugabe, Takawira, Malianga, Muchachi, and Sithole); one opposed, Moyo; and one abstaining, Msiko." Sithole reported that Chitepo, Shamuyarira, Chinamano, and Chidzero would also join.

More importantly, Sithole explained the reason for the split. Far from being something the Americans had created, Sithole described how the executive had "long dissatisfaction with his [Nkomo's] indecisive leadership and poor management of [the] party." The last straw, as has been given in most accounts of the split, was Nkomo's sending the executive to Dar es Salaam in April 1963 with instructions to form a government-in-exile.[52] Sithole explained how Nkomo had led the others to believe that Nyerere had approved of the plan, but when they arrived in Tanganyika, Nyerere was quite upset and against the idea, as he

considered government-in-exile foolish so long as political and constitutional avenues still open and that [the] only country in Africa that would conceivably recognize Nkomo's Government-in-exile was Ghana. He [Nyerere] had curtly told [the] entire executive in his first meeting with them that if they insisted on government-in-exile they could go to Ghana.[53]

The most likely reason for the guarded secrecy was Sithole's request of Leonhart to keep the upcoming announcement of the "leadership changes" a secret until Sithole announced them on "July 11 or 12." Sithole also explained, "There would be no Government-in-exile until all political and constitutional possibilities for movement toward majority rule had proved unavailing." The new leadership's strategy was to return to Southern Rhodesia "roughly in order of [the] severity of charges pending against them in SR courts." Once the executive had returned, they would "raise [the] political consciousness of SR Africans by [a] series of nonviolent political actions."[54] Leonhart's concluding comments to the State Department were positive, expressing the belief that Sithole's plans were "moving very swiftly . . . and in [a] constructive direction." He thought if a proposed

Commonwealth Commission could "materialize, it now seems likely SR nationalists will be represented by their most responsible leaders."[55] And indeed, from a Cold War perspective in the summer of 1963, the overtures to the United States from Takawira, Sithole, and Chitepo for assistance and support would have been quite comforting. As Larry Bowman observed, it was an open secret that ZANU "was well financed by Nkrumah's Ghana, Malawi, Algeria, Tanzania, and (to Nkomo's outrage) by the Organization of African Unity Liberation Committee."[56] Nkomo continued to receive support from Egypt and Nigeria. The diplomacy involved in getting the party off the ground with American support failed, however, to realistically assess the power and support for the Nkomo group in ZAPU. As in Irving Brown's overly optimistic reading of Jamela's SRTUC's prospects, the Americans in Southern Rhodesia and Tanzania were not willing to more realistically assess the power of Nkomo, his supporters, and the logic of "sellout" politics.

Nkomo's main supporter, James Chikerema, made the "imperialist stooge" charge the center of his campaign against the breakaway group. Chikerema, who had previously been on good terms with Geren, stated by the end of July that the African nationalist movement "will have nothing to do with the Americans." According to Geren, Chikerema angrily stated, "The American plot against us and the Zimbabwe people has been uncovered."[57] Chikerema claimed to have allegedly obtained some "200 letters" from the Americans to Sithole, letters that would give the specific details of the link between Sithole and American imperialist goals. This accusation came as somewhat of a surprise to Geren, who reported, perhaps somewhat sardonically, that "Nkomo and Chikerema had lunch at the [American consul's] Residence on July 26, at which time no mention was made by them of these allegations against the U.S."[58] It is worth considering how the "sellout" rhetoric became the focal point of Nkomo's group. It was not simply the continuation of a type of politics used successfully against Jamela; it was also a much older form of political mudslinging that Mzingeli had used whenever his monopoly on power was challenged.

Chikerema's public accusations against the Americans must have also seemed incongruous to Geren because of the good relationship built over the years between Geren, Nkomo, and Chikerema. Geren describes a productive meeting with Chikerema and the Americans in Salisbury on April 24, 1963, in which he speaks highly of Chikerema and suggests that perhaps Chikerema would take over "as a candidate for the lead role" in ZAPU. At the meeting, Chikerema had "reiterated the plea made in February to Governor Williams that the United States come all-out for African nationalism in Southern Rhodesia." The occasion for the meeting was a luncheon hosted by the consul general for Hans A. Ries of the Continental Ore Company of New York. Accompanying Chikerema was Peter Mutandwa and Boniface Gumbo. Mutandwa had just been released from nine months in jail, and Gumbo is described as the "former Highfield branch chairman of the NDP."[59]

News of the ZAPU-ZANU split, and the charges against American meddling, was taken seriously in Washington. William Brubeck sent a confidential memorandum to National Security Advisor McGeorge Bundy at the White House in order to brief President Kennedy on the split. Brubeck may have thought it necessary to send this information to the White House because Julius Nyerere, president of Tanganyika, was due to arrive for an official visit with Kennedy. Brubeck's memorandum explains the recent events around the leadership split, indicating the seriousness of the issue and the uncertainty of the outcome.[60] It also elaborated on the charges against American influence. Brubeck wrote how the consulate general in Salisbury, Geren, had heard from a "reliable source" that the Nkomo group had accused the American Embassy at Dar es Salaam of being "responsible for the ZAPU split." According to the memorandum, "The Consulate General at Salisbury has asked this 'reliable source' to tell Nkomo that the United States was not involved in this internal struggle of ZAPU. Salisbury has commented that Nkomo might wish to charge U.S. involvement in an effort to smear his opponents as tools of 'imperialism.'" The memorandum concluded by lamenting the split, as it had "seriously weakened" the African nationalist movement right when the Federation was being dismantled. It is an open question whether the memorandum expressed the true sentiments of the African Affairs Bureau of the State Department or the line considered more useful for President Kennedy in preparation for talks with President Nyerere. As the next chapter demonstrates, both Geren and Leonhart had become more trustful of Sithole and Robert Mugabe and seemed to have lost patience with Nkomo, Chikerema, and Silundika. Equally important, Americans back in Washington, including Brubeck and Mulcahy, had developed a great respect for the leaders of the new group who had come to Washington, in particular Reverend Sithole and Dr. Herbert Chitepo.

7

The ZAPU-ZANU Split and the Battlegrounds of Harare and Highfield

This chapter examines the leadership split in the nationalist movement and the subsequent ramifications in Harare and Highfield. The decision by the breakaway executive of ZAPU to form a new party in the summer of 1963 led to a struggle that would culminate in intramovement violence. This development was welcomed by the Southern Rhodesian state, especially as the Rhodesian Front took advantage of the political violence to legitimate its draconian measures to "maintain law and order," while actually using these laws to divide and dismantle the leadership of the nationalist movement. In addition, given the physical layout of the townships and their relative isolation from European residential areas, the government could allow factions to battle against each other at the cost of township residents with little complaint from white voters.

Eugene Wason, the editor of the *Daily News* from 1962 to 1964, was among a small but vocal group of Europeans critical of this policy, and he would later describe how it was the state's policy to carry out sweeps of the townships every six months or so to make arrests, but otherwise the authorities were content to watch as the two factions used intimidation, petrol bombs, and beatings in their own attempts to take control of the townships. The factionalism also allowed the government's Special Branches to arrest leaders at will or, at other times, to covertly participate in the township violence and make it appear as part of the daily reality of political violence. American political scientist Larry Bowman, who worked as a professor of politics in Salisbury at the time, later described the split as the start of "a sad, wasteful, and useless struggle" in which "little attention was paid to the putative enemy—the local settlers—who were free to pick off the nationalists as they pleased."[1] Bowman provided statistical evidence of the magnitude of arrests, detentions, and restrictions in these years. Arrests under the Law and Order (Maintenance) Act (LOMA) increased from roughly

1,000 a year during 1961–63 to 4,435 in 1964 alone. Similarly, detentions increased from 495 in 1959 to 690 in 1964.[2] This chapter will explore further the implications of the factional violence on township life.

The official launch of the Zimbabwe African National Union (ZANU) occurred on August 8, 1963. Reverend Ndabaningi Sithole had left in early August for Salisbury in order to organize the new party and begin the campaign of nonviolent political actions he had proposed. Four days later, American consul general Paul Geren traveled to Dar es Salaam to discuss this development with Mugabe. Geren indicated the personal confidence he had in Mugabe: "We have a high estimate of Mugabe's analytical powers, his political sense, and his resolve for political action."[3]

In his interview with Mugabe, Geren sought to gauge Mugabe's opinion of the impact Nkomo's new anti-American rhetoric was having on the nationalist movement. No doubt annoyed by Nkomo's and Chikerema's quick reversal of their relationship with the Americans, he asked Mugabe for his views on Nkomo's sudden shift. According to Geren, "Mugabe believes that the charges of identification between the Sithole faction and the U.S. by the Nkomo faction do little harm with the masses, much less than a charge of collusion with the British or the Rhodesian Whites would do."[4] This nonchalant attitude toward Nkomo's rhetorical critique of ZANU leaders as "sellouts" to the Americans was in stark contrast to the violent campaign that would greet Sithole and others in ZANU in Harare and Highfield shortly afterward.

Funding issues were paramount on Mugabe's mind, and when Geren asked Mugabe to predict when the Sithole faction would take over the nationalist movement from ZAPU, Mugabe hesitated to give a timetable but told Geren, "The Sithole group needs money above all." What money they did have was frozen in the ZAPU accounts at Grindlays Bank in Dar es Salaam. At the time of the split, according to Mugabe, there was a balance of "£2,900," which represented mainly the donations of a group of "American friends" who had pledged to give £500 a month to ZAPU and had recently remitted in one sum covering several months' pledge. At that time the account required four signatures for operation—those of "Nkomo, J. Z. Moyo, Mugabe and Malianga, the former two signatories in the Nkomo faction and the latter two in the Sithole faction." Mugabe showed Geren

an old bill for £500 from the *Hotel Internationale* in Dar es Salaam, and spoke of similar bills outstanding in Dar, London, and New York. He also mentioned that the executive committee members were supposed to receive a £25 monthly allowance, which had not been paid for several months. Mugabe admitted that the claims of the Sithole faction to a part of existing ZAPU bank accounts would probably suffer from the creation of the new party ZANU.[5]

After the conversation, Geren observed, "Mugabe in shirt sleeves and sandals gives the impression of a most impecunious politician."[6] As a strategy for dealing with the Americans and gaining further financial backing, Mugabe's approach may have been convincing. There were, however, a number of other alleged funding sources for ZAPU besides these "American friends." According to Maurice Nyagumbo, for example, "Nkomo had just received ten thousand pounds from Nigeria which was used to transport many thousands of people from all over the country."[7] Nyagumbo also claimed "Egypt made a point of giving ten thousand pounds to Nkomo every month."[8] Nyagumbo related how the money was spent to target ZANU supporters: "Throughout 1963, the destruction of houses and property and the molestation of ZANU members were systematically carried out in townships throughout the country."[9] It was in this atmosphere that the new ZANU leaders desperately sought out funding from both sides in the Cold War gamble for influence among African nationalists.

As Mugabe's detailed description of financial problems showed his trust in Geren, Mugabe also appeared to trust Geren as a messenger to Sithole back in Salisbury. Geren indicates that Mugabe wanted to get word to Sithole to tone down appeals to nonviolence.

> Mugabe is worried about Sithole's favor for a program of "positive action" which is his name for what Sithole is describing as "non-violent" action. Mugabe believes this argument may fail to win the masses who want a more radical policy than that followed by ZAPU. He seeks to get word to Sithole to go easy on "non-violence" in his public speeches.[10]

As well as displaying Mugabe's trust in the American diplomat, his message also indicated Mugabe's skills at reading public sentiment and defining the party's rhetoric accordingly. That such sentiment demanded greater rhetoric about violence and self-defense versus Sithole's continuation of the strategy of nonviolence shows how far events in the early 1960s had moved toward a violent confrontation, not just between the African nationalists and the Southern Rhodesian government, but also in the relationship between the nationalist leadership and their social base of support. Similarly, ZAPU leader Joshua Chinamano had told Geren in April 1963 that nonviolence was no longer possible. Chinamano explained to Geren how the Northern Rhodesian United National Independence Party (UNIP) chair, Solomon Kalulu, had advised him and others "to adopt passive resistance especially [the] mass strike." Chinamano told Geren, "African nationalists in the north did not appreciate [the] extent [of] police control and surveillance in Southern Rhodesia."[11] The weakness of the trade union movement given the split in 1962 had also made the possibility of mass strikes less likely.

Sithole was the first of the new ZANU leaders to experience a backlash upon his return to Salisbury in early August to address a meeting of ZANU supporters in Highfield. Sithole, Nkala, and "200 supporters" required the protection of the Rhodesian police in order to hold their meeting. Geren reports that a "milling pro-Nkomo mob of [a] thousand threatening death to 'sellouts'" remained outside the meeting, and Sithole's and Shamuyarira's cars were stoned as they left the meeting. The next day, "Sithole acknowledged [the] miscalculation of Nkomo's mass strength," as Nkomo was even stronger in Harare and Mufakose townships.[12] Maurice Nyagumbo, who along with Sithole and Nkala organized the first ZANU meetings in the townships, would later describe the violent reception ZANU supporters received in August 1963, as he and other ZANU leaders "were finding difficulties in holding meetings. Each time we called one, Nkomo and his men fielded hundreds of thugs who would go about intimidating people and prevent them from attending. As it was not possible to protect every party member, those who could not protect themselves soon resigned and joined the Nkomo group."[13] According to Nyagumbo, Nkomo made statements against specific ZANU members, calling for their "elimination . . . from African society."[14] Afterward these individuals, including Nyagumbo and Shamuyarira, had their houses stoned by ZAPU supporters.

A month after Geren met with Mugabe in Dar es Salaam, the American consul general would call on Reverend Sithole and ask him to explain why the new ZANU representative in China, Tranos Makombe, was making anti-American statements over Chinese radio. Sithole, who was already under serious stress over the difficulties he and the others in ZANU faced in organizing against the established ZAPU, expressed his "frustrations" with the Americans for not providing funds to help him and ZANU in their battle against Nkomo and his supporters. According to Geren, Sithole made the following points:

The U.S. would help only in situations where communism threatens.

He (Sithole) having studied in the United States and having many friends there is reckoned by American authorities as "safe" and it is out of the question that he should be identified with communism. Consequently, no aid is offered to him.

Officers in the Department of State talk big and with encouragement but when it comes to acting to help a cause like Sithole's they cannot deliver.[15]

Sithole's previous attempts to gain greater financial support from the United States appeared to have been insufficient by September 1963, particularly as the American funds raised earlier while Sithole was still part of ZAPU were frozen in the Dar es Salaam account. This was a crucial period for ZANU, and while his new party was under attack from Nkomo's supporters and the

Rhodesian state, financial support from America and elsewhere was essential. Robert Mugabe, still in Tanganyika, continued to discuss with U.S. Ambassador Leonhart the importance of American financial backing for his trip to New York to address the United Nations and for European travel. Mugabe also told Leonhart of the need for funds to provide transport, food, and beer at ZANU rallies, just as Nkomo was reportedly doing with the funds he allegedly received from Egypt and Nigeria.[16] Leonhart cabled the State Department:

> Mugabe called yesterday to discuss his UN petitions and European Travel. UN appearances had provided him valued opportunity [to] clarify SR issues and make new contacts. ZAPU's Silundika [was] staying in New York and hoped [to] open office there. Mugabe said ZANU must find [a] way [to] finance [a] permanent representative [in] New York, [the] "single most important location in world."[17]

While Mugabe was exclaiming the value of New York City, the scene in the townships was not so enticing. Violence in Harare and Highfield between pro-ZAPU and pro-ZANU supporters started almost immediately after the announcement of ZANU's formation. The contrast between local politics and what John Day critically referred to as Zimbabwean "international nationalism" was therefore quite starkly drawn.

By August 14, 1963, both Nkomo and Sithole were denouncing the factional violence in the African press, but little in what both leaders said indicated they were capable of stopping it. Both sides said they would find whoever was involved and "see that the culprits are brought to book."[18] Nkomo blamed the violence on ZANU supporters, claiming that his supporters were using "self defence against a group of power-hungry people who have failed to gain public support." Viewing such factional infighting as unfortunate, Sithole said he had "a group of well-disciplined officials who can control the youngsters." Nkomo thought the "police must intervene, and right away, if the situation is not to deteriorate." Sithole reiterated that his supporters were under control and that "violence will not take us anywhere and I call on all who support me not to take notice of violent elements organized to move the clock back."[19] During a speech at the National Club in Salisbury in mid-August, former prime minister Garfield Todd expressed his frustrations over the decision by the African Heads of State Meeting in Addis Ababa, Ethiopia, to "not rest until changes are made in Southern Rhodesia, South Africa, and the Portuguese territories."[20] Observing the extremist element in the Rhodesian Front moving to take advantage of the now divided nationalist movement, Todd warned of future bloodshed and proclaimed, "How stupid Whites are. . . . We are living in terrible days and we don't realize the depths to which we are sinking."[21]

ZAPU Character Attacks

When Ndabaningi Sithole held the first ZANU press conference in Southern Rhodesia on August 22, 1963, he told the press, "When the party came to power it would repeal the Land Apportionment Act. It would also repeal the Land Husbandry Act and replace both by a new land redistribution law." In addition to land redistribution, Sithole promised, "A Bill of Rights would be entrenched in the constitution guaranteering [*sic*] the rights and freedoms of every citizen." He also reassured the reporters that "his party is non-racial and people who share a common destiny and democratic rule by the majority, regardless of race, colour, creed or tribe, could be accommodated."[22] The relatively quick announcement of a ZANU platform was heralded in the press, and particularly so given the lack of a comprehensive platform from ZAPU. The new platform also echoed the "rights of man" rhetoric of earlier nationalists, along with Reverend Sithole's commitment to nonracialism.

Rather than entering into a public debate over future platforms or tactics, ZAPU continued to respond to ZANU in a style dominated by character "assassination," a style reminiscent of African nationalist politics from Mzingeli's time straight through to the present. The ZAPU representative in Dar es Salaam, Benjamin Madlela, wrote and distributed a press release entitled "Information on the men behind the plot to unseat Nkomo." Madlela went further than Chikerema's earlier and somewhat vague pronouncement that ZAPU had unearthed the "American plot" to undermine Nkomo. Madlela's propaganda sought to link each of the key ZANU personalities with the Americans through brief biographical background sketches. Reverend Sithole was, according to Madlela, the most clearly implicated given his relationship with the American Methodist School, a relationship Madlela claims Sithole had developed "for the convenience of going to the United States of America. There for over three years, he was ordained in religion and imbibed American culture. Whilst in the United States and from that angle he wrote his book on African Nationalism."[23] Enos Nkala was singled out for allegedly having accepted American money to buy a car. Madlela suggests that the Americans made a deal with Nkala, paying a £225 fine to get him released from prison and, after his release, buying him a car.[24] As this particular accusation became widely circulated by ZAPU speakers, Nkala responded by threatening to bring Nkomo to court.[25]

Madlela's collective charges waged against the new ZANU leadership revealed a specific class issue involved with the split. Many of those who remained in ZAPU had been with the SCYL and SRANC right from the beginning. They viewed those in the ZANU leadership as representing the latecomers, those educated men who had been involved in multiracial organizations during the Federation period, but who had jumped on the nationalist bandwagon only in the early 1960s. Madlela describes the common characteristics shared by the ZANU leaders: they were all multiracialists; they all belong to "one tribal group which is not Joshua Nkomo's (Enos Nkala excepted)"; and they represented "*'intellectuals'* in a colonialist sense. This means it is comprised in the main of Africans who, by the privilege of their education, in our circumstance, regard themselves more identified to the European ways of life."[26] The longer-serving leadership of Nkomo, Chikerema, and Nyandoro allowed Madlela to conclude, "The difference runs directly along the lines of the founders of African nationalism and those collected from the wayside at a late stage." Rather than enter into a more meaningful debate on tactics and goals, Nkomo's camp adopted this claim to authenticity, which along with linking ZANU with the Americans, became a key rhetorical strategy. There are parallels here with Mzingeli's old rhetorical claims that certain leaders, particularly those associated with the Congress, were too closely aligned with European ways to understand the demands of the majority of less formally educated urban residents. In addition, similar to examples where younger men challenged Mzingeli's leadership role, ZAPU was now chastising the ZANU leaders for not having been there from "the beginning."

Nkomo took the anti-American rhetoric even further in his speeches in September 1963, suggesting that the Americans were planning to take over the country and that Sithole and Mugabe were their agents. Geren described Nkomo's speech to a crowd of two thousand supporters at Fort Victoria:

> Nkomo said the United States will "help us get the whites out" but with the aim afterwards of exploiting the country's minerals resources. . . . Nkomo said, "The minerals are here, but so is the cheap labor. . . . Patrice Lumumba died because he refused to sell the Congo to America. . . ." Nkomo added, "It does not matter about Sithole or Nkomo; but who is going to get our country back and not sell it to someone else?" He asked the crowd if they wanted money from Britain, America or Russia, to which the crowd roared: "No."[27]

This xenophobic rhetoric echoed a similar refrain coming from white Rhodesian politicians in their claims that the African nationalists were part of a larger communist (or perhaps American) strategy of foreigners attempting to take over Rhodesia from the white minority government. In November 1963 William J. Harper, minister of internal affairs in the Rhodesian Front government, spoke in Bulawayo against African nationalism, telling his supporters how "this is the time for us to close our ranks. Surely we have the wit and the skill, as well as the courage to defend our heritage, our land and our people against an alien 'aggressor.'"[28] It is usually considered that such sentiments referred to Communist influence on African nationalism, but the Rhodesian Front was also wary of American involvement. Commenting on Nkomo's anti-American speech, Geren added that Nkomo's rhetoric "with respect to the plans of U.S. business to displace the present whites" sounded curiously similar to what he was hearing from certain quarters of "the Southern Rhodesian business community."[29]

The ZAPU strategy to discredit the ZANU leaders based on their relations with Americans also appeared in the African press based on personal accounts and accusations. As Shamuyarira explains, the sale of the *Daily News* to the Thomson Publishers in 1962 had a direct impact on the editorial decisions of the paper. After Shamuyarira had resigned and the new ownership took over, the Thomson newspapers hired a Scottish editor, Eugene Wason, who would later write a revealing account of the *Daily News* in these years.[30] The *Daily News* was meant to become a paper for European as well as African readers, and the change is noticeable, with a mix of wire stories from Britain and the United States, and local stories on Rhodesian politics and township violence.

Shamuyarira claims that the *Daily News* became solidly pro-Nkomo in these years, and Wason's account confirms the newspaper's greater support of Nkomo. It did publish occasional editorials by ZANU supporters, or at least opponents to ZAPU, such as Edson Sithole. But the vast majority of articles and editorials were pro-Nkomo after the split. A large reason for this was the presence of pro-Nkomo Matthew Wakatama as a columnist. Wason also appears to have decided to support Nkomo and ZAPU because he agreed with others that Nkomo would be the leader most likely to work with Europeans. The campaign against ZANU was therefore a large part of the "news."[31] In September 1964, for example, the *Daily News* quoted Jane Ngwenya, the PCC/ZAPU secretary for women's affairs, as having told a trade union congress that the leaders of ZANU "were given more than £3 million to oppose Joshua Nkomo."[32] She also claimed that J. Z. Moyo had heard from "a certain American" that the Americans had held "secret talks with Sithole" and this, according to Moyo, had been the start of the split.[33] In October, according to Geren's reports, Chikerema told a rally attended by twelve thousand people held by the People's Caretaker Committee (PCC), which was the name of ZAPU inside Southern Rhodesia after it was banned in August 1963, that their beloved Dr. Banda from Malawi was now an "imperialist agent and puppet" for his support of the Sithole group. Chikerema claimed Sithole was a "stooge of the Americans," as the Americans were responsible for giving him the idea of forming a new party.[34] By November 1963 the fighting in the townships between ZAPU and ZANU supporters had increased in scope and intensity, leading to the first death when a government messenger and a member of the PCC was "beaten and killed by three ZANU youth."[35]

The divided loyalties between Nkomo's supporters and those supporting the Sithole group—whether in Highfield, Harare, or elsewhere—began to take on a more deadly and violent tone. This political infighting made it much easier for the Rhodesian state to more systematically use informers and surveillance in order to identify leaders and organizers for both ZAPU and ZANU. The leadership, in turn, put the blame for the violence on the Rhodesian state. A key example of this occurred in October 1963, when Nkomo was arrested for making the following "subversive statement" directed at the minister of law and order, Clifford Dupont: "Whatever is happening, be it violence or so-called hooliganism, is a direct natural reaction by the people against the Nazist and Fascist Regime that prevails in this Unfortunate Country—A regime of which you are a minister."[36] Nkomo's rhetoric echoed Mzingeli's choice of words from the 1940s, even as violence was destroying the chances for political alternatives, as the combination of factional violence and state repression reduced the scope of the public sphere. Public meetings were made illegal, and throughout 1960–64 arrests of leaders and supporters were extremely common. At one point in 1964, there was an average of ninety cases a week of LOMA violations in the Salisbury magistrate's court.[37]

The Rhodesian Front government's harassment and arrests of Nkomo, Sithole, Mugabe, Takawira, and others were relentless, following a pattern similar to the apartheid South African government's use of arrests and violence to shut down the ANC, the PAC, and their clandestine military organizations.[38] Nkomo was arrested in October and December 1963 and again in January and April 1964. Sithole was imprisoned in May 1964. The police would arrest leaders on the slightest provocation, usually with charges related to "subversive statements." The police tape-recorded the leaders' public speeches in order to use as evidence in court. Leopold Takawira, for example, was arrested in Que Que for having told a police superintendent to "shut up." Takawira lost his appeal in the Salisbury High Court in August 1964 and was sentenced to one and a half months in jail "plus a four-month suspended sentence." The incident began when Takawira was addressing a meeting and "moved a distance of about 15 feet away from the microphone" attached to the police tape recorder. The officer in charge, a Superintendent Jones, asked him to speak into the microphone, to which Takawira replied: "Shut up, shut up . . . when I am speaking this is not your platform . . . this is not a concert." The High Court upheld the magistrate's conviction "on a charge of stating something likely to undermine the authority of a police officer."[39] The humiliation of these arrests tested the patience of men such as Takawira. He would die tragically in prison in 1970, as his wardens failed to provide adequate medical attention for his diabetes.[40]

Joshua Nkomo recalled in his autobiography an incident of frustration involving Maurice Nyagumbo, James Chikerema, and himself. The three men were eating dinner at a house of a supporter in the town of Rusape. The police detachment assigned to watch them waited outside. After a while, according to Nkomo,

The young officer in charge came rushing into the room where we were eating and officiously told us that we had no authorisation to spend the night in that township; we must finish our dinner and get out of there so that he could go off duty. Foolishly he had come in alone, leaving his black constables outside. Nyagumbo lost his temper and pulled the young chap down with a smash onto the plates on the table. Then Chikerema waded in and they gave the police a real beating. He was quite a mess when he went out to his men.[41]

Nkomo goes on to describe how his lawyer, Leo Baron, managed to have the charges dropped. The symbolism of this vignette was clear enough: after years of Chikerema and others verbally standing up to the injustices of a police force that harassed and hounded them, the leaders themselves responded in a manly fashion to this particular insult.

Township Violence and the End of Democratic Space

Harare and Highfield were, by the beginning of 1964, much more chaotic and violent than leaders of ZAPU and ZANU were willing to admit to their international supporters. The divisiveness that developed in 1962 around Jamela and the category of the "sellout" had become even more politically and rhetorically charged. In November 1963, for example, the "Talk of the Town" column in the *Daily News* reported the coincidence of the death of a trade unionist, Tembe Chiweshe, on the same day as the assassination of American president John F. Kennedy. The columnist relates how Chiweshe had been a "trade unionist and a politician, a jocular fellow who was dedicated to his principles." What was most troubling, however, was how a number of his fellow politicians and trade unionists, even those who had been his neighbors in the Zwimba Reserve, were unable to attend his funeral out of fear of violence. The columnist concluded, "If this is politics today, that even in death you cannot recognize your relatives and neighbour, the whole thing becomes stupid."[42] The treatment of Jamela at Parirenyatwa's funeral and the fear it had invoked meant funerals were no longer safe from political violence.

Fay Chung's account of township violence in 1964 succinctly captures this dynamic at work:

> Groups of youths roamed the townships demanding party cards from all and sundry. The petrol bombing of each other's houses was becoming a daily occurrence. It was believed that the violence was initially instigated by ZAPU, using the slogan that it was essential to destroy the "snake inside the house," meaning ZANU, before destroying the "snake outside," meaning the colonial-settler regime of Ian Smith.[43]

The violence between ZAPU and ZANU made it difficult by January 1964 to organize the type of public showings of support that had been orchestrated in the era of mass rallies in 1960–61. The PCC attempted to show support for Nkomo during his January trial in Umtali, but the combination of tougher police tactics and factional violence had taken its toll on people's ability to participate in strikes and demonstrations. When Nkomo returned to Highfield after being released from jail in Umtali in mid-January, he was met by both his own supporters and members of ZANU trying to disrupt his welcome. Positioned between these groups were the police who used tear gas and dogs to break up the crowds awaiting Nkomo. Nkomo's car was late in arriving, so people in the crowd started to stone cars and buses along the Ardbennie Road, a common scene during this period. The police diverted traffic but a bus had its windows smashed "as stoning got out of hand."[44] Nearby, in Harare township, "a gang forced their way into the home of an African police reservist, took out his uniform and burned it." Eventually, Nkomo did arrive but was unable to enter the township and had to use "back roads" to make his way to Highfield. Stone throwers broke the streetlights and stoned cars along his route.

Signs of exhaustion and distrust, as well as increased worker insecurity over employment, reduced the ability of leaders to call for political strikes. The initial response to a called political strike at the end of January 1964 was very poor. Because of this lack of turnout, according to *Daily News* coverage, "young girls aged from 12 to 15 years walked into the houses of all the six sections of Highfield and told the women, "You must all go to Machipisa [Shopping Centre]. We want to show them. If you remain, anything can happen to your house." Once the women arrived at Machipisa, riot police used tear gas to disperse the crowd, and these reluctant participants returned home without food because most of the shops had closed early in the morning. During the evening, groups of young men went around "intimidating workers further but to no avail"; as a result, "the strike did not materialize on Tuesday either."[45] Police presence was high during the morning and afternoon of the first Monday of the strike as workers came and returned to work. But the Umtali magistrate's court decision on that same Monday finding Nkomo guilty caused a real outpouring of violence and destruction of property in protest. Nkomo had been charged with "making an act without lawful excuse, likely to engender feelings of hostility towards the police" for having told a gathering at the Sabi Bridge: "The torture that goes on during these investigations [by the police] . . . my Blood is boiling inside me when I see what is going on. I am saying to you your children are under torture. Unless and until you save this country from the fear-ridden settlers you must be prepared for this torture."[46]

A new strike call was issued for Tuesday, and this time workers who ignored the strike "were badly beaten-up," according to the *Daily News*. The reporter described how both Harare and Highfield "were smouldering with resentment against the gangs of unemployed thugs who began yesterday's rioting." A car carrying four Africans was "heavily stoned at Highfield" until the police arrived. Once the police appeared, the stoning intensified, and according to a police statement, the security forces "were forced to open fire 'to save their lives.' "[47] Two African men were killed by the police, including a twenty-five-year-old unemployed man. The reporter's disdain for the rioters is hardly contained as he describes middle-class African men forced from their cars by "thugs" who turned the cars over and set them on fire. A *Daily News* photographer "saw scores of women being 'rounded up' by intimidators and made to throw stones and attack other Africans returning from the city." The police tried to crack down, with loudspeaker vans driving around the township warning in ChiShona "that anyone arrested for stone-throwing could be imprisoned for 20 years."[48] In August 1964 a young man arrested under these laws for throwing stones at an off-duty police reservist in Highfield received a twenty-year sentence. According to the court proceedings, the young man and others threw stones at the police reservist while shouting, "Hit that Tshombe." In September in Harare township, a crowd on a football field beat two African reservists, one of whom died from the wounds.[49] The intimidation campaign against African policemen also had an impact on the ranks of the Rhodesian police force. Although Brigadier A. Dunlop reported to Parliament that the police "had admirably succeeded in containing in Harare and Highfield" the "subversive activities" of the two banned political parties, Dunlop also had to report that there had been 201 resignations from the force in 1964 and it was 103 officers "under strength."[50]

Now that there was a constant threat of informants helping the Special Branch of the police to arrest and evict residents for holding political meetings in their homes, Highfield residents, whether they supported the PCC or ZANU, were forced to organize "underground." An eviction from state-owned homes was a real threat and a reminder of the invasive nature of the state in the townships. Nathan Shamuyarira characterized the precarious situation for those who were reluctant to join or support the nationalists: "Most of them feel unable to make the sacrifices which nationalism demands of them—taking part in a demonstration could cost them everything . . . job, house, their children's schooling, their entire livelihoods." In contrast to these residents, Shamuyarira claimed the majority of "the activists are drawn from rural men and the jobless young townsmen."[51]

To be politically active took skill and the knowledge of evasive tactics. One Old Highfield resident, a married man who lived throughout these years across the street from a police compound, explained some of the tactics used to evade arrest:

> We used to ask people what they felt about politics. Those who said party-politics was a thing of the past were left alone, but those who were willing to discuss

politics were given an up-date of the struggle. We would work "underground" though. This way, we could convert many people in all parts of the location. In 1962, when people were detained at Gonakudzingwa, not many people were still active in politics, because the "intelligence" then really beat up people. If we had football matches, we used to have meetings afterwards. . . . We wrote down names of football players on a piece of paper. We called this "Yellow Press." Wherever we had a match, we would discuss politics if the police were not within earshot. If, however, we were raided, we would say we were a football team, and each member would say out his name and his number (on the team). The police then told us to carry on . . . but this stopped after some people who worked in the government informed on us.

The clearing of beer halls became a political act as well. Drinking establishments in Harare and Highfield were no longer places to escape violence, but targets of stoning and intimidation. On one January evening in 1964, the popular bars in Harare, including Vito's tavern, Matapi beer hall, Mapitikoti beer hall, and Marengenya tavern were all stoned on the same night, with youths breaking the windows.[52] The beer halls in Harare and Highfield were cleared on a Sunday in January to prepare residents for the general strike called for Monday. A European township official, expressing his dismay in the *Daily News*, asked how "thousands" of beer drinkers were capable of completely abandoning the beer hall and how they could be "afraid of small gangs of thugs and 'meekly obey their orders.' "[53] He, of course, did not have to live in the township and thus misread the levels of intimidation involved.

Factional intimidation and violence also made its way to the university campus in the European suburb of Mount Pleasant. The ZANU publication *Battle Cry* described an attempted speech by ZAPU (PCC) leaders in March 1964:

A number of PCC puppet leaders, including Mr. and Mrs. Chinamano, Messrs. Enoch Dumbetshena, Wakatama, Savanhu and Joseph Msika and a group of thugs imported from Highfield were shamefully chased from the Salisbury University College by the strong ZANU university students. . . . The culprits were chased away like dogs before they even uttered a word and had to bolt away from the University grounds faster than they had come in. The students sang ZANU songs as they chased the revisionists.[54]

Intimidation was showing up everywhere, and it was setting a tone for public violence and harassment that empowered those carrying it out. As this pro-ZANU account of the University College scene indicates, the split also represented an emerging class divide, with the ZANU supporters represented by the university students versus the old guard supporters of ZAPU who still had the loyalty of many people in Highfield and Harare.

Attacks against "Modern Girls"

As the politics of the mass nationalist period fundamentally challenged the earlier populist models, violent forms of cultural censorship appeared that combined party discipline with physical attacks on those seen to represent "sellout" tendencies. The mass meetings organized by ZAPU in the early 1960s, at a time when such meetings were still legal, were known for their creative uses of tradition in music and dance, but these rallies also made a call for complete subservience to the nationalists. The tough antisellout tactics displayed by the SCYL became a common characteristic as groups of young men and women targeted women just as during strike actions such as the 1948 General Strike and 1956 bus boycott. Young women were targeted for the style of clothes they wore or were ridiculed for wearing modern styles of clothes and hairstyles.[55] A *Daily News* account from October 1963 described the scene:

> Highfield gangs of young thugs are on the march again, threatening young women and girls with violence if they don't obey orders to "stop using make-up." Girls who have straightened their hair to try to look smart have been warned. "All girls who try and imitate Europeans in this way will be attacked." . . . The latest campaign follows threats last week to young girls wearing short skirts.[56]

As a *Daily News* editorial in that month suggested, "the campaign against the girls is a culmination of an extensive plan to subject the public to the rule of thuggery." The editors pointed out how the campaign has only appeared after the split in the nationalist movement, and that "although they [the *Daily News* editors] would be the last to say our women should be immodest in their dress. . . . We take the strongest exception to the idea of their being subjected to the humiliation and insults being meted out to them by these hooligans."[57]

For Edna Mathende, the hypocrisy of these attacks on girls in Western-style clothes and makeup by men in Western clothes deserved comment. In what was a rather strongly worded editorial on the *Daily News* Woman's Page—which was usually limited to praising the modern African woman or girl for either her fashion sense or her service to community, and at times both—Mathende's response lashed out at the illogic of a harassment campaign based on women's hair, makeup, and choice of clothing. Mathende reminded readers that the "very people who are carrying out these campaigns against women do so while wearing trousers, shirts, shoes, socks, and smoking cigarettes." Mathende then extrapolates this hypocrisy to politics in general:

> The African man in this country realises there is no party that can succeed without the support of the women and makes the greatest play of "our women must come with us." Yet when the women come, he does not share the planning and policy making with them. This image of the African woman being used as a tool dates back

to the old days. A man sought the opinion of his wife behind closed doors and then presented what he liked of it at the "all-male" caucus without giving the woman any credit. He does not think of her as an equal or a friend. She is his property.[58]

Similar assessments of the contradictory trajectories of nationalism for different groups and individuals appeared in the African press. Such letters demonstrate how some women were not accepting the paternalistic rhetoric of men protecting women.

A pro-ZANU letter to the editor written to the *Daily News* in February 1964 provides a more strongly worded criticism of the mistreatment of girls and women and the futility of the ZAPU-ZANU power struggle. Written by E. Kawanza of Mufakose township, the letter expresses a high level of frustration with the nationalist rhetoric when compared to the realities in the townships. Kawanza wrote:

> We as mothers of Zimbabwe notice our daughters beaten up in the streets for being smart, our homes are petrol bombed every now and then and so eventually we will live in perpetual fear of these brutalities in the land of our birth. Freedom can only be achieved by confrontation and determination. Praying [to] a man and kissing his feet will never get us anywhere. This will merely reflect our morals and as such, we as mothers of Zimbabwe must be careful to set perfect examples for our sons and daughters.[59]

In attending to the contradictions between male and female roles during the military phase of the liberation struggle, it is worth noting how clearly and forcefully women such as Kawanza and Mathende articulated these contradictions, while there was still a public forum for such discussions.

At the same time, the women in the leadership of the PCC were not spared from the detentions and imprisonments of the Rhodesian Front's campaign to contain and disrupt African nationalist organizations. Trade unionist Jane Ngwenya and community activist Ruth Chinamano were two prominent leaders who were arrested; Jane Ngwenya was sent to Wha Wha Prison, where she was given a separate cell, and Ruth Chinamano was sent with her husband, Josiah Chinamano, and the other leaders of the PCC, including Joshua Nkomo, to the desolate internment camp at Gonakudzingwa, located in the southeast part of the country near the Limpopo River. The arrest of these two women prompted a protest march involving 200 women from the townships into the Salisbury city center. A *Central African Examiner* reporter who witnessed the protest, which resulted in the arrest of 120 women, made a special point of indicating the women were acting on their own initiative and were not forced to participate by threats. "Not only were no 'thugs' following, but the slower marchers at the back were making obvious efforts to catch up with the main body, and none were drifting off into side streets as they might so easily have done."[60]

Figure 7.1. Protester and police officer, Salisbury city center, 1964. Cover photo from the *Central African Examiner*, May 1964.

The cover photograph from the *Central African Examiner* quite effectively captures the tensions and extremes such public marches by women created in the city center. The need, however, for the reporter to defend the protesters as acting independently of the dominant intimidation makes it difficult to assess a separate women's political influence in this period marked by youth violence and intimidation targeted against township women. Jane Ngwenya would later recall how " 'In politics, I don't think anyone wanted women to be there.' "[61] Ruth Chinamano, known for her speaking abilities at NDP and ZAPU rallies, nonetheless had to go out of her way to explain to Joshua Nkomo that she had been detained at Gonakudzingwa because of her own work and not because she was Josiah's husband.[62] If women at the leadership level were not able to advance a more progressive agenda, township violence in the early 1960s forced many politically active women to abandon temporarily their roles in the social services and the social welfare work they had traditionally done since the 1940s.

One of the more difficult protests for many residents in the township was the decision to enforce a boycott of township schools. The teachers were divided on this tactic, and the intimidation used to enforce the boycott brought out animosities between the respectable teachers and parents versus the "thugs" that they saw as "envious" of their using education to improve their lot. This fight over the school boycott brought out many of the underlying class tensions that had been heightened by the nationalist split. A "Harare Teacher" wrote to the *Daily News* in August 1964 expressing indignation over the ". . . Nationalist thugs threatening to murder anyone who dare to defy their orders by going to school. Is this Nationalism?" The author sympathized with the thousands of students who had hoped to "to sit for examinations at the end of the year" but who were "likely to fail because of the boycott which had already lasted for more than three weeks." The teacher then asks the rhetorical question of whether the underlying motive was not so much nationalism as "pure envy in the hearts of those thugs which makes them beat up children smaller than themselves," concluding that nationalist leaders "who really love their people should stop those criminally-inclined of their followers from frightening and endangering the lives of Africans of Zimbabwe."[63]

The school boycott did not seem to have the official sanction of either ZAPU or ZANU leadership. It was more of an indication of how those carrying out the violence and discipline in the townships had begun to set their own agenda, particularly with the arrests of large numbers of leaders. Nathan Shamuyarira, writing in *Crisis in Rhodesia*, does not mince words in his description of this divide: "The schools' boycott in Salisbury and Bulawayo in 1964 was largely the work of unemployed thugs. . . . The point to underline is that most of these thugs were primary or secondary school school-leavers."[64] Pointing out that this group consisted of "80,000 to 100,000 urban would-be workers roaming the streets without jobs, or any future prospect of one," Shamuyarira explains how "they are feared by Africans in the townships where they exert influence far greater than their numbers warrant. They are articulate debaters."[65] The high levels of intimidation made it very difficult for community leaders to step in and resolve the boycott.

The ability of the leadership to discipline their followers or to maintain control over tactics and targets needs further research involving interviews with participants in order to reconstruct the command structure of each party's youth wing in detail. Some evidence from interviews of participants and observers indicates the difficulties for organizers and those trying to remain outside of the conflict. One longtime resident of Highfield, who in his profession as a wood seller had to interact with his customers and party youth, remembered how "those years were nasty. There was what was known as '*Madhunamutuna*'. . . . It means 'one does not know what one is doing,' and as such, you just went along, even if this meant falling into a pit and hurting yourself. A '*dhunamutuna*' was someone who had no sense."[66] The severe demands of factional violence meant that extreme caution had to be used when traveling in the townships. According to local testimony, residents from Harare township were wise to avoid Highfield or Mufakose, and vice versa. Drinkers going to and from the beer halls had to weigh their interests there with the risk of running into youth from the other party.

> If you got caught, you were beaten to death. If you failed to prompt party slogans you were also beaten up. There were two party-slogans, so if you said the wrong one to the right people you got into serious trouble. If you supported ZAPU, you saluted the ZAPU way, and if you supported ZANU, you saluted the ZANU way. If you saluted the ZANU way to ZAPU people you were beaten up, to discourage you from supporting ZANU.

Older residents remember that the routine of having to call out the proper "password" was particularly troublesome for non-ChiShona speakers as the passwords would frequently change and could be tricky. For example, the word for "chicken" might work one day and the next it had been changed to "chick."

Another man gave an alternative definition of "*dhunamutuna*," claiming it was the name given to someone responsible for recruiting youths for military training outside the country. This source explained how the youth were intentionally kept separate from the political meetings of older men.

> At our meetings we arranged demonstrations and even the petrol-bombing of places. We arranged this secretly. We told the youths to emulate the Mau Mau of Kenya. The local white people did not want to see reason so we had to fight them clandestinely. They would never cede the country through dialogue. Petrol bombs were also used to destroy homes of rival party supporters. Top party officials were almost always targets, and they suffered a lot.

A growing fear and loathing in Highfield and Harare townships is portrayed in the numerous brief letters by residents to the editor of the *Daily News* stating that they were in fact ZAPU supporters who had been falsely accused of supporting ZANU. They wanted people to stop spreading these rumors and sometimes the bolder writers would threaten anyone who attempted to damage their property with either physical violence or a lawsuit. Wason later recalled how Africans from Highfield and Harare began to come to the *Daily News* office on Saturdays and personally deliver their letters to him. He remembered mostly how frightened they were after having received threats against themselves, their families, and their homes. Wason agreed to publish the first batch of letters and then it became twice a week—the initial group headed "Not ZANU" and the following ones headed "Nor Me." Sometimes there would be as many as a dozen headed "Not Me." These letters raised an interesting ethical dilemma for Wason, as he was "faced by five terrified Africans and asked to publish letters that they were certain were untrue. Truth is important, but so is compassion."[67] Wason provides an example of the letters: "Sir,—There are rumours circulating that I am ZANU. I would like the public to know that I am not ZANU and I don't intend being one. I am with the people in the PCC. Who am I to go against the wishes of the people?"[68] In such an environment, it was more than likely that some township residents would use the split to settle old scores. Individuals could either inform on their neighbors to the police or start rumors that their neighbors or prominent township businesspeople were supporting ZANU. In either case, there was likely to be a counterresponse, and this began to express an element of class conflict.

The lack of safety for township residents began to take its toll on collective action and people's willingness to attend rallies, strikes, and protests. In February 1964 "small gangs of youth knocked at the doors of houses and told people to stay home" to protest police shootings in Highfield. The youth made their rounds from three o'clock until five o'clock in the morning, but Highfield residents ignored the youths' demands, and by 6 a.m. the buses to the city center were full as usual.[69] Residents' patience with the youth had worn thin by then, and as Fay Chung writes in her autobiographical account, the chaos of the split also involved the seeking of revenge: "Jealous neighbors would report each other to the colonial authorities. Since these allegations were difficult to prove or disprove, this practice was a way of ensuring that rivals would be incarcerated without trial, with all their property permanently confiscated."[70]

The level of intimidation and violence in Harare and Highfield reached a peak in 1964. For example, on a single weekend in January 1964, police responded to complaints of house stoning, beatings, and assault in Harare and Highfield that had led to fifty-four arrests. In the Egypt section of New Highfield, two residents reported being confronted by "a group of 20 people carrying stones and were asked to what political party they belonged." In Harare, near the *mapitikoti* (petticoats) beer hall, two women were approached "and told not to wear tight clothing." Even Patrick Pazarangu, the postmaster for Harare township and Mzingeli's longtime supporter and friend, "was stopped near the Runyarare Hall and beaten up by a group of 20 people." The crowd dispersed only after they found out that Pazarangu's friend in the nearby car was an off-duty police officer.[71] Pazarangu, who had a reputation for toughness when he was younger—someone not afraid to throw a punch if someone insulted the RICU or Mzingeli—was now seen as just another old man, a sellout, who deserved be "roughed up."

Closing Down the *Daily News*

The Rhodesian Front had used its censorship powers to further restrict coverage of its campaign against African nationalism. As Elaine Windrich observed, the RF had effectively pressured the main papers in Southern Rhodesia to follow the party line.[72] The real thorns in the RF's side were the *Daily News* and the *Central African Examiner.* Both of these periodicals were strongly opposed to the RF's draconian measures against the African nationalists. As Eugene Wason described it, the two most popular themes in the *Daily News* were stories about the Rhodesian Front's plans for a unilateral break from Britain and stories about township violence. He noted that at first Africans living in the townships were not pleased about the coverage, but as the violence became increasingly worse, those threatened by it welcomed the coverage given by the *Daily News*. Wason and his staff kept up the pressure on the RF for its failure to protect township residents from violence. The RF, from its international public relations viewpoint, wanted to stop the *Daily News* from publishing stories about the RF's plans for the unilateral declaration of independence and about township violence.

One day before the state of emergency was declared in Highfield, on August 26, 1964, and following a 24–18 vote in Parliament, the RF government succeeded in its goal of banning the *Daily News* from publication. The parliamentary debate lasted until almost midnight, as opposition MPs argued against the ban. The minister of law and order, Mr. Lardner-Burke, gave an hour-long speech justifying the ban on the grounds that the *Daily News* had "become the mouthpiece of the nationalists and what was written in it was accepted by nationalists as orders from their leaders." He argued that the *Daily News* had as "its policy to spread subversion against constitutional government and that its activities are contrary to the interests of security but I regret that, for security reasons, I cannot make these public."[73] Opposition to the ban included the argument from J. R. Nicholson, MP, who suggested the ban had more to do with strong opposition on the part of the *Daily News* to the proposed unilateral declaration of independence—something his party, the Rhodesia Party, also opposed. Nicholson remarked that the *Daily News* "had consistently advocated that there should be an end to the struggles in the townships between the rival African nationalist factions."

University students responded to the planned vote to close down the *Daily News* with a protest on the morning of August 26. The interracial protest was noted during the debate by an opposition MP from Borrowdale, Mr. P. H. Grey, who remarked that "it was most disturbing to see young people of both races being carried away by the police. 'I believe these people are fighting for

Figure 7.2. Demonstration outside Parliament, Salisbury, against the banning of the *Daily News*. Front row: left, Judith Todd; right, Wendy Clarke. The photo caption reads: "Demonstrators had placards snatched from them before an incident outside Parliament yesterday. They were bustled into vehicles and taken to Salisbury police station." *Rhodesia Herald*, August 27 1964, 5. *Rhodesia Herald*, Copyright Zimbabwe Newspapers 1980/Ltd.

something which is a basic belief—freedom of the individual and of the press.'"[74] The *Rhodesia Herald* ran a photo of the protesters the following day, showing some of the seventy protesters sitting down in front of Parliament holding up copies of the *Daily News*. The *Herald* made a point of noting the protesters included "two European girls." The photo shows the two women prominently in the front of the protest, with everyone holding up copies of the *Daily News* with the headline "Chikerema Calls for End to Violence." A. E. Abrahamson, the Rhodesia Party MP from Bulawayo East, challenged the RF government on the proposed ban. After saying he had looked for any precedents in Africa for the banning of a newspaper, Abrahamson asked Parliament, "Are we really showing an example of the maintenance of standards and upholding a civilised way of life by emulating what Ghana has done?"[75] Part of the irony of the *Daily News* headline "Chikerema Calls for End to Violence" was that Wason had tried to get Nkomo to make a similar statement earlier but Nkomo, now in Gonakudzingwa, "felt he was unable to denounce violence" in August 1964. Wason then sent a reporter to Lusaka, Zambia, to locate Chikerema and ask him to publicly denounce the violence in the townships.[76] It is therefore possible to contemplate that the nationalist leaderships in both ZANU and ZAPU would not have been completely opposed to the banning of the *Daily News*.

The timing of the vote to ban the *Daily News* was significant, as it occurred the day before the imposition of a state of emergency in Highfield. Elaine Windrich suggests that the RF "proclaimed the Daily News a prohibited publication in terms of the Law and Order (Maintenance) Act, allegedly because they could not 'permit the much prized ideal of press freedom to be used for spreading subversion.' "[77] The more self-serving motivation of the RF is captured in Windrich's quotation of Prime Minister Ian Smith's commentary on the issue: " 'When people talk about the freedom of the press, of course, it is impossible to liken the position in this country to any other country in the world.' "[78]

By removing the *Daily News*, the Rhodesian Front had managed to close down one of the few remaining sources of news and political criticism in Salisbury. More importantly, the closing of the *Daily News* meant there would be less critical coverage of the state of emergency announced for Highfield the following morning. The government used sweeping powers to arrest ZANU and PCC leadership and the physical layout of Highfield to monitor and control the nationalist parties.

Townships under a State of Emergency

A state of emergency was announced on August 27, 1964, in the early morning hours, which included the banning of ZANU and the People's Caretaker Council. ZANU and PCC offices in town were blocked off in the early morning, and those who appeared at the offices were asked to give up their keys. The leadership was expecting this action, and most of them were out of town or already in prison when the banning occurred.[79] For residents in Highfield, the morning of the state of emergency presented quite a sight. From his house in Old Highfield, one man remembers watching as the police surrounded Highfield with rolled barbed wire and went about setting up checkpoints for people to enter and exit. All residents had to show their work certificates and legal addresses at the checkpoints, and workers were given stamps on their hands permitting them to reenter the township in the evenings after work.[80] The mayor of Salisbury described the state of emergency as a protective measure: "What has been done is in the interest of the inhabitants. Before, normal family life did not exist. The people lived in daily fear of their lives."[81] The language of the official notices posted around the township for residents to read expresses the professed paternalistic protection for residents:

> This letter is to tell you that the area of Highfield Township has become an area which is required to be looked after by police and soldiers because the way of living of the people in this area has become bad these days. Highfield Township has been noted as an enclosed area (emergency area). Police and soldiers have been placed in the area of Highfield so that they may sort out those people who are worrying you.[82]

Two months later, a state of emergency was declared for Harare township on October 8, 1964. As with the Highfield sweep, "police officers can arrest any person without a warrant, 'if he reasonably suspects that such a person—among other things—has acted or is about to act in a manner prejudicial to the public safety, or to the maintenance of public order.' "[83] Harare township was not completely surrounded with barbed wire as Highfield had been, but residents there experienced similar house-to-house searches and workers were required to get marks on their hands to proceed to and from their place of employment.

After the imposition of these states of emergency in the townships, and with the majority of the nationalist leadership either imprisoned, detained, or in exile, the Southern Rhodesian government had managed to suppress, for the time being, a viable African political movement. By August 1964, Joshua Nkomo, Ndabaningi Sithole, Robert Mugabe, and many other nationalists were in custody and would not be released for ten years.[84] The movement's focus now shifted to the clandestine work of organizing a campaign of sabotage and disruption throughout the country in hopes of creating, as Norma Kriger has written, "such chaos inside Rhodesia that Britain would intervene and negotiate African majority rule." The uprising never materialized, so the leadership was forced to concentrate on the difficult tasks of mobilizing and training for a direct military conflict.[85] By October 1964 the RF government proclaimed the "police round-up of hooligans" as a success in Highfield. The government's estimation of "success" in containing African violence in the townships reflected only part of the story, as the situation had called for a new strategy. Unfortunately, the arrests of the ZANU and ZAPU leaders and the imposition of a state of emergency were not enough to end the factional division between the two groups; they would remain divided and keep their forces separate during the war of liberation.

The township violence over the previous two years had taken a heavy toll in terms of the effectiveness of the nationalists. It had also created a situation

Figure 7.3. Ndabaningi Sithole, Leopold Takawira, and M. Washington Malianga at Sikambela, 1965. Photograph from the National Archives of Zimbabwe.

in which the state, by first standing aside and letting the factions fight each other, was now in a position to "restore order" within the township, therefore granting some legitimacy to the RF government among township residents. The nationalists had failed to keep their militants disciplined, and the result was a fear among many residents of being victimized or being falsely accused of being on the wrong side. The ability of factions to control different areas in the townships resulted in a new display of power, but this factionalism meant that groups on both sides remained relatively ineffectual in terms of the larger battle against the settler state.

Conclusion

This book has sought to weave together a linear narrative while at the same time unraveling many of the complexities contained within such concepts as African nationalism and the local, national, or international interests in Zimbabwean history. A fundamental theme has been to examine how nationalist leaders channeled their personal and localized frustrations with the humiliations of white racism, economic and political discrimination, and residential segregation into political action. It would be a mistake to assume that such channeling of discontent should automatically lead to a coherent nationalist politics, and as this narrative has shown, it was not a linear or "natural" progression. It was instead a struggle that at a fundamental level had less to do with competing visions of the nation than with who would ultimately lead the nationalist movement. This book, especially the second half, has focused on the ways the acceptance of violence toward rivals as well as specific groups in society, such as socially mobile women and men, represented a sharp break from the democratic practices developed in the early period. To illustrate the unfolding of this trajectory, I have documented Charles Mzingeli's use of imperial working-class citizenship as his conception of democratic politics and how this continued with Reuben Jamela's commitment to defending the independence of the trade union movement from nationalist control. The narrative examined the SCYL and the SRANC in their bids to continue the populist rhetoric of Mzingeli while expanding it from its local urban roots into a nationalist movement. These leaders, such as George Nyandoro and James Chikerema, made progress but changed tactics and strategies as the ruling white minority decided to confront them and other nationalist leaders with arrests, banishments, harassments, and violence. By 1960, however, as the stakes became higher, nationalist politics became less about expanding ideas of reciprocal nationalism and more about defending a core leadership against state repression *and* against rival leadership factions and their followers. In what was to be a short span of time the nationalist visions held by many of a more democratic and progressive political future gave way to a siege mentality, in which the disciplining of supporters and attacks against nonmembers became the overarching concern. In the process, the concept of the nation and of citizenship changed from earlier community-based visions to a nationalist struggle where rights to state power were more important than the rights of individuals.

In making this distinction, the preceding chapters have demonstrated how the shift to a more violent politics concurrently involved reinventing roles for women and nonelites within nationalist and revolutionary rhetoric. Mzingeli's earlier attempts to extend the notion of citizenship to poorer women and men were all but ignored by the 1960s, with only traces of his populism implied in post-1960 radical rhetoric. The breakdown of the cross-class alliances of Mzingeli's RICU in the late 1940s and 1950s by the more confrontational factionalism of the 1960s not only reshaped leaders' attitudes toward women as political allies but also allowed for a greater disregard for the urban working class and poor. The shift to violence and harassment to assure participation in protests and political strikes changed the rules of urban politics—and, by extension, national politics.

It is important to point out that this process is not unique to African nationalism or progressive movements, as comparisons can be drawn to other places and times where more inclusive "grassroots" movements achieve initial successes only to find their leaders and most active members—most often women—pushed out of their leadership roles. Anna Clark demonstrates this in her work on radical politics in nineteenth-century England. Clark suggests the successful pressure of the Chartist movement to reform labor laws in the early 1840s was a direct result of women's participation in strikes and mobilizations. The Chartist movement was to fail, however, some ten years later in its attempts to mobilize around the issue of universal suffrage. "By this time, physical force had been detached from its roots in the united action of communities and had become an all-male affair. The large demonstrations Chartists thought would intimidate Parliament into granting them manhood suffrage failed, undermined by lack of enthusiasm and suppressed by efficient state coercion."[1] Mzingeli's RICU campaigns in the 1940s and 1950s and the ensuing protests by the City Youth League can be similarly interpreted as more effective than the protests of the early 1960s precisely because the earlier protests incorporated township residents' specific grievances—women's demands, access to affordable urban housing, and improved wages and working conditions.

The factionalism in the Zimbabwean nationalist movement, initially around trade union loyalty, then led to a split in the leadership, which inadvertently served to assist the state's efforts to weaken the opposition. John Day cynically described the outcome: "Civil war between PCC [ZAPU] and ZANU was the outstanding feature of the nationalist movement during the period when the Government tolerated their existence, between August 1963 and August 1964."[2] Most importantly, the "backlash" against "modern girls" and against those township residents involved in upward economic and social mobility—the attacks on people with cars or those commuting to their jobs in the city center, for example—were accepted by the leadership as part of the mobilization of forces against their competitors.[3] Such violence against those who were intricately involved in the running of township life, such as social workers, teachers, nurses, and shop owners, created an extremely difficult situation in the townships—and often in rural areas. If this had been a temporary situation created in the crisis of the early 1960s, it would perhaps be no more than a brief chapter in Zimbabwean history. Unfortunately, as readers familiar with postindependence Zimbabwe are aware, this recourse to political violence has remained a key strategy to intimidate and harass voices of opposition and has become a means for the ruling party to maintain control in the urban areas.[4]

Another theme woven into the narrative reflects the contingent nature of international influence on the formation of nationalist politics and the destruction of alternative nationalist visions. The simultaneous abandonment of Jamela and courtship of ZAPU and then ZANU by their American "friends" shows how difficult it is to define one party as imperialist or pro-American while defending the other group or individuals as legitimately "Zimbabwean." Simple anti-imperialist interpretations are insufficient as the evidence reflects a more nuanced interaction of personal ambitions that were often draped in the rhetoric of national honor. The history of U.S. involvement in Zimbabwean nationalism also sheds light on the role of American and foreign interests more generally. What the United States likely saw as relatively "small" investments in individuals and movements had disproportional consequences for those who received American support and backing. The American sources discussed in this book reveal how essential these international contacts were in legitimating trade union as well as nationalist leadership, even if the funding rarely met the needs of those who were counting on it.

Reuben Jamela's story is particularly clear on this point, but it will be important to research further to better understand how American financial support for ZANU influenced the factionalism at the township level in the 1960s. Nkomo and ZAPU did everything possible to portray the ZANU leadership as "sellouts" and "imperialist stooges," but the impact of these accusations within the context of the factional battles in the townships remains unclear. It was, however, the case that just when ZAPU had decided to cease using urban strikes and demonstrations because they had become less effective, the factional conflict with the SRTUC and then the ZAPU-ZANU split caused urban political violence to detract and hinder the success of nationalist strategy.

As with so many elements of Zimbabwean political history, starting with Mzingeli's own inability to cooperate with other leaders, the ZAPU-ZANU split was a costly example of intransigence. At the same time, it is worth questioning the impact of Cold War politics on this propensity toward nationalist disunity. For example, to what extent did the availability of U.S. support encourage Sithole, Mugabe, and their colleagues to leave ZAPU? What about promises of military training and assistance from China and elsewhere? The interactions between the Americans and the Zimbabwean nationalists reveal diplomatic theatrics where the official line from Washington expressed caution and recognition of Britain's lead role in mediating the crisis, while diplomats in Salisbury and Dar es Salaam remained preoccupied with making sure they had gained the trust and confidence of the "winning side." Understanding the potential impact of U.S. financing, African nationalists did what they could to take advantage of this lack of coordination between Washington and "the field" in order to channel what funds were available to help launch ZANU and compete with ZAPU. With hindsight, the ruling ZANU-PF's current obsession with outlawing "outside influences" in Zimbabwean politics reveals the leadership's historical understanding of the crucial role American funding played in launching ZANU at a time when ZAPU was better positioned in the urban areas. Such evidence is crucial for deconstructing what Terence Ranger has called "patriotic history."[5]

A third theme of this book has been the changing nature of the public sphere. The first half of the narrative emphasized the intellectual commitment among African politicians and journalists to define a separate African press and then to use the limited space available to promote a lively and democratic public sphere. The final chapters have explored the closing down of this space carried out in part by the inherent logic of "sellout" politics. By the end of the period, a nationalist politics preoccupied with settling scores and carrying out character assassination no longer encouraged a free press or open dialogue. Staying clear of any real debate over issues of leadership and governance, the ZAPU and ZANU leaders only wanted publications they themselves could control to proclaim others "enemy of the people." As the political divide between the NDP/ZAPU and Jamela's SRTUC heated up in 1962, both sides attempted to use the *Daily News*, but the paper was unsuccessful at remaining neutral in the conflict. As the split between ZAPU and ZANU translated into battles in the townships, the ZANU leaders were already convinced of the pro-Nkomo slant of the *Daily News*, while the leaders of ZAPU were seldom enthusiastic about press coverage of factional violence, including stories of violence against schoolchildren and community leaders, which did not help their international reputation or their competition over funding and legitimacy.

The closing down of the public sphere also corresponded with the shift from community leaders with extensive experience to the dominance of competing party leaders in the townships. In the process, politicians with little experience leading communities usurped the democratic impulses of earlier urban politics and used "sellout" rhetoric and violence to remove and discredit those existing leaders powerful enough to stand in their way. In order to build an army of local militants, they accepted the violence of those who were acting on very different short-term strategies. The class and gender tensions in the township that surfaced in the name of defending "the people" from "sellouts," provided a convenient cover for the nationalist leadership from criticisms of their own specific class interests.

Although the historical context had changed, this style of politics did not disappear with the attainment of the nationalists' goal. After 1980, the ruling party in Zimbabwe continued to use political violence in order to discipline township residents and to remove potential political rivals and movements. Judith Todd, in her recent book *Through the Darkness: A Life in Zimbabwe*—a valuable book for understanding the nature of post-1980 Zimbabwean power politics—quotes from a May 29, 1994, front-page article in the *Sunday Mail* entitled "Go House to House, President Urges Party Youth":

> President Mugabe yesterday called the members of the youth wing of the ruling party to undertake a "house to house action" campaign to mobilize support for ZANU (PF) in preparation for next year's elections. . . . He said the party had now to resort to the methods used in the early 1960s where party cadres moved from one house to another recruiting membership. . . . He said the youth and women's leagues were the real wings of the party. "It is these two which will send a message to the opposition, to those little parties that think the opportunity is ripe to take over and destroy the revolution. Make them think twice before doing that," he told the cheering crowd.[6]

In addition, Norma Kriger's work investigating ZANU-PF's use of intimidation around elections beginning in the 1980s lends support to the notion that it was the conscious decisions of leaders to rely more on the power of youth-wing violence than the effectiveness of their own party to govern.[7] As Vesta Sithole has shown, the attacks on rival political groups have consistently remained within the rubric of "sellout" politics after 1980.[8] Likewise, the survival of the "sellout" logic in Zimbabwean politics, defined as the ever-present threat of those who would "destroy the revolution," has been used to attack urban populations, particularly those who were most vulnerable, and to forcibly remove an estimated seven hundred thousand urban residents from Harare, Bulawayo, and other towns in 2005.[9]

It is important to remember that the urban roots of democracy were not completely severed by the political violence of the early 1960s. Many brave and committed individuals continued to work within township advisory boards and residents' associations in order to keep the local tradition of self-help and community politics alive. Enos Msindo's research on the continuity and defiance of township advisory boards in Bulawayo during the early 1960s is an important example of the type of historical work needed for advisory boards in Harare, Highfield, and other townships.[10] These histories will most likely show the resilience and strength of local initiatives as urban leaders faced both harassment from the nationalists and an intransigent white administration. The history of the opposition to ZANU-PF rule over the past two decades will also reveal bravery and commitment similar to that shown by so many women and men discussed in this book. The organizing of popular protests from within the trade unions, community groups, women's organizations, and universities will once again confirm the urban roots of democracy in Zimbabwe.

As scholars increasingly turn to the history of the postindependence period and the post-2000 crisis, it is also worth considering the great deal of historical work still to be done in the 1940–64 period. Further explorations of other nationalist visions and their impact on local forms of participatory democracy in this period would be beneficial. The histories of different nationalist trajectories in rural areas, as well as in nonracial or multiracial contexts, and the links between more progressive democratic participation in other political spaces need to be examined with greater specificity in order to build an expanded historiography of these traditions. In addition, the political biographies of other individuals, many of whom are only mentioned in passing in this narrative, need to receive further attention by historians. Hopefully, the history presented here will help to remind students of Zimbabwean history of the strong nonviolent, participatory, and democratic political traditions that originated in the urban townships of present-day Harare.

Lastly, Charles Mzingeli, and the women and men who worked with him in the 1940s and 1950s, provide a formidable group of urban political activists who stand as an example of just how strong the fight for democracy and expanded notions of rights and social justice has been in Zimbabwean history. Some current schools of history would like to forget their contributions toward the creation of Zimbabwe, but the history of Mzingeli's and his contemporaries, and Rueben Jamela and his contemporaries, remain as inspiration to the many brave men and women, young and old, working today to build a better future for Zimbabwe.

Notes

Introduction

1. William Saidi describes the flavor of Harare township life in his novel *The Old Bricks Lives*. "Old Bricks" was the first section of Harare township built first for men only but later occupied by women and families. For all the hardships Saidi's characters experience, there remained a sense of community and a township way of life worth defending against the impersonal, commoditized lifestyle of the European suburbs that became available to those who could afford to move out of the townships by the late 1960s. William Saidi, *The Old Bricks Lives* (Gweru: Mambo Press, 1988). Lawrence Vambe's account of life in Harare, in his book *From Rhodesia to Zimbabwe*, explores the dynamics of mission-educated men like himself who had few options but to live in a township along with migrant workers, beer brewers, prostitutes, and others. Vambe's writings as a journalist for the African press in the 1940s convey the excitement and uniqueness of township life, while also expressing the outrage of segregation laws that applied to all irrespective of educational or cultural attainment. Vambe and his counterparts often faced humiliating inspections, police harassment, and regulations that shaped their view of the settler state as much as the economic discrimination they faced in the city center. Lawrence Vambe, *From Rhodesia to Zimbabwe* (Pittsburgh: University of Pittsburgh Press, 1976).

2. See Joyce Jenye Makwenda, *Zimbabwe Township Music* (Harare: Storytime Promotions, 2005), and Thomas Turino, *Nationalists, Cosmopolitans, and Popular Music in Zimbabwe* (Chicago: Chicago University Press, 2000).

3. Jocelyn Alexander, JoAnn McGregor, and Terence Ranger, *Violence and Memory: One Hundred Years in the "Dark Forests" of Matabeleland* (Portsmouth, NH: Heinemann, 2000), 85.

4. See Geoff Eley, *Forging Democracy: The History of the Left in Europe, 1850–2000* (Oxford University Press, 2002), 17–18.

5. Joane Nagel summarizes Enloe's argument: "She [Enloe] argues that women are relegated to minor, often symbolic, roles in nationalist movements and conflicts, either as icons of nationhood, to be elevated and defended, or as the booty of spoils of war, to be denigrated and disgraced. In either case, the real actors are men who are defending either their freedom, their honor, their homeland, and their women." Cited in Joane Nagel, "Nation," in *Handbook of Studies on Men and Masculinities*, ed. M. S. Kimmel et al. (Thousand Oaks, CA: Sage Publications,

2005). Original quote from Cynthia Enloe, *Bananas, Beaches, and Bases: Making Feminist Sense of International Politics* (Berkeley: University of California Press, 1990).

6. For a useful discussion of these developments, see Ida Bloom et al., introduction to *Gendered Nations: Nationalism and Gender Order in the Long Nineteenth Century*, ed. Ida Bloom et al. (Oxford: Berg, 2000); Sita Ranchod-Nilsson and Mary Tetreault, "Gender and Nationalism: Moving beyond Fragmented Conversations," in *Women, States, and Nationalism: At Home in the Nation?* ed. S. Ranchod-Nilsson and M. A. Tetreault (London: Routledge, 2000), 1–17.

7. As Alexander et al. pointed out in 2000, Zimbabwean nationalism itself can no longer be viewed as a unified ideological or social fact: "In Zimbabwe today, it almost goes without saying that a critical history of nationalism is essential: many of the fundamental issues which affect Zimbabwean society arise out of the promises, the disputed character and the failures of nationalism. Elsewhere in Africa it may be true that not only 'nationalist history' but the history of nationalism have to be discarded—because the nation was never imagined; because nationalist rhetoric has proved to be empty; because the nation state has withered away." Alexander, McGregor, and Ranger, *Violence and Memory*, 83.

8. Teresa Barnes, *"We Women Worked So Hard": Gender, Urbanization, and Social Reproduction in Colonial Harare, 1930–1956* (Portsmouth, NH: Heinemann, 1999). Elizabeth Schmidt, *Peasants, Traders, and Wives: Shona Women in the History of Zimbabwe, 1870–1939* (Portsmouth, NH: Heinemann, 1992); Diana Jeater, *Marriage, Perversion, and Power: The Construction of Moral Discourse in Southern Rhodesia* (Oxford: Clarendon Press, 1993); Michael O. West, *The Rise of an African Middle Class: Colonial Zimbabwe, 1898–1965* (Bloomington: Indiana University Press, 2002); and Tsuneo Yoshikuni, "Black Migrants in a White City: A Social History of African Harare, 1890–1925," (PhD diss., University of Zimbabwe, 1989). See Frederick Cooper, "Conflict and Connection: Rethinking Colonial African History," *American Historical Review* 99, no. 5 (December 1994): 1516–45, and Achille Mbembe, *On the Postcolony* (Berkeley: University of California Press, 2000), esp. p. 5. In addition to Barnes's *"We Women Worked So Hard,"* the following works, among others, on women's experiences during the Liberation War period have developed a common theme in Zimbabwean nationalism and gender: Norma Kriger, *Zimbabwe's Guerrilla War: Peasant Voices* (Cambridge: Cambridge University Press, 1992); Josephine Nhongo-Simbanegavi, *For Better or Worse? Women and ZANLA in Zimbabwe's Liberation Struggle* (Harare: Weaver Press, 2000); Tanya Lyons, *Guns and Guerrilla Girls: Women in the Zimbabwean National Liberation Struggle* (Trenton: African World Press, 2003); Wendy Urban-Mead, "Religion, Women, and Gender in the Brethren in Christ Church, Matabeleland, Zimbabwe, 1898–1978," (PhD diss., Columbia University, 2004). The majority of these works share a view of Zimbabwean nationalism as an ideology unwilling or unable to go beyond a rhetorical promise toward women's demands. This argument is made quite explicitly by Horace Campbell in *Reclaiming Zimbabwe: The Exhaustion of the Patriarchal Model of Liberation* (New York: African World Press, 2003), 268–98.

9. Barnes's approach provides an alternative to the development trope of gender and nationalism, moving beyond studying women's participation in politics as a demographic question and instead looking at how gender transformed African nationalist politics more specifically. Diana Paton, in her work on postemancipation Jamaica, offers a similarly sensible view of historical gender analysis: "Gender is also

a central category for this book, even though the most pressing questions addressed here are not about the construction of gender, nor do I assume that gender is always the central method of marking difference and power. Men's and women's experiences of the events and processes discussed differed, although this is often occluded in the sources, which frequently present men's experiences as the norm. . . . But more than simply exemplifying existing gender hierarchies, the processes studied here contributed to the reformulation of gender difference." Diana Paton, *No Bond But the Law: Punishment, Race, and Gender in Jamaican State Formation, 1780–1870* (Durham: Duke University Press, 2004), 16. Another work outside of African history that helped formulate the historical argument in this book is Anna Clark, *The Struggle for the Breeches: Gender and the Making of the British Working Class* (Berkeley: University of California Press, 1995).

10. Tsuneo Yoshikuni, "Gender and Urban History," review of "*We Women Worked So Hard": Gender, Urbanization, and Social Reproduction in Colonial Harare, 1930–1956* by Teresa A. Barnes, *Journal of Southern African Studies* 27, no. 1 (March 2001): 172–74, quote on 174.

11. William Beinhart, "Political and Collective Violence in Southern African Historiography," in *Political Violence in Southern Africa*, ed. William Beinhart (special issues), *Journal of Southern African Studies* 18, no. 3 (September 1992): 455–86.

12. T. Dunbar Moodie with Vivienne Ndatshe, *Going for Gold: Men, Mines, and Migration* (Berkeley: University of California Press, 1994); Glen Elder, *Hostels, Sexuality, and the Apartheid Legacy: Malevolent Geographies* (Athens: Ohio University Press, 2003).

13. An example of how the analytical sensibility of the concept has improved since Bienhart's initial criticism is Robert Morrell, ed., *Changing Men in Southern Africa* (London: Zed Books, 2001).

14. Benedict Anderson, *Imagined Communities: Reflections on the Origin and Spread of Nationalism* (London: Verso, 1983); Jürgen Habermas, "The Public Sphere," in *Becoming National: A Reader*, ed. Geoff Eley and Ronald Grigor Suny (New York: Oxford University Press, 1996), 21–26.

15. Habermas, "Public Sphere," 22–23; Jürgen Habermas, *The Structural Transformation of the Public Sphere: An Inquiry into a Category of Bourgeois Society*, trans. Thomas Burger (Cambridge: MIT Press, 1991). According to Giovanna Borradori, Habermas views the increasingly powerful news and advertising media creating a situation where "mass culture thus imposes its own rules of democratic participation: namely, utilitarian rules serving private interests rather than universal rules serving the public interest." Giovanna Borradori, *Philosophy in a Time of Terror: Dialogues with Jürgen Habermas and Jacques Derrida* (Chicago: University of Chicago Press, 2003), 58.

16. Editorial, "African Nationalism," *Chapupu*, July 20, 1957, 4 (Hoover Institute Microfilm S57).

17. Ibid. The more radical rhetoric was also built on a racial and sometimes ethnic solidarity. In this regard, the SRANC's leaders were very conscious of the need to connect the past to an authentic nationalist movement: "African Nationalism is conceived and to this end shall it rebuilt [*sic*] the lost heritage and destroyed shrines of that which pleased God to make us a people." Ibid.

18. A late-1960s analysis and critique that highlighted the international emphasis of African nationalists can be found in John Day, *International Nationalism: The*

Extra-Territorial Relations of Southern Rhodesian African Nationalists (London: Routledge and Kegan Paul, 1967).

19. The logic of sellout politics has a historical parallel in the art of radical rhetoric expressed in the writings of the Abbé Sieyès during the French Revolution. Abbé Sieyès argued that France would be better off without the parasitical aristocrats who were sapping the real strength of the French bourgeoisie and working classes. William H. Sewell Jr., *A Rhetoric of Bourgeois Revolution: The Abbé Sieyes and What Is the Third Estate?* (Durham: Duke University Press, 1994), 203.

20. An interesting influence on Mzingeli's early career with the ICU was a female community leader, Martha Ngano, who Mzingeli suggests helped to form the ICU and create the basis for African protest politics in Southern Rhodesia. Mzingeli claimed she was a member of almost every organization in Bulawayo, a pattern he would repeat in Salisbury. For Martha Ngano see West, *African Middle Class*, 128–29. For the ICU in Southern Rhodesia, see Terence Ranger, *The African Voice in Southern Rhodesia, 1898–1930* (Evanston: Northwestern University Press, 1970); and Richard Gray, *The Two Nations: Aspects of the Development of Race Relations in the Rhodesias and Nyasaland* (Westport, CT: Greenwood Press, 1974 [1960]).

21. For personal accounts by nationalist leaders and analyses by Zimbabweans during this period, see especially Nathan Shamuyarira, *Crisis in Rhodesia* (London: A. Deutsch, 1965); Ndabaningi Sithole, *African Nationalism*, 2nd ed. (London: Oxford University Press, 1968); Maurice Nyagumbo, *With the People: An Autobiography from the Zimbabwe Struggle* (London: Allison and Busby, 1980); Joshua Nkomo, *Nkomo: The Story of My Life* (London: Methuen, 1984); Lawrence Vambe, *From Rhodesia to Zimbabwe* (Pittsburgh: Pittsburgh University Press, 1976); and Eshmael Mlambo, *Rhodesia: The Struggle for a Birthright* (London: C. Hurst and Company, 1972). See also David Martin and Phyllis Johnson, *The Struggle for Zimbabwe: The Chimurenga War* (London: Faber and Faber, 1981).

22. For the continuity of these problems facing trade unionism in Zimbabwe, see Tefetso Mothibe, "Organized African Labor and Nationalism in Colonial Zimbabwe, 1945–71" (PhD diss., University of Wisconsin–Madison, 1993); Lloyd Sachikonye, "Trade Unions: Economic and Political Development in Zimbabwe since Independence," in *Keep on Knocking: A History of the Labour Movement in Zimbabwe, 1990–97*, ed. Brian Raftopoulos and Ian Phimister (Harare: Baobab Books, 1997), 107–28; and Freek B. Schiphorst, "Strength and Weakness: The Rise of the Zimbabwe Congress of Trade Unions (ZCTU) and the Development of Labour Relations, 1980–1995" (PhD diss., Universiteit Leiden, 2001). For the AFL-CIO involvement in Southern Rhodesia, see Yvette Richards, *Maida Springer: Pan-Africanist and International Labor Leader* (Pittsburgh: University of Pittsburgh Press, 2004), 227–33; and *Conversations with Maida Springer: A Personal History of Labor, Race, and International Relations* (Pittsburgh: University of Pittsburgh Press, 2004), 240–47.

23. The strongest Pan-Africanist opposition came from Ghanaian trade unionist John Tettegah. See John C. Stoner, "Anti-Communism, Anti-Colonialism, and African Labor: The AFL-CIO in Africa, 1955–1975" (PhD diss., Columbia University, 2001).

24. Cooper, "Conflict and Connection," 1545.

Chapter 1

1. I have used the term "imperial working-class citizenship" to emphasize the difference between what Mzingeli saw as possible for a wide range of urban Africans compared with the more elitist view of "Imperial citizenship" that was marked by attaining European attributes of civility and wealth. See Ann Stoler and Frederick Cooper, eds., *Tension of Empire: Colonial Cultures in a Bourgeois World* (Berkeley: University of California Press, 1997), 1–3.

2. Michael West has described the history of voter qualifications, noting that from 1898 suffrage was open "to all males twenty-one years of age or older who met certain qualifications, namely, personal ownership of immovable property valued at £75 (which, significantly for Africans, excluded both cattle and communally owned land), or an annual income of £50, plus the ability to write one's name, address, and occupation in English." West also notes "as late as 1948 there were only 258 blacks compared with approximately 48,000 whites on the voter rolls." West, *African Middle Class*, 126–27.

3. Geoff Eley, *Forging Democracy: The History of the Left in Europe, 1850–2000* (New York: Oxford University Press, 2002), 30.

4. Terence Ranger, *Are We Not Also Men? The Samkange Family and African Politics in Zimbabwe, 1920–64* (Portsmouth, NH: Heinemann, 1995); West, *African Middle Class*.

5. See Helen Bradford, *A Taste of Freedom: The ICU in Rural South Africa, 1924–1930* (New Haven: Yale University Press, 1987), and William Beinhart and Colin Bundy, *Hidden Struggles in Rural South Africa: Politics and Popular Movements in the Transkei and Eastern Cape, 1890–1930* (London: James Currey, 1987).

6. Information about Mzingeli's early life comes mainly from three sources. First, there is Lawrence Vambe's biographical chapter on Mzingeli in his book *From Rhodesia to Zimbabwe*. Vambe became close to Mzingeli beginning in the 1940s and had a great deal of respect for him. The admiration was mutual, as Mzingeli would later recall that of all the educated Africans in Harare township Lawrence Vambe was the only one that "was with us," reflecting Mzingeli's disdain for most of the educated leaders at the time. Second, there is the "Interview with C. L. Mzingeli Harare Township," Harare, September 15, 1970, by Prof. Ray Roberts, Murray Steele, and Tobias Mapuranga (University College of Rhodesia) (copy of transcript in "Industrial Commercial Union, Rhodesia (T.U.)" file, Institute of Commonwealth Studies Library, University of London). Third, Edwin Munger, "Charles Mzingeli: Leader of Southern Rhodesian Africans? A Letter from Edwin S. Munger," *American Universities Field Staff Reports*, December 6, 1952, Central and Southern Africa Series, vol. 1, no. 5 (Federation of Rhodesia and Nyasaland) (New York: American Universities Field Staff, 1956), 41–47. In addition, Ngwabi Bhebe refers to Mzingeli as "a Karanga from Plumtree." Ngwabi Bhebe, *B. Burombo: African Politics in Zimbabwe, 1947–1958* (Harare: College Press, 1989), 40. While Mzingeli told the National Native Labour Board (NNLB) in 1952: "I come from Bulalima-Mangwe in Matabeleland. I came in 1929. I am indigenous. My home language is Sindebele." "NNLB Evidence" (1952), 164. National Archives of Zimbabwe [NAZ] S2809/3320(c).

7. Italics added. Munger also adds, "Mzingeli had a sister who died recently and has a brother who has been in the Criminal Investigation Department for many years." Munger, "Charles Mzingeli," 41–47.

8. Ibid.

9. Vambe, *From Rhodesia to Zimbabwe*, 94. Vambe had also attended school at a Catholic Mission school located at the Chishawasha Mission near Salisbury. Vambe describes how as a young man, even before meeting Mzingeli, Mzingeli's reputation preceded him. "Since my early days at Chishawasha, the name Charles Mzingeli had been well-known among well-informed men and women in the Mission. The things he was reported to have said and done and the sufferings he had undergone in championing the cause of African freedom had always stamped him in my mind as an extraordinary individual." Vambe, *From Rhodesia to Zimbabwe*, 93.

10. For a more detailed discussion of the ICU's early days in Southern Rhodesia, see Ranger, *African Voice in Southern Rhodesia*.

11. Beinhart and Bundy, *Hidden Struggles*; see esp. the chapter entitled "The Union, the Nation, and Talking Crow: The Ideology and Tactics of the Independent ICU in East London," 270–320.

12. Interview with Tobias K. Nhapi, by author and Joseph Seda, National Section, Mbare, May 6, 1992. The generational connection continues, as Mr. Nhapi's nephews, Fidelis Nhapi and George Nyandoro, were both brought into the RICU at an early age by Tobias, reading literature at Mzingeli's office/shop during school holidays. Both men later went on to establish the Salisbury City Youth League. The interesting recollection of Tobias Nhapi that Mzingeli was rumored to be an African American fits well with general rumors in southern Africa in the 1920s that Marcus Garvey and his army of African Americans were going to come to liberate southern Africa from white settlers. See Michael O. West, "Seeds Are Sown: The Garvey Movement in Zimbabwe in the Interwar Years," *International Journal of African Historical Studies* 35, nos. 2–3 (2003): 335–62.

13. Vambe, *From Rhodesia to Zimbabwe*, 85.

14. Carol Summers, *Colonial Lessons: Africans' Education in Southern Rhodesia, 1918–1940* (Portsmouth, NH: Heinemann, 2002).

15. Tsuneo Yoshikuni, "Notes on the Influence of Town–Country Relations on African Urban History, before 1957: Experiences of Salisbury and Bulawayo," in *Sites of Struggle: Essays in Zimbabwe's Urban History*, ed. Brian Raftopoulos and Tsuneo Yoshikuni (Harare: Weaver Press, 1999), 113–56.

16. There was also a more practical reason for a falloff in Mzingeli's achievements as an RICU organizer. After large crowds attended his initial RICU meetings on Sunday afternoons, the European Native Affairs authorities took notice and tried to create alternative activities on weekends to Mzingeli's popular meetings. The white-controlled Native Welfare Society—an organization Mzingeli would remain at odds with for most of his career—worked to provide soccer matches and leagues on Sunday afternoons, and the municipality's Native Affairs Department organized boxing matches. These events drew attendance away from Mzingeli's meetings. For the more educated young men living in the township, football teams became a rite of passage into the more respectable and elite circles in the township and colony as a whole. See Ossie Stuart, "'Good Boys,' Footballers, and Strikers: African Social Change in Bulawayo, 1933–1953" (PhD diss., School of Oriental and African Studies (SOAS), University of London, 1989).

17. Mzingeli told Munger that the Chief Native Commissioner had intentionally set up the rival group to put Mzingeli out of business and that "no one was convicted

of the murder" even though, Mzingeli said, "it was easy to find the murderer if they wanted to." Edwin Munger, "Charles Mzingeli," 4.

18. Munger concludes, "He actually served nine months with time off." Quoted in ibid., 4–5.

19. Interview with Charles Mzingeli, by Roberts, Steele, and Mapuranga, June 20, 1971.

20. As Michael West has shown, the rise of an African middle class was largely predicated on the distinctions around alcohol consumption, dress, and speech. West, *African Middle Class*; see also Timothy Burke, *Lifebuoy Men, Lux Women: Commodification, Consumption, and Cleanliness in Modern Zimbabwe* (Durham: Duke University Press, 1996).

21. Transcript of interview with L. C. Mzingeli, by T. M. P. Mapuranga (of University of Rhodesia), Harare, June 20, 1971, 7.

22. Ibid., 1.

23. Quoted in Munger, "Charles Mzingeli," 4.

24. According to Mzingeli, he approached Colonel Walker, the Labour Party MP for Salisbury South, who "happened to be a socialist." He took Mzingeli's views seriously and brought Mzingeli to meet with the general secretary of the Labour Party, Gladys Maasdorp. Interview with Mzingeli, by Mapuranga, 10–11.

25. Colonel Walker provided another account of how the African Headquarters Branch was formed. He suggested the view at the time was that since there was no color bar in the constitution of the party, he welcomed the five or six Africans who became party members. They could not, however, attend the Salisbury South Branch meetings so they formed their own group, with a chairman and secretary. They kept minutes of their meetings, and kept the white parliamentary members informed of "matters of concern to Africans." The number of African SLRP members had grown to seventeen by 1941, and Mzingeli applied to register the group as a party branch. Colonel Walker, "Draft Memo on African Headquarters Branch," May 1944, NAZ SR 9/1/1/6, Southern Rhodesia Labour Party (SRLP).

26. D. J. Murray, *The Government System in Southern Rhodesia* (Oxford: Oxford University Press, 1970), 180, 256. See also James Barber, *Rhodesia: The Road to Rebellion* (Oxford: Oxford University Press, 1967), 9–11. Barber describes Huggins's "confined political circle" in which "there was no mass electorate to please, no great party machine to be organized. For the potential leaders it was important to mix well, to be known, liked, and trusted within the circle." Barber, *Rhodesia*, 9. See Ian Phimister's description of how industrialists and agricultural interests dominated Southern Rhodesia's Parliament, in Ian Phimister, *Wangi Kolia: Coal, Capital, and Labour in Colonial Zimbabwe, 1894–1954* (Harare: Baobab Books, 1994).

27. Murray, *Government System in Southern Rhodesia*, 332–36.

28. The conflict between Mzingeli and Ibbotson continued over a number of years. Percy Ibbotson to Sir Godfrey, May 15, 1947, NAZ S482/709/39, vol. 3. Thanks to Michael West for providing me a copy of this letter.

29. Godfrey Huggins, "Natives in Urban Areas," reprinted in Southern Rhodesia, *Hansard*, November 23, 1944, 4, NAZ S1361/65.

30. For the origins of the use of Locations to control African workers and separate them from European and other groups, see Charles van Onselen, *Chibaro: African Mine Labour in Southern Rhodesia, 1900–1933* (London: Pluto Press, 1976).

31. Lt. Col. G. H. Walker, SRLP MP from Salisbury South, was also present during the meeting. D. J. Ranthokoana and E. K. Chitiyo, both branch members, and D. B. Ntuli, the branch secretary, attended as well.

32. African HQ Branch Memorandum on meeting with the prime minister, October 11, 1945, NAZ SR 9/1/1/6, SRLP, 1.

33. Ibid., 2.

34. Ibid.

35. These newspapers included the South African communist paper *Nkululeko*, for which Mzingeli claimed to be a contributing editor, when testifying to the strike commission in 1948. He related how he was responsible for distributing about four dozen copies per week of the *Guardian*, out of Cape Town, and an equal number of *Nkululeko*. When asked suspiciously by the commission if he gave the unsold copies away for free, he replied, "No . . . I use them in my shop for wrapping parcels." Southern Rhodesia, Commission of Inquiry into Native Disturbances, "Oral Evidence," Salisbury, July 21, 1948, NAZ ZBZ 1/1/1.

36. Nobel laureate Doris Lessing worked closely with Gladys Maasdorp and therefore got to know Mzingeli well and wrote of him in her novels (particularly *Landlocked* and *A Ripple from the Storm*) and in her autobiography. They would have been political associates from 1944 to 1947. After Lessing moved to London, she met him again as she helped to bring him around London to meet various trade union and political contacts. On March 27, 1946, Lessing was elected as an alternate representative of the African Branch to the National Executive Committee as it was proposed to have a European alternate elected to the post. Lessing had been nominated for the position a year earlier at the meeting of July 5, 1946. The executive elected at the 26 March 1947 meeting included Mzingeli as chair, D. J. Ranthokoana as vice chair, D. B. Ntuli as honorary secretary, Patrick Pazarangu as assistant secretary, Mzingeli as representative to the national executive, and M. D. Lessing as alternate.

37. Doris Lessing, *Under My Skin: Volume One of My Autobiography to 1949* (New York: Harper Perennial, 1994), 306.

38. Doris Lessing, "Hunger," in *African Stories* (New York: Simon and Schuster, 1951), 404–519.

39. Lessing, *Under My Skin*, 307.

40. For a description see Doris Lessing, *A Ripple from the Storm* (London: M. Joseph, 1958), 237–39. A less dramatic reading of what was likely the same meeting is found in Mzingeli's minutes of the "African Branch of the Labour Party Congress" held at the Township Recreation Hall in February 1944. Here again Maasdorp was present, as were the other leading members of the more radical, nonracist group of whites who worked with her. These minutes may have been written up by Lessing, as her name appears last under visitors and spaces were left for the spelling of some African names. The visitors included Mrs. Maasdorp, Mr. Isaacson, Mr. McCoun, Mr. P. Ibbotson, Mr. Allen, Mr. Collins, Mr. Gilson, and Mrs. Lessing. Mzingeli read apologies from "Colonel Walker, Mr. Pelham, Mr. North, who is ill, Miss D. Schwartz, who had gone to the Union, and Mrs. Lieberman." Minutes of the Congress of the African Branch of the Labour Party Held at the Jabula Hall on the Afternoon of Saturday, February 18, 1944, NAZ SR 9/1/1/6.

41. For details of Creech-Jones's attempts to redefine British colonialism after the war, see Frederick Cooper, *Decolonization and African Society: The Labor Question in French and British Africa* (Cambridge: Cambridge University Press, 1996), 64–66.

42. Mzingeli to Creech-Jones, April 12, 1946, Rhodes House (RH) Fabian Colonial Bureau (FCB) 106/1 ff 57. Doris Lessing also remembers Mzingeli's continual references to British veto powers: "He was always asking us to remind the British Parliament of its obligations. We were always sending off letters, copies of minutes, notes of resolutions, relevant parts of the Constitution to Members of Parliament in Westminster supposed to be 'good' on colonial issues, but if we got a reply at all, it would be a polite refusal. It was the war, we told Charles, people in Britain did not have time for anything but the war. 'They did not have time before the war,' he might remark, smiling as usual." Lessing, *Under My Skin*, 306.

43. Rita Hinden to Mzingeli, June 20, 1946, RH FCB 106/1 ff 58. Other examples of Mzingeli's appeals include Mzingeli to Arthur Shearly Cripps, July 22, 1945, and Mzingeli to Creech-Jones, British Secretary of State for the Colonies, April 12, 1946, RH Mss. Perham, 605/1 f 51, 106/1 f 157.

44. Hinden to Secretary of State Addison, September 13, 1946, RH FCB 27/1 ff 85. In another letter, Hinden suggested to Addison that the "present arrangements whereby HMG retains a responsibility over which it is almost impossible for the British Parliament and the British public to exercise any effective control, are basically unsatisfactory." Hinden to Secretary of State Addison, "Discriminatory Legislation in Southern Rhodesia," RH FCB 27/1 ff 32.

45. In his reply, Lord Addison tells Hinden how the Southern Rhodesia government informed him that the Fabian Colonial Bureau had "insufficient appreciation of the condition under which natives live in the towns, or the state of affairs which the Act purports to relieve." He points out that the SR government designed the N(UA)ARA "to enable a relatively inefficient worker, who is married, to live a decent life, and not live apart from his wife as he had to now because she remains in the Native Reserves." Lord Addison to Rita Hinden, November 21, 1946, RH FCB 27/1.

46. Colin Leys, *European Politics in Southern Rhodesia* (Oxford: Oxford University Press, 1959 [reprint, Greenwood Press, 1982]. See chapter on the Labour Party, 178–89, and specifically 182–83 where Leys describes the presence of an African Branch as part of political mudslinging within the leadership in 1944.

47. Mzingeli to Hinden, March 11, 1946, RH FCB 99/1.

48. Ibbotson writes, "The interview was naturally of a rather stormy nature, but I fortunately did not lose my temper, though I must confess I was filled with righteous indignation!! Dr. Hinden revealed that she was completely ignorant of many of our problems, and her knowledge of the Colony left very much to be desired. I think it is possible that the interview has done some good, and I hope there will be less interference in the future." Ibbotson to Sir Godfrey, November 4, 1946, NAZ S482/163/41. Thanks to Michael West for providing me a copy of this letter.

49. Ibbotson was not alone among white administrators of "Native Affairs" who had developed a strong sense that they alone understood what was best for Southern Rhodesia's Africans. See Diana Jeater, *Law, Language, and Science: The Invention of the "Native Mind" in Southern Rhodesia, 1890–1930* (Portsmouth, NH: Heinemann, 2007).

50. African Branch, SRLP, "Memorandum on the Danger of Segregation Policy as Applied in the Colony of Southern Rhodesia under the Provisions of Native Pass Acts, Land Apportionment Acts, re: Enforced by the Urban Areas Act, 1946," November 29, 1946, NAZ Records NAS L2.

Chapter 2

1. David Johnson, *World War II and the Scramble for Labour in Colonial Zimbabwe, 1939–1948* (Harare: University of Zimbabwe Publications, 2000). On Rhodesian African troops in World War I, see Timothy J. Stapleton, *No Insignificant Part: The Rhodesia Native Regiment and the East Africa Campaign of the First World War* (Waterloo: Wilfrid Laurier University Press, 2006). See also Gregory Mann, *Native Sons: West African Veterans in the Twentieth Century* (Durham: Duke University Press, 2006).

2. Reformed Industrial and Commercial Workers Union of Africa, "Reformed ICU, Minutes of a Public Meeting held at the Recreation Hall, Municipal Native Location, Salisbury, on Sunday September 22, 1946 at 3:30 p.m.," NAZ SR 9/1/1/6, pp. 2–3.

3. See Lisa Lindsay, *Working with Gender: Wage Labor and Social Change in Southwestern Nigeria* (Portsmouth, NH: Heinemann, 2003), 77–105; and Cooper, *Decolonization and African Society*, 131–41.

4. Ian Phimister, *An Economic and Social History of Zimbabwe, 1890–1948* (London: Longman, 1988), 263–64.

5. Ken Vickery, "The Rhodesia Railways African Strike of 1945, Part 1: A Narrative Account," *Journal of Southern African Studies* 24, no. 3 (September 1998): 545–60; and Vickery, "The Rhodesia Railways African Strike of 1945, Part 2: Causes, Consequence, Significance," *Journal of Southern African Studies* 25, no. 1 (March 1999): 49–71.

6. Vickery, "Rhodesia Railways Strike, Part 2," 61.

7. Pazarangu and Mzingeli to Kabell, November 5, 1945, NAZ SR 9/1/1/6, 1. This passage has been quoted often in secondary sources as proof of the "awakening" of elite links with working-class issues. See, for example, Vickery, "Rhodesia Railways Strike"; Phimister, *Economic and Social History*; Ian Phimister and Brian Raftopoulos, " 'Kana sora ratswa ngaritswe': African Nationalists and Black Workers—the 1948 General Strike in Colonial Zimbabwe," *Journal of Historical Sociology* 13, no. 4 (August 2000): 289–324.

8. Ranger, *Are We Not Also Men?*, 110. Original quote appeared in the *Bantu Mirror*, March 2, 1946.

9. Pazarangu and Mzingeli to Kabell, November 5, 1945, 2, NAZ SR 9/1/1/6.

10. Many years later, Savanhu explained that he worked so hard for the Bulawayo union that he "had little sleep and hardly time to eat which contributed to my succumbing to an attack of tuberculosis and I was admitted to hospital in April 1946." After his recovery, he went to work for the African press as a reporter and by 1951 he had become editor of the *Bantu Mirror* in Bulawayo. Savanhu commented on Mzingeli's unilateral move to start his own union in Salisbury even though Savanhu had already helped to launch one in Bulawayo: "Apparently Mr. Mzingeli being a born leader was not able to co-operate and started the Trade union movement here [Harare] which he called the Reformed ICU, the re-formation of his old movement and went ahead. For

that reason the movement we had started in Bulawayo was restricted to Bulawayo only." Interview with Jasper Zengeza Savanhu (b. 1917–d. July 14, 1984), by Dawson Munjeri, February 28, 1977, NAZ Oral History Collection, AOH/5.

11. ChiManyika is a language spoken in eastern Zimbabwe, primarily around Mutare (Umtali preindependence). The relationship between languages, Benedict Anderson's notion of "print-languages," and ethnic identity in Zimbabwe is explored by Terence Ranger in "Missionaries, Migrants, and the Manyika: The Invention of Ethnicity in Zimbabwe," in *The Creation of Tribalism in Southern Africa*, ed. Leroy Vail (Berkeley: California University Press, 1989), 142–43. Ranger has addressed the question of Manyika identity in Bulawayo, in particular reference to violence, in Ranger, "The Meaning of Urban Violence in Africa: Bulawayo, Southern Rhodesia, 1890–1960," *Cultural and Social History* 3, no. 2 (April 2006): 3.

12. RICU, "Ndaba Tree Salisbury," February 1946, NAZ SR 9/1/1/6, 1.

13. Ibid., 2.

14. Ibid., 3. The Atlantic Charter was discussed in other forums and meetings as well. One of the more telling readings of the Charter came from Captain Bertin, who served as minister of Native Affairs in early 1944. In a speech to the Bulawayo Native Welfare Society meeting, he responded to a question about the Atlantic Charter and its applicability to Africans. Bertin suggested that those "not reading the Charter carefully assumed that it referred to everyone." He suggested that it might have "in a broad sense" applied to everyone but that Churchill and Roosevelt "had in mind the peoples of countries with an older civilization than Rhodesia." He agreed, however, that Africans fell under the category of those who should "live in freedom from fear and want." Elaborating further, he thought "Africans did live in freedom from fear in Southern Rhodesia." "Colony's Plans for Natives: Study of the Atlantic Charter Urged," *Rhodesia Herald*, January 21, 1944.

15. "A Grand Salisbury Wedding," *African Weekly*, January 29, 1947, 8.

16. "A Ibid.

17. For the overlooked history of South African township advisory boards, see Gary Baines, "The Contradictions of Community Politics: The African Petty Bourgeoisie and the New Brighton Advisory Board, c. 1937–1952," *Journal of African History* 35, no. 1 (1994): 79–97.

18. Rev. Percy Ibbotson, "Location Advisory Boards," Bulawayo, February 16, 1943, NAZ RH 16/1/1 1942–43, vol. 2, 336.

19. "Native Advisory Board for Harare African Township: Eight Members Elected to Serve One Year," *African Weekly*, November 5, 1947, 1; "Harari Advisory Board Elected," *African Weekly*, November 3, 1948, 1.

20. Bhebe, *B. Burombo*, 57.

21. Mzingeli to Rita Hinden, April 27, 1948, RH FCB 99/2ff., 67–68.

22. An important reappraisal and account of the strike is Phimister and Raftopoulos, "'*Kana sora ratswa ngaritswe.*'"

23. Lawrence Vambe recounts how he himself ignored these barriers, and how, after the first day returning back to his home in the Location, the police stopped him and told him he wouldn't be allowed out the following day: "I said I was going to work and they realised that I was not a stupid African and they left me." Lawrence Vambe, "Oral Evidence, Commission of Inquiry into Native Disturbances," Salisbury, 1948, NAZ ZBZ 1/1/1.

24. Maasdorp writes of her cook who lived in the township with his wife and child: "[He] was afraid to leave the township, partly because of hooliganism and partly because of the repercussions should he do any work. He has worked for me about 16 out of 22 years." Her other two servants, the "houseboy" and "garden-boy," lived behind the house in their *kia*. Gladys Maasdorp to Rita Hinden, Salisbury, April 27, 1948, RH FCB 99/2 ff 57–59.

25. Commission to Investigate into Native Strike (Hudson Commission), *Report of the Commission*, Salisbury, September 1948, NAZ S482/114/8/48.

26. Reformed Industrial and Commercial Workers Union of Africa (RICU), "Second Annual Conference," Salisbury, September 11–13, 1948, RH FCB 99/2 ff. 79–89. See also "Oral Evidence, Commission of Inquiry into Native Disturbances," Salisbury, 1948, NAZ ZBZ 1/1/1.

27. Hudson Commission, *Report*.

28. For a useful narrative of the strike and the events leading up to the strike in Bulawayo, the city where the strike began, see Bhebe, B. *Burombo*, 44–72, and Phimister and Raftopolous, "'*Kana sora ratswa ngaritswe,*'" 289–324.

29. Maasdorp to Rita Hinden, April 27, 1948, RH FCB 99/2 ff 57–59. Maasdorp goes on to say that she could not confirm the truth of the statement about Mzingeli but was "told by one of his friends that he was in great danger." According to Mzingeli, on the Thursday after the strike, the CID raided his house and took all of his papers and personal correspondences. RICU, Mzingeli to Rita Hinden, April 27, 1948, RH FCB 99/2 ff 67–68.

30. Mzingeli to Hinden, April 27, 1948, RH FCB 99/2 ff 67–68. Ian Phimister and Brian Raftopoulos have analyzed this issue and the debate it has created over the years among historians. Much of the writing about the general strike has been to recast it as a "leaderless" strike that showed the "true" working-class spirit of those involved, and the "petty bourgeois" character of leaders such as Mzingeli and the many others in Bulawayo who have been seen as involved but not leading the strike. Phimister and Raftopoulos argue that a too narrow focus on the leadership of the strike misinterprets the meaning of the strike more generally and in particular the complex politics of urban African township residents at this point in time. See "'*Kana sora ratswa ngaritswe,*'" 316.

31. Interview with Reuben Jamela, by author, Cranborne Park, Harare, June 24, 1992.

32. "Federal Council of All Progressive African Organisations," letter by Mzingeli, *African Weekly*, July 7, 1948, 10.

33. "Harari Doings," *African Weekly*, August 11, 1948.

34. "Salisbury News," *African Weekly*, November 17, 1948, 10.

35. George Ballenden, "Oral Evidence, Commission of Inquiry into Native Disturbances," Salisbury, July 22, 1948, NAZ ZBZ 1/1/1.

36. "A Lesson for African Leaders," *African Weekly*, April 28, 1948, 6.

37. George Hartley, "Policy: Relations between the Native Advisory Board and the City Council," December 10, 1948, NAZ Records 12/7/13.

38. Native Advisory Board, Minutes of the 23rd Ordinary Meeting, December 21, 1949, NAZ Records 12/7/13.

39. Minister of Justice, in *Hansard*, quoted in B. J. Mnyanda, *In Search of Truth: A Commentary on Certain Aspects of Southern Rhodesia's Native Policy* (Bombay: Hind Kitabs, 1954), 143.

40. Ibid., 144.

41. Mnyanda writes: "As a result of the recommendation of the Hudson Commission, the Subversive Activities Act of 1950 was enacted by Parliament. But it is a barbarous piece of legislation going far beyond its professed objects and calculated to embitter racial feelings . . .," Mnyanda, *In Search of Truth*, 142.

42. Ibid., 148–50.

43. Mzingeli, "Subversive Act," NAZ Historical Manuscripts (HM) SRLP 9/1/5/13, 2.

44. Ibid.

45. Hardwicke Holderness, *Lost Chance: Southern Rhodesia, 1945–1958* (Harare: Zimbabwe Publishing House, 1985), 74.

46. Holderness describes Mzingeli as "lightly built, bespectacled, earnest, sensitive and—as I came to understand—touchy and probably quite lonely" (ibid., 73). His experience with Mzingeli led Holderness to ask, "Was it not true that if whites proved unable to take seriously and sympathetically someone like Mzingeli they would be asking for leaders like him to be replaced by much more implacable ones, and ones who might really have something sinister about them?" Ibid., 77.

47. Charles Mzingeli, Reformed ICU Newsletter 1, no. 5 (November 1950), NAZ HM RH 16/1/3/4.

48. See Penny M. Von Eschen, *Race against Empire: Black Americans and Anticolonialism, 1937–1957* (Ithaca: Cornell University Press, 1997), for the far-reaching impact of anti-communism within Pan-African politics in this period.

49. NAZ HM SRLP 9/1/5/13, Subversive Act, 1. Mzingeli quotes the Official Report, vol. 31, no. 34, col. 1903, 2.6.50 (*Hansard*), which links the Subversive Activities bill (now an act) with the 1948 General Strike. The minister opening up the debate stated: "The origin of the measure goes back to 1948. The House will recollect that early in 1948 there was a series of more or less serious Native disturbances through the colony, known now as the Native general strike." Ibid.

50. RICU, "Minutes of Second Annual Conference," 79–89.

51. Edward Roux, *Time Longer than Rope: A History of the Black Man's Struggle for Freedom in South Africa* (Madison: University of Wisconsin Press, 1964).

52. Ranger, *Are We Not Also Men?*, 121. Mnyanda's letter to Thompson Samkange is dated March 21, 1947; Aaron Jacha's letter to Thompson Samkange is dated August 7, 1947.

53. *African Weekly*, November 30, 1949, 11.

54. *African Weekly*, November 23, 1949.

Chapter 3

1. George Ballenden, "Report to the Native Administration Committee, Salisbury City Council: RE: The N(UA)ARA Act No. 6 of 1946," Salisbury, December 13, 1946, NAZ RC TC 11/181.

2. "Police Raids on Married Women," *African Weekly*, April 19, 1950, 9.

3. For a more in-depth discussion of *mapoto* wives and women in the informal sector, see Barnes, "*We Women Worked So Hard*," and Terri Barnes and Everjoyce Win, *To Live a Better Life: An Oral History of Women in the City of Harare, 1930–70* (Harare: Baobab Books, 1992).

4. "*Imba Kuzara ne zivo mukadzi*," *African Weekly*, June 20, 1945, 2 (letter in ChiShona, trans. Simba Handiseni).

5. Interview with Topias Nhapi, by author and Joseph Seda, National Section, Mbare, June 1, 1992.

6. Charles Mzingeli, "Oral Evidence to the National Native Labour Board Commission of Inquiry into the Employment of African Women," Salisbury, 1953, UZ Godlonton Collection.

7. "Self-criticism by Africans," *African Weekly*, October 5, 1950, 5. Such topics fit well with Mzingeli's emphasis on the dignity of labor and the need for Africans to create a culture of cooperation in the township in order to make better demands for political and economic recognition. But given the demographics of the township, the potential audience for this message was not extremely large.

8. Charles Mzingeli, Minutes of the RICU General Meeting, Salisbury, June 3, 1951, NAZ Records (RC) Native Administration Department (NAD) R7.

9. Ibid.

10. Quoted in *African Weekly*, April 5, 1950, 1.

11. See Schmidt, *Peasants, Traders, and Wives*, Jeater, *Marriage, Perversion, and Power*, and Barnes, "*We Women Work So Hard*."

12. Charles Mzingeli, Reformed ICU Newsletter, July 1951, NAZ HM RH 16/1/3/4.

13. "The Long Arm of the Law," *African Weekly*, August 24, 1949, 4.

14. Charles Mzingeli to Director of Salisbury Native Administration Department, Salisbury, June 1951, RC NAD RI.5.

15. Charles Mzingeli, Reformed ICU Monthly General Meeting, Salisbury, September 7, 1952, RC NAD R7.

16. Ibid., March 2, 1952, RC NAD R7.

17. The municipality was worried by Mzingeli's capacity for organizing a campaign. Mzingeli recalled that once a woman went into labor and gave birth during a raid in which she was arrested, Mzingeli was called and he told the husband he would look into the matter. Before he could raise the issue with the authorities, the municipality responded by providing the couple with their own house, and telling them to stay away from Mzingeli. Interview with C. L. Mzingeli Harare Township," by Roberts, Steele, and Mapuranga.

18. "Immorality at Harari: Native Board's Denial," *Sunday Mail*, March 30, 1952, NAZ Records R7. Mzingeli goes on to argue that since Africans were not able to build their own homes, it was the responsibility of the "powers that be" to build homes "for every African who lives in Harari."

19. *African Weekly*, February 6, 1952.

20. Interview with Mrs. Johanna Scott, by author and Joseph Seda, Old Highfield, October 18, 1991.

21. Regarding housing conditions, Wilkins continues: "In the Union [South Africa] you have shanty towns in many of the cities. We have not got shanty towns here but we have worse overcrowding in parts of Harari than they have got in the Union. We must not blind ourselves that because we have not got shanty towns we are doing a grand job of work and being successful. We are not. What we have managed to do is hide the problem but it is still there." Dr. A. J. W. Wilkins, "Oral Evidence to the Urban African Affairs Commission," Salisbury, 1957, NAZ S51/2.

22. D. M. Barbour, ibid. Government publications equated this high turnover with the number of "single" men in the city. A figure based on questionable 1956 census data shows 100,000 African men working in the city, of whom 88,000 are "single" and 12,000 have their families with them. This was the basis for saying "88% of the African labour force is migratory." Southern Rhodesia, *African Housing Schemes of the Southern Rhodesian Government* (Salisbury, 1956). Data on those housed in the Salisburg City Council's townships (Harare and Mabvuku) in October 1953 had 22,222 tenants, of whom 4,754 rented married accommodations, giving them a ratio of 1 married to 3.67 single. "Salisbury City Treasurer Department to Chief Native Commissioner," Salisbury, October 23, 1953, NAZ S2809/4329E.

23. The Joint National Council, a powerful group of industrial interests, including representatives from the Chamber of Mines of Rhodesia, the Federation of Rhodesian Industries, the Federated Chambers of Commerce, the Mining Federation, the National Farmers' Union, etc., called for an investigation into the employment of African women in 1951. It is not surprising that the Joint Council, representing diverse aspects of employers' interests, wanted the government to take a more interventionist role in getting women to work, most notably to "free up" male labor (especially those working as domestics) for industrial and farm employment. The council begins its memorandum with a typical colonial stereotype of the urban woman as less industrious than the rural peasant woman: "It appears that the majority of African women living in Locations or townships, unlike those living in the Reserves, have little with which to occupy themselves and from this aspect alone it appears that employment of some kind would be beneficial." Joint National Council, Race Relations Committee, "African Women in Industry," Salisbury, September 18, 1951, NAZ S2788/19. Official accounts of the female population remained low. In 1951, according to the testimony of Col. George Hartley, the director of Salisbury's African Affairs Department, the population of the municipality and commons was 75,663; this total included 60,533 men, 5,033 women, and 10,097 children. (By 1956 these figures had increased to the admittedly low estimate of 100,000 men, 12,000 women, and 36,000 children. Southern Rhodesia, *Report of the Urban African Affairs Commission* (Plewman Commission) (Salisbury, 1958), 18.

24. Native Advisory Board, board minutes of meeting, January 16, 1952, NAZ S2824/5/2; "Appointment of an NNLB . . . concerning the employment of African women in Industry," 2.

25. George Hartley, "Oral Evidence to the National Native Labour Board's Enquiry into the Employment of African Women," Salisbury, 1952, UZ Godlonton Collection, 193.

26. Mr. S. E. Aitken-Cade, "Oral Evidence to the National Native Labour Board's Enquiry into the Employment of African Women," Salisbury, 1952, UZ Godlonton Collection.

27. See Barnes and Win, *To Live a Better Life*, 79–83.

28. "African Women to Form Helping Hand Club: Only needy Cases will benefit," *African Weekly*, September 2, 1953, 1. See Barnes and Win, *To Live a Better Life*. The women of the 1960s generation, including South African–born Ruth Chinamano and others, were more involved directly in the politics of protest, and after the arrest of the NDP leadership in 1960, they became the central focus of protests demanding the release of the detained leadership. Chinamano's work with her husband at the

Highfield Community School needs further attention by historians, as it offers an alternative to both mission and state-run schools.

29. From a purely economic view, African domestics often got higher wages from the new immigrants, especially from the RAF personnel. Mr. Chibisa-bira, who worked at the RAF Cranborne Hostel in supplies, remembered watching the British pilots and their wives go from an initial period when they paid decent wages, socialized with their servants, and often ate food and drank European liquor with them at the same table. It was only a matter of time until Rhodesian whites would coach them in the "proper" way to treat their domestic servants. Interview with Mr. Chibisa-bira, by author and Joseph Seda, New Highfield, May 25, 1992. The Southern Rhodesian government pamphlet *Your Servant and You* (Salisbury: Government Printers, 1946), which was primarily addressed to the newly arrived housewives, explained the taboos of eating together at the same table, and most of all of paying too high a wage.

30. The prejudices of white administrators against the African women working in their homes is captured in the following remarks: "The great majority of female servants are employed as nurse maids to children and as such their duties consist of pushing a perambulator to the park and sitting and watching children at play. For such duties many of these girls demand wage in excess of the cook employed in the same household, uniform and in addition insist upon food from the employer's table. The number of native women who have experience as house maids is still limited and due to the comparative ease with which posts as nurse maids are obtained and the simplicity of the duties expected of the latter, the majority prefer this type of employment. Their point of view was succinctly expressed recently by the remark of a woman made at a meeting held in Harare: 'First we want good wages and second we should be supplied with long handles so that we do not hurt our knees.'" Salisbury Native Administration Department, *Report, 1951–1952* (Salisbury, 1952), 49.

31. Native Commissioner, Salisbury, "Report for the Year Ended 31st December 1952," Salisbury, 1953, NAZ S2827/2/2/2.

32. Charles Mzingeli, "Oral Evidence to the National Native Labour Board's Enquiry into the Employment of African Women," Salisbury, 1952, UZ Godlonton Collection.

33. Interview, Tobias Nhapi, National Section, Mbare, June 1, 1992.

34. Charles Mzingeli, Minutes of Reformed ICU Public Meeting, Harare, October 19, 1952, NAZ RC NAD R7.

35. The results: "Mr. Mzingeli (RICU) 237 votes; Mr. Patrick Pazarangu (RICU) 180 votes; I. H. Samuriwo (HRP) 174 votes; Jameson Moyo (HRP) 174 votes; B. J. Mnyanda (HRP) 164 votes; J. P. Bassoppo (HRP) 164 votes; L. Takawira (HRP) 162 votes; P. G. Phiri (HRP) 162 votes" "Record Poll in Harare Board Election," *African Weekly*, December 20, 1950.

36. This point is made by Gary Baines in his discussion of township advisory boards in South Africa:; see "Contradictions of Community Politics," 79–97.

37. "Record Poll in Harare Board Election."

38. Lawrence Vambe describes how a Catholic priest, "Reverend Father Burbridge, S. J.," who headed "St. Peter's, the Catholic African mission at the edge of Harare Location," had attempted to convince Mzingeli to transform the ICU into "a Catholic trade union, subject to the direction and control of the Catholic Church." According to Vambe, Mzingeli told Father Burbridge "he would give no Church or priest the

executive right to control his union. Not even the Holy Father the Pope could per-
suade him to alter one word of this [the ICU's] constitution. Burbridge lost his temper and told Mzingeli that from now on he could consider himself to have been
excommunicated from the Church. The African leader was shattered by such intolerance from a man whose concern with the lot of the black people he had admired."
Vambe, *From Rhodesia to Zimbabwe*, 102–3.

39. Charles Mzingeli, Minutes of Meeting of the Reformed ICU, Salisbury, October
7, 1951, NAZ Records NAD, RI.5.

40. According to Hannan's *Standard Shona Dictionary* (1959 [1987]), 848, the verb
-pipa translates as "producing untoward effects through magic [Zezuru]." *African
Weekly*, December 6, 1950, 11. Letter signed L. C. Mzingeli, April 6, 1951. Writing in
the RICU newsletter in 1950, Mzingeli criticizes Chingattie, a Jan Hofmeyr graduate
in "native social welfare work," who was also Secretary of the Nyasaland Students
Association. He writes, "He started his secretaryship in the Harare Township where
he was appointed, and it ended in the Magistrate's Court, when he was cautioned and
discharged for assaulting his chairman." Mzingeli, "Reformed ICU Newsletter," vol.
1, no. 6, April 1951, NAZ HM RH 16/1/3/4. Chingattie had likely studied magic
with another young social worker with the railways, Joshua Nkomo, who was based in
Bulawayo. Nkomo was reported to have "caused uncontrollable excitement and anx-
iety when he demonstrated that he was a great conjurer." "Social Worker Performs
Magic," *African Weekly*, March 24, 1950(?), 11.

41. Mzingeli, "Reformed ICU Newsletter," vol. 1, no. 6, NAZ HM RH 16/1/3/4.

42. "Mr. Mzingeli Rejoices at Board Results," *African Weekly*, December 26, 1951,
Board Elections: Statements by HRP and RICU, Salisbury, NAD RI.5.

43. "Farewell Reception for Mr. Mzingeli" *African Weekly*, October 28, 1951,
Clipping Files, Salisbury, NAD RI.5.

44. See Sir Frank Walcott, *Frankly Speaking* (St. Michael, Barbados: Barbados
Workers' Union, 1991).

45. *African Weekly*, January 6, 1954.

46. It was common to express wages in shillings and pence, rather than
pounds/shillings/pence. In the previous quote, therefore, 35/- would equal
£1/15s/od per month. Mzingeli, Minutes of Reformed ICU Public Meeting, Harare,
October 19, 1952, NAZ RC NAD R7.

47. According to Tobias Nhapi, Eleanor Solomon served on the RICU executive.
She was the only woman to serve on the executive and was, according to Nhapi, quite
skilled at organizing, bringing a number of women workers into the RICU in the
early 1950s. But Nhapi considered her to be sometimes too radical for the RICU:
"She was quick to call for a strike each time things went wrong." Nhapi recalls a time
when he himself spoke at a spontaneous meeting of Harare residents over the issue
of electricity. There was some confusion in the early 1950s about the removal of electricity from some of the homes in the Old Bricks section of Harare township. A gathering took place at the Boxing Grounds, and Nhapi explained to the crowd that the
municipality's excuse that the wires were worn-out was false, because who had ever
heard of copper wire rusting? He told the crowd that since Africans were now working willingly—unlike in the early days when they were forced to by the whites—there
was no justification for turning off the power. "In a way this was tantamount to chasing us away . . . so if we were no longer required we could as well go back to our home

areas." While Nhapi had only implied that a protest action would come, Eleanor Solomon called out for an immediate strike, which, according to Nhapi, was not what the RICU had planned: "The thing is, I had addressed the meeting and threatened that there would be an exodus of people to their home areas if this disconnection continued, but this woman [Eleanor] had even outlined the date we intended to have the strike." That evening Mr. Brock, the Chief Native Commissioner, apologized over the radio (loudspeaker), telling people to refrain from striking, as it had been a mistake. The next morning the power was turned back on.

Nhapi remembered Solomon as coming from Umtali and living alone most of the time—being continuously employed in European homes. Her leadership was perhaps symbolic of the difficulty the RICU had in combining the potentially radical politics of women in the township with the approach of Mzingeli and other men who witnessed the frustrations and anger of these women but were more cautious to act, as they had more vested in both European and African respectable society. Solomon may have perhaps seemed to Mzingeli and others on the executive as always potentially threatening, but her militancy was not lost on the SCYL, and when the bus boycott was called for at a public meeting in 1956, it was Solomon who stood up and urged township residents to refuse to ride the buses.

48. Mzingeli, Minutes of the RICU General Meeting, November 2, 1952, NAZ RC NAD R7. For this notion of the "struggle for the breeches" in nineteenth-century British history, see Clark, *Struggle for the Breeches.*

Chapter 4

1. In 1954 a comparison of the elected officials in the Harare advisory board and the Salisbury and District African Welfare Society shows the same RICU members dominating both organizations. Mzingeli won the 1954 advisory board election with the most votes (608), followed by Patrick Pazarangu (271) and J. P. Bassoppo-Moyo (208). The top five vote getters were RICU executive board members. The first three names nominated to be on the Welfare Society board were Mzingeli, Pazarangu, and Bassoppo-Moyo. *African Weekly,* January 6 and 27, 1954.

2. Michael West has shown the campaign against Federation as one of the very few occasions Mzingeli was able to work with other African leaders in a concerted campaign. West, *African Middle Class,* 184–92.

3. Charles Mzingeli, "Man of Principle," *Central African Examiner,* August 1963, 19. See also "Interview with C. L. Mzingeli Harare Township," September 15, 1970, by Roberts, Steele, and Mapuranga, 5.

4. The Harare Civic Association (HCA) made demands similar to the RICU's in the 1940s: lowering of rents, further electrification of the township, and better police protection for residents. The HCA was originally established by the RICU to nominate RICU candidates for the local advisory board elections. It was also meant as a public forum where residents could bring their problems, which the HCA then passed on to the local advisory board. However, it would seem, based on Mzingeli's minutes, that many people did bring their problems directly to Mzingeli at his shop/office.

5. "Harare Civic Association," *African Weekly,* February 24, 1954.

6. Quote from a Castle Beer advertisement reproduced in Barnes, "*We Women Worked So Hard*," 157. There is an interesting link between Mukarakate and his wife's role as the leaders of the "Highfields Creche." The Castle ad includes a personal testimony by Mukarakate to the benefits of a "cold Castle" as follows: "'My boys may sometimes get beaten in the ring, but you can't beat a cold Castle when the occasion calls for a cool refreshing drink. After a game of tennis I'm always happy to serve Castle Beer to my friends, then I have an excuse to enjoy one myself. My wife has a busy and harassing time running the Highfields Creche, and she too finds there is nothing like a cold Castle to pull her together at the end of a tiring day." Advertisement from 1958. Mukarakate had resigned as leader of the Employed Women's League in 1955.

7. "Women's League Holds Function," *African Weekly*, July 14, 1954.

8. Interview, Tobias Nhapi, National Section, Mbare, July 6, 1992.

9. "Women's League Holds Social Evening in Harare," *Bantu Mirror*, Bulawayo, July 10, 1954.

10. Ibid., 2.

11. Ibid. Other dignitaries included A. Mukarakate, the general secretary and founder of the league; J. Z. Savanhu, MP; and the "Expensive Bantu Choir." By 1960–61, according to the Harare township superintendent's report, "the Southern Rhodesia African Women Workers union 'functioned spasmodically' and had a paid membership of 257. Its members are identifiable by a plastic badge they wear, particularly when seeking employment. Their male president resigned his office in October 1955." Director of Native Administration, City of Salisbury, "Annual Report of the Director of Native Administration for the Municipal Year 1st July 1955 to 30th June 1956, Salisbury, 1956" (G. H. Hartley), RH Mss. Perham Box 625/5 item 1.

12. "Harare Women Protest to Advisory Board," *African Weekly*, November 3, 1954, 6.

13. Letter to editor, signed Charles Mzingeli, *African Weekly*, June 2, 1954.

14. Brian Raftopoulos, "Nationalism and Labour in Salisbury, 1953–1965," *Journal of Southern African Studies* 12, no. 1, *Special Issue: Urban Studies and Urban Change in Southern Africa* (March 1995): 79–93, quote on 81.

15. Ibid., 92.

16. Interview with Reuben Thomas Jamela, Harare, African Oral History Collection NAZ AOH 63, 20.

17. The estimated membership of African political organizations as of 1952 indicates the variety of political choices available, although Mzingeli's RICU remained the most important in Salisbury's African townships until the shift described below. These membership numbers are from the All-African Convention founding meeting in 1952 and are therefore probably inflated estimates: SRANC (5,000), British African National Workers Union (6,000), Federation of Southern Rhodesian African Workers Union (4,300), Matebele Home Society (500), African Farmers Union (1,000), S.R. African Association (10,000), Reformed ICU (2,000 in Salisbury), and the African Artisans Guild [Union] (1,000). Cited in Directory of Salisbury Native Affairs, "Annual Report for the Year 1953," NAZ.

18. Interview, Mr. Reuben Jamela, Cranborne Park, Harare, June 24, 1992.

19. "Contracts Offered to African Builders," *African Weekly*, March 3, 1954. Jamela's skills were further evidenced when the National Industrial Council of the Building Industry—the organization that administered the Industrial Conciliation

Act for European builders—responded to the city council's decision by requiring African builders to register as employers. Jamela's response was to call an emergency meeting of the African Artisans Union, at which he passed his resolution advising all members to not fill in the forms sent to them by the National Industrial Council until such time as Africans were included in the Industrial Conciliation Act in the definition of "employee." "African Artisans Required to Register as Employers," *African Weekly*, March 24, 1954.

20. Letter to editor from P. P. J. Kadzutu, Organizing Secretary TUC, Mashonaland and Manicaland Provinces, *African Weekly*, March 24, 1954.

21. Letter to the editor from L. C. Mzingeli, *African Weekly*, April 7, 1954.

22. Brian Raftopoulos, "Labour Internationalism and Problems of Autonomy and Democratisation in Southern Rhodesia, 1951–1975," in Ranger, *Democracy and Human Rights in Zimbabwe*, 2:61.

23. In 1956, at the same meeting where James Chikerema was elected president of the SRANC, the decision was taken to create branches in Highfield as well as in Harare. Edson Sithole was the chair of the Harare branch, while Herbert Munagatire chaired the Highfield branch, as he had moved out of the *Daily News* quarters and bought into the homeownership scheme. The Highfield executive of the SCYL, according to Nhapi, included himself, Munagatire, and Henry Hamadziripi. Mr. Nhapi recalls how before the ANC was banned in 1959 official business would be discussed openly at Paul Mashonga's shop at Machipisa Shopping Centre in Highfield. After Joshua Nkomo took over as president of the SRANC, the headquarters were moved into town. Interview with Fidelis Nhapi, by author, Mabelreign, Harare, April 10, 1992.

24. With the completion of New Highfield in 1954, many men, especially foreign migrants, moved from Harare township and brought their wives to live in New Highfield. A significant number of single men became lodgers in the 4,000 units in New Highfield. The lodger system was seen as a way to help the Highfield homeownership participants subsidize their payments. By 1957 the population of New Highfield was estimated at 21,000. Survey data from that year indicated that even with a lodger system to help pay the rents, more skilled and educated people moved to Highfield and that the residents there "are in general a wealthier class of African than those elsewhere." Southern Rhodesia, *Report of the Urban African Affairs Commission*, Appendix N, 188.

25. Interview, Fidelis Nhapi, National Section, Mbare, March 12, 1992.

26. See John McCracken, "Democracy and Nationalism in Historical Perspective: The Case of Malawi," in Ranger, *Democracy and Human Rights in Zimbabwe*, vol. 2, 47.

27. Vambe, *From Rhodesia to Zimbabwe*, 275–76.

28. Interview, Fidelis Nhapi, National Section, Mbare, March 12, 1992. Nhapi describes how, in the formative period, every day and every evening the three men—Fidelis Nhapi, Edson Sithole, and Thompson Gonese—would get together to discuss the new party. Gonese and Sithole would come from the *African Daily News* and pick up Nhapi from St. Peter's School in Harare, where he was teaching. At the time, Sithole was not yet as educated as the other two, but he managed to put himself through school, attending St. Peter's through Standard VI, and then obtain his junior certificate and later a university degree. According to Nhapi, these men

formed the nucleus of the Youth League, which they launched in August 1955 from their shared bachelor's quarters.

29. George Houser, *No One Can Stop the Rain: Glimpses of Africa's Liberation Struggle* (New York: Pilgrim Press, 1989), 221. Houser praises the actions of the SCYL, and sees its program as "reminiscent of the non-violent civil rights movement of the United States." Houser writes: "I was fascinated by the incidents of civil disobedience Chikerema and Nyandoro described to me, such as using the toilets at the native commissioner's office, encouraging the preparation of the African home brew called 'chukuba,' and encouraging Africans to cultivate a potato crop on private land, all in defiance of regulations." 222.

30. Interview, Fidelis Nhapi, Mabelreign, Harare, April 10, 1992.

31. Raftopoulos, "Nationalism and Labour in Salisbury, 1953–1965," 88.

32. Interview, Fidelis Nhapi, Mabelreign, Harare, April 10, 1992.

33. "Mabvuku Becoming 'Heart' of Congress," *Daily News*, November 10, 1958, clipping from NAZ Records NAD R1/7. Women were present as leaders of the SRANC's separate women's branches starting in December 1958. The Mabvuku Women's section was headed by Mrs. A. Katiyo, while the Highfield women's branch was led by a committee of seven women headed by a thirty-five-year-old "Nyasaland woman," Mrs. Mupandamwara. The SRANC's women's branch had an eleven-member national executive committee, and perhaps as an indication of Highfield's importance, Mrs. Mupandamwara was the chair of the executive committee. Other members included Mrs. E. Mushonga, Mrs. Murape, Mrs. Makwangara, Mrs. Chavunga, Mrs. Chiota, and Mrs. Kadani. Elections in December 1958 added Mrs. George Nyandoro, wife of "the vociferous Secretary General of the Congress," Mrs. Augustine Mutyambizi, Mrs. Mwaera, and Mrs. Mugadza. "ANC Forms 2 Women's Branches," *Evening Standard*, December 30, 1958.

34. Interview, Tobias Nhapi, National Section, Mbare, June 1, and July 16, 1992.

35. Vambe, *From Rhodesia to Zimbabwe*, 274.

36. Ibid., 275.

37. West, *African Middle Class*, 238; original quote from *Bantu Mirror*, January 5, 1947, in West, 291n6.

38. Ibid., 291.

39. Interview, Tobias Nhapi, National Section, Mbare, June 1, and July 16, 1992. Tobias Nhapi had, like Mzingeli, contributed a great deal to prepare Nyandoro's generation to take on the challenge of political organizing. He remembered that throughout these years he "favoured all causes that addressed the plight of black people, although I feared arrest." He, like many others of the older generation, continued to work behind the scenes for the Youth League, and he eventually became a local unit chairman for the ANC and NDP. Nhapi's house was subjected to searches, and he was detained and arrested for his connection to Nyandoro and others. On one occasion, in the late 1950s, he had a large sack of mealie-meal dumped on the ground because the authorities believed he had "the typewriter belonging to the NDP." His white employers (the government), upon hearing the story, made the police refund him for the mealie-meal.

40. Fidelis Nhapi remembers the difference between the SCYL's original state of mind compared with the later, more encompassing message of the ANC: "When you start off something, you have ideas, which, with the passage of time, become modified.

When we started the organisation, we never meant to have the full loaf; we just wanted to have a share. We wanted political recognition. At that time we were completely cut off from job opportunities, education and the provision of land." Interview, Fidelis Nhapi, Mabelreign, Harare, April 10, 1992.

41. "Stone Throwing Incidents," *African Weekly,* January, 26, 1955, Native Administration Department (Salisbury), "Crimes: Violence Press Cutting," NAZ Records NAD C8/4.

42. "Absence of stoning in Colony," *Rhodesia Herald,* November 1, 1955, ibid.

43. *Sunday Mail,* February 26, 1956, ibid.

44. Shamuyarira concludes the passage with the following: "If I seem to labour over the point, it is because many Europeans deliberately misinterpret the reasons for some of the ugly incidents which occur whenever there is a riot. To others the incidents may seem inexplicable, but there is always some reason like the one I have outlined above behind the incident." Nathan Shamuyarira, *Crisis in Rhodesia* (London: A. Deutsch, 1965), 43.

45. Nyagumbo, *With the People,* 105.

46. Boycott Action Committee, Memorandum Submitted to the Minister of Roads, Local Government, and Housing, Salisbury, September 1956, NAZ S2819/9.

47. Johnny Maoko, a manual laborer employed by Lever Brothers at the time, remembers walking to work in the morning from the hostel in Harare and seeing new people being hired to replace those who stayed away during the boycott. After work, he would hurry home and join the gangs of protesters who would beat up men who had gone to work. Interview with Johnny Maoko, by author and Joseph Seda, National Section, Mbare, February 24, 1992.

48. Interview with Fidelis Nhapi, by author and Joseph Seda, Mabelreign, Harare, April 10, 1992.

49. *Daily News,* September 17, 1956.

50. *Daily News,* September 18, 1956. The same edition carried a small item that represented Mzingeli's demise and the animosity of the *Daily News* staff toward him: "Mzingeli Supports Boycott," which quoted him as saying, "I regret that the decision to boycott the buses was taken in my absence . . . but I associate myself with the boycott," adding, "Mr. Mzingeli was away from Salisbury for the weekend and the first time he knew anything about it was this morning from the daily press." Ibid.

51. Ibid.

52. George Nyandoro, "Letter" (n.d.), as quoted in Miriam Green, "The Salisbury Bus Boycott," *History in Zambia* 13 (1983): 1–17.

53. *Daily News,* September 18, 1956. The Salisbury Native Administration Department listed the material damage at the hostel as "233 window panes broken, 47 doors smashed and locks broken 10 door panels broken, 25 vent grills broken . . ." and so on, Salisbury Native Administration Department, "Annual Report for the Year 1956–57," Salisbury, 1957, 65.

54. "Shona War Song at Sacking of Girl's Hostel: Court told of Riots," *Rhodesia Herald,* October 2, 1956. See also "High Court Verdict on Harare Rioters," *African Daily News,* December 13, 1956: "Of the 21 Harare Africans, charged by violence during the Harare riots, on September 19, 1956, 6 were found guilty in the Southern Rhodesia High Court this afternoon. . . . All the others were found not guilty." "Five-Year Sentence for Harari Rioters—Some Are Discharged," *Rhodesia Herald,* January 5,

1957: "In a separate trial, this time heard by Mr. Justice Morton, in the Salisbury High Court, two Africans charged with public violence for the destruction of a hot-dog stand, got sentences of five years with hard labor and six cuts with the cane." Therefore the Court gave the same sentence for rape as it did for destroying a hot-dog stand.

55. "Harari Rioters in Court: Stallholders and Women Describe Night of Terror," *Rhodesia Herald*, March 10, 1956. In Salisbury Magistrates Court: "Five African women—two of them under 19—told the Court that they had been raped when rioters broke down the doors of their rooms at the Carter Women's Hostel. Four said they were hiding under beds, and the fifth said she was in a cupboard. One of the women said she was held on her bed by five men and was raped by three of them. When she was about to be raped by a fourth, the police arrived."

56. *African Weekly*, September 20, 1956. The original Shona phrase was not included in the article, only the English equivalent.

57. *African Weekly*, October 8, 1956.

58. "Chikerema to Call Off Boycott If Government Will Negotiate," *Daily News*, September 19, 1956, NAZ S2819/9.

59. "Interview with C. L. Mzingeli Harare Township," September 15, 1970, by Roberts, Steele, and Mapuranga. See Terence Ranger's discussion of perceptions in Bulawayo of Manyika and violence. Ranger, "Urban Violence in Africa," 3.

60. "Mr. Mzingeli Replies to Mr. Chikerema," *African Weekly*, October 10, 1956, 1.

61. Shamuyarira credits the formation of "a civic organization which was primarily concerned with matters of Harare and Highfield townships." Nyandoro and the others began to challenge Mzingeli openly at public meetings and they "never hesitated to shout down their opponents at public meetings, to discredit Mzingeli's reputed strength." In addition to Nyandoro and Chikerema, Shamuyarira credits Edson Sithole, Henry Hamadziripi, and Thompson Gonese as the most vocal in their attacks on Mzingeli and the RICU in 1956. Shamuyarira, *Crisis in Rhodesia*, 40–41. He also credits Dunduzu Chisiza for pushing himself and the other intellectuals to join up with the Youth League based on their reading, in 1955, of a pamphlet on "Self-Determination" that had been given to Chisiza by the Indian High Commissioner at that time, Nirmal Singh.

62. Acongen, Salisbury to State, January 10, 1957 745c.00/1-1057, "Youth League Victory in Harare Township Advisory Board Elections," 2.

63. Ibid.

64. George Nyandoro, ed., *Chapupu*, June 1957, NAZ S/CH275.

65. Ibid., August 3, 1957.

66. Angelina Mhlanga, "Major Matters for 'Minors,'" *Central African Examiner*, June 1962, 9.

67. For a discussion of rape in the urban culture during this period, see Joyce Chadya and Koni Benson, "*Ukubhinya*: Gender and Sexual Violence in Bulawayo, Colonial Zimbabwe, 1946–1956," *Journal of Southern African Studies* 31, no. 3 (September 2005): 587–610.

68. Italics in original. *Chapupu*, Highfield, June 1957, no. 1, 6.

69. Ibid.

70. Gossip by "Murumbo Munhu" and "African Women Forced to Work on the Roads," both in *Chapupu*, October 19, 1957, 5.

71. "Mrs. Chinamano Sailing to England in October," *African Weekly*, September 7, 1955. At the time she had been in Rhodesia for four and a half years, having met Josiah Chinamano when he was studying in South Africa. She returned with him and was teaching Standard IV at Waddilove School.

72. Ruth Weiss with Jane L. Parpart, *Sir Garfield Todd and the Making of Zimbabwe* (London: British Academic Press, 1999), 98.

73. Doris Lessing, *Going Home* (London: Panther, 1968 [1957]), 88.

74. Holderness, *Lost Chance*, 222.

75. Ibid., 223–25.

76. Ibid., 230.

77. Ian Hancock has described Whitehead as the choice of the established elite, comprising "the Argus press, the mining companies and manufacturing firms, the banks and finance houses, senior civil servants and heads of statutory bodies, wealthy ranchers and gentleman framers." They thought he represented an acceptable middle ground between Todd on the one hand and the "segregationist right" on the other. Ian Hancock, *White Liberals, Moderates, and Radicals in Rhodesia, 1953–1980* (London: Croom Helm, 1984), 82.

78. See Adam Ashforth, *The Politics of Official Discourse in Twentieth-Century South Africa* (Oxford: Oxford University Press 1990).

79. Southern Rhodesia, Legislative Assembly, *Hansard*, col. 310, July 22, 1958.

80. Ibid.

81. Ministerial statement on African housing, Legislative Assembly, *Hansard*, col. 1207 February 3, 1959.

82. Mr. Aitken-Cade, Legislative Assembly, *Hansard*, col. 522–23, July 24, 1958.

83. Richard W. Murphy, "Report of Conversation at Home of Mr. Lawrence Vambe, Sunday evening, March 2, 1958; enclosed as an attachment in AmConGen, Salisbury to Department of States, Despatch no. 376 USNA 745c.00/3-758, March 7, 1958, Microfilm 93/347, Reel 2.

84. Ibid.

85. Ibid.

86. Ibid. Chikerema's public attacks on Sir Patrick Fletcher were not unlike a tactic used by Mzingeli in the 1940s against the Chief Native Commissioner, whom he called a "thief" rather than chief. Chikerema later was charged and went to court for his public verbal attacks on Fletcher.

Chapter 5

1. The Sharpeville massacre occurred March 21, 1960. Philip Frankel's *An Ordinary Atrocity: Sharpeville and Its Massacre* (New Haven: Yale University Press, 2001) is an excellent historical analysis of Sharpeville. Six months before the Sharpeville massacre, the police in Windhoek, South-West Africa (Namibia), killed sixteen nonviolent protesters in September 1959, when a crowd refused to leave after police tried to remove three "pickets" outside of a municipal beer hall. See Ruth First, *South West Africa* (Harmondsworth, U.K.: Penguin Books, 1963), 210–11.

2. Mlambo, *Rhodesia*, 133.

3. Ibid., 134.

4. Ranger, *Are We Not Also Men?*, 183.

5. Stanlake Samkange, *Samkange Newsletter,* July 27, 1960, cited in Ranger, *Are We Not Also Men?*, 183.

6. Terence Ranger, "The Terrible Mistake Policy," *Dissent,* no. 22, October 20, 1960, 5. The *Sunday Mail's* account had emphasized the chaotic atmosphere on the evening of October 8, as "the fierce glow of burning buildings lighting the locations, police opened fire with Greener riot guns. Order was given to fire low at the rioters . . . and first casualties were at the main beerhall." *Sunday Mail* (Salisbury) October 9, 1960, 1. *Dissent* also included a firsthand account of the Saturday October 8 Harare riot "told by an African worker," a man who lived in the Nenyere hostels—and was on his way home from the city centre at around 5:30 p.m. when he found the protest in full swing at the hostels. From his hostel room window he watched as African workers threw stones at a European police truck and when the truck stopped someone set it on fire.

The author describes what happened later in the evening when "the police fired tear gas at us where we were standing outside the hostel. I ran away towards the Makabusi River. As I was coming to the river I saw five boys armed with empty quart beer bottles, sticks and iron bars. It was getting dark and they could not see well. They called out to ask me if I was African or European. They told me they would have killed me if I were European and if I were African and had loot they would have taken it from me. They told me they would murder me unless I went with them to loot the Magaba stores. I asked them why they wanted to steal things because they would be searched. They said they did not care because if they were sent to prison it would be better because there they would have something to eat. When we were going to that place I got behind the group and I immediately ran away from them. I didn't look back to see if they were chasing me. I just was sure I had to run very fast. Then I went to my uncle's house and stayed the night." "The Day of the Riots (Harare, October 8, 1960), Told by an African Worker," *Dissent,* no. 22, October 20, 1960.

7. West, *African Middle Class,* 223.

8. Harold Macmillan, the British prime minister, had referred to the "winds of change" sweeping through Africa during a visit to Cape Town on February 3, 1960.

9. A. Z. Murwira, "The Petrol Bomb, Its Advent and Effect," *Daily News,* July 24, 1962, 4.

10. For a clearer picture of the meaning of cultural nationalism in this period, see Thomas Turino, *Nationalists, Cosmopolitans, and Popular Music in Zimbabwe* (Chicago: University of Chicago Press, 2000). See esp. 88–89, where Turino quotes from interviews with township residents who explain the use of intimidation to make sure township residents attend rallies.

11. The Association for Diplomatic Studies and Training Foreign Affairs Oral History Project, Ambassador Edward W. Mulcahy, interviewed by Charles Stuart Kennedy, March 23, 1989 (ADST, 1998).

12. Maida Springer's initial role in establishing AFL-CIO ties with the SRTUC and African nationalists is detailed in Richards, *Maida Springer.*

13. Ignatius Takaidza Chigwendere, "White Aristocracy with a Black Proletariat," presented to a ZANU Seminar, Lusaka, September 1975, NAZ 22–23.

14. The article concludes: "Such an observation did nothing to reassure Africans, who now conclude that the Congress leaders are being held as hostages for the good behaviour of 3,000,000 Africans in SR." Also, from the same article: "Mrs. Victoria

Chitepo, wife of Southern Rhodesia's only African barrister, planned to call a meeting of the women of Salisbury this weekend to discuss means by which they might plead for the immediate release of the 13. One proposal was that hundreds of women should walk the 50 miles from Salisbury to Marandellas and remain quietly outside the prison gates until the prisoners were freed. But at the last minute the meeting was cancelled because it was thought that it might give the Government the opportunity of taking repressive action." "No Release Yet for Africans: Anniversary of Emergency," *Manchester Guardian*, February 28, 1961.

15. For a detailed analysis of this period, and a provocative revision of its importance, see David Leaver, "Multiracialism and Nationalisms: A Political Retrospective on 1950s Southern Rhodesia ('Colonial Zimbabwe')," *Journal of Third World Studies* (Fall 2006). See also Mlambo, *Rhodesia.*

16. Nkomo attended as NDP president, Ndabaningi Sithole as treasurer-general, and George Silundika and Herbert Chitepo as advisers. See Mlambo, *Rhodesia*, 153.

17. Ibid., 153. Original quote cited from the *Rhodesia Herald* and the *Daily News*, February 8, 1961. See Mlambo, *Rhodesia*, 163n33.

18. Interview with Reuben Jamela, by author, July 1, 1992.

19. Edson F. C. Sithole, "Real Reason Why ZAPU Expelled Jamela," *Daily News*, August 2, 1962, 4. The other leaders Sithole lists as being opposed to the decision were K. S. Mhilzha, J. T. Maluleke, and D. N. Madzimbamuto; all of these men, as well as Sithole, had been detained and were held at Marandellas Prison at the time of the 1961 constitutional debate.

20. Sithole, "Real Reason Why ZAPU Expelled Jamela," 4.

21. Martin and Johnson say that Nkomo called Takawira a "Tshombe" and "imperialist" for openly criticizing his decision to support the new constitution. Martin and Johnson, *Struggle for Zimbabwe*, 68.

22. Interview with Rueben Jamela, by author, July 1, 1992, 19–20.

23. Mlambo, *Rhodesia*, 159.

24. Interview with Terence Ranger, by author, Oxford, 1996.

25. Michael Mawema, "Why I Resigned from the NDP to Join the Zimbabwe National Party, Salisbury, September 1961," reprinted in Christopher Nyangoni and Gideon Nyandoro, *Zimbabwe Independence Movements: Selected Documents* (New York: Harper and Row, 1979), 48–50, quote on 49.

26. "Nkomo Take-Over in 12 Months," *Times* (London), May 1, 1962, 9.

27. NDP External Affairs Office, "ZAPU Policy for the Masses," *Radar* 1, no. 6 (June 16, 1962), Fox-Pitt Papers, PPMS 6/6/4 Box 9 School of Oriental and African Studies (SOAS) Archive.

28. See Mlambo, *Rhodesia*, 164–87.

29. Shamuyarira, *Crisis in Rhodesia*, 110.

30. Paul Mushonga, the former NDP member who broke off with Nkomo to form the Zimbabwe National Party (ZNP), provided the British Trade Union Africa representative, Ian Page, a different interpretation in July 1961; excerpts of his comments follow: "There is no contact between the ZNP and Reuben Jamela, President of the TUC." "Jamela is nervous of his position, the pro-NDP faction in the TUC threatened to get rid of him if he supported the ZNP. The detainees, led by Maluleke, have sufficient support and standing to take over the leadership of the TUC if they were to be released. Nkomo realises this, hence the lack of pressure for their release. There

are two of the detainees who are definitely left-minded. They are Maluleke and Mhiza." "The recent strike in S. Rhodesia was a failure mainly owing to bad organization. Nkomo tried to get Jamela to take responsibility for organizing the strike, but Jamela, having agreed to do so, did very little—and even not until the last moment. Nkomo completely lost all respect." Paul Mushonga (ZNP, SR), discussion with Ian Page, Thursday July 27, 1961, MCF COU 122(a) SOAS Archives.

31. Interview, Reuben Jamela, June 24, 1992.

32. Chigwendere, *White Aristocracy with a Black Proletariat*, 31.

33. Interview with Jamela, June 24, 1992. The U.S. evidence supports Jamela's contention that his decision to call off the September 1 General Strike was within the bounds of NDP directives, and it may have been in line with Nkomo's wishes. Emmerson's interpretation of the events of September suggest Nkomo and Jamela were more closely in line than the subsequent NDP-SRTUC fallout would suggest. Emmerson to Dept. of State, December 5, 1961, United States National Archives (USNA) Record Group (RG) 59, Box 2506 845c.062/12-561, 2. Emmerson, the American consul in Salisbury, telegraphed Washington requesting Jamela be informed during his visit to the United States that Mswaka's announcement of the postponement of the General Strike had not gone over well, particularly with the Commercial [African] Workers Union (CAWU), and that "Jamela leadership [was] reportedly under attack." Emmerson to Secretary of State, August 29, 1961, USNA RG 59, 845c.062/8-296, and Emmerson to Secretary of State, September 12, 1961, USNA RG 59, Box 2506 845c.062/9-1261.

34. T. E. M'swaka to Brother Reuben Jamela, September 4, 1961, George Meany Memorial Archives, RG 18-001, Irving Brown Papers, 1956–1962, Box 12 File 9.

35. Brown described what he saw as "a general difference of opinion between the African political leaders of the National Democratic Party (NDP) and trade union officials. The former apparently resented Jamela's reluctance to use the trade union movement for political purposes. Mr. Brown felt that this difference of opinion contributed to the failure of the NDP pre-July 26 referendum campaign." Emmerson to State Department, September 9, 1961, USNA RG 59, Box 2506 845c.062/9-1961 (entitled: "Memorandum of Conversation between Irving Brown, AFL-CIO Representative in Europe; John K. Emmerson, American Consul General; and Clifford R. Nelson, American Consul [Salisbury]").

36. Emmerson to State Department, September 9, 1961. Maida Springer's relations with Nkomo are explained in Richards, *Maida Springer*, 227. Springer later told Richards that she "surmised that he [Nkomo] might have had difficulty accepting a woman as an equal."

37. Terence Ranger, "Whitehead's Short-Term Victories," *Central African Examiner*, August 1961, 5–6. For a detailed discussion of the relations between the Whitehead government and African nationalists, see Leaver, "Multiracialism and Nationalisms."

38. Ranger, "Whitehead's Short-Term Victories," 5.

39. AmConsul Salisbury to Department of State, October 13, 1961, USNA RG 59, 845c.062/11-1561.

40. Before leaving for Dakar, Jamela, in an interview with the *Daily News*, stressed how he "had no intention to import trade union brands, stock, lock and barrel [*sic*] from other older countries. We have to fit our trade union struggle within the framework and format of the problems akin to the African Continent." He also pointed out

that while he was against the white government setting up "dummy unions," he also believed that there should be "free democratic and independent trade unions based on Pan-Africanism." "Jamela Off to Dakar: Says Unions and Politics Not Separate," *Daily News,* January 9, 1962, 4.

41. Telegram Purvis to Brown, January 17, 1962, George Meany Memorial Archives, RG 18-001, Irving Brown Papers, 1956–1962, Box 12 File 9.

42. "Petrol Bombed House," *Daily News,* January 4, 1962.

43. Charles Mzingeli, "Qualified Responsibility," *Central African Examiner,* December 1961, 17.

44. Mlambo, *Rhodesia,* 160.

45. Ibid., 161.

46. Nathan Shamuyarira, "NDP's Future: Quickening Conflict Out of Deadlock," *Central African Examiner,* December 1961, 7.

47. Ibid.

48. "Jamela Hits Out at Labour Laws," *Daily News,* 1, 3.

49. Richard Jeffries, "Populist Tendencies in the Ghanaian Trade Union Movement," in *The Development of an African Working Class: Studies in Class Formation and Action,* ed. Richard Sandbrook and Robin Cohen (Toronto: University of Toronto Press, 1975), 271.

50. Mulcahy elaborated on the function of these parties: "The labor leaders, the teachers, and the journalists, the people who are still the leaders today, the first generation of Rhodesian political leadership, were at our houses. It was a matter of principle that we never gave a representational affair without having blacks there. We always had blacks at our cocktail parties and dinner parties. Some people turned down our invitations because they knew they'd run into blacks but it was de rigueur with us. You say this is a mixed racial society, we will treat you as a mixed racial society." Interview with Edward W. Mulcahy, by Charles Stuart Kennedy, March 23, 1989, Association for Diplomatic Studies and Training Foreign Affairs Oral History Project, 1998.

51. Mulcahy goes on to recount Mugabe's conversation: "Mugabe recalled that Jamela had attended a labor conference at Dakar earlier this year. According to Mugabe, this conference was initiated by the ICFTU with the view of creating in Africa a strong pro-West trade union movement. Mugabe stressed that by attending and participating in such a conference Jamela had deviated completely from the proper course of Pan-Africanism." "In conclusion, Mugabe opined that although the Russians were friends of the Africans, the people of Africa would not accept the Russians as masters. He said it would be foolish for the Africans to sacrifice their freedom at the altar of communist ideology. He emphasized that Africans wanted to be masters of their own country and that the 'Communists will not be substituted for the British imperialists.'" AmConsul Salisbury to State, April 18, 1962, A-134, USNA RG 59, 845c.062/4-1862 XR 745c.00.

52. Paul Geren to State, "Third Annual Labor Report," February 13, 1963, 7, A-682, USNA RG 59.

53. Mulcahy reported Jamela making "several strong public statements in the past two weeks condemning the SRATUC as being Communist inspired." Edward Mulcahy, American Consul, Dispatch no. 1014, June 14, 1962, USNA RG 59 845c.062/6-1462 Box 2506, 3.

54. *Zimbabwe Labour News,* June 2, 1962; vol. 1, no. 18, 8, MCF COU 122(a) SOAS Archives.

55. Ibid.

56. Mulcahy added that although the "ZAPU extremists" believed that the SRATUC was under their control, it was well known that Maluleke was not "willing to play second fiddle." Mulcahy, Dispatch no. 1014, June 14, 1962.

Chapter 6

1. Southern Rhodesia Information Service, "Our Fight against Hooliganism and Thuggery: Victims' Stories of Intimidation, Fear, and Arson and Their Struggle against Racialist Extremism," 19. Fox-Pitt Papers, PPMS 6/6/4 Box 9 SOAS Archives. This source contains no date but includes newspapers titles and stories from August to September 10, 1962.

2. City of Salisbury, Annual Report of the Director of African Administration for the Year Ending 30th June 1962 (Salisbury, 1962), 40. Mothibe has also suggested that the early 1960s were seeing a growing number of unemployed urban workers, thus employers were not as desperate to hold on to their workforce as they had been during previous strike actions. See T. H. Mothibe, "African Labour in Colonial Zimbabwe in the 1950s: Decline in Militancy or a Turn to Mass Struggle?" *Labour, Capital, and Society* 26, no. 2 (November 1993): 226–50.

3. Paul Geren, American Consul, August 10, 1962, Airgram A-94, USNA RG 59 845c.062/8-1062 Box 2506 (Mugabe's letter is an unclassified attachment to Airgram A-94).

4. Edson F. C. Sithole, "Real Reason Why ZAPU Expelled Jamela," *Daily News,* August 2, 1962, 4.

5. Geren to State, September 28, 1962, USNA RG 59 845c.062/9-2862.

6. Mulcahy to State, March 23, 1962, A-121, USNA RG 59 845c.062/3-2362.

7. Geren to State, February 13, 1963, "Third Annual Labor Report," 7.

8. Jamela interviewed by author and Joseph Seda, July 7, 1992, 27. See Vambe's interview description in Brian Raftopoulos, "The Labour Movement in Zimbabwe, 1945–1965," where Vambe described Jamela: "He was a very strong person, and so the white people planned to use him, but I do not think he wanted to be used. The way they offered him certain favours and the way they spoke of him, made people think he was being used. The government authorities would say, for instance, 'if all the leaders were like Jamela . . .' Unfortunately that made people think he was a sell-out. And so when the poor man decided to go and bury his friend Parirenyatwa, innocently, he did not realize that he was on the wrong side of the people." In Raftopoulos and Phimister, *Keep on Knocking,* 83–84.

9. Vambe, *From Rhodesia to Zimbabwe,* 287.

10. "TUC Will Meet Force with Force—Jamela," *Daily News,* August 20, 1962, 1. Jamela goes on to describe the event: "'On my way in,' he said, 'I passed a group of people who were sitting in the veranda. They included Mr. Joshua Nkomo and Miss Jane Ngwenya. Whilst I was still inside the house a message arrived to say that my presence had provoked the gathering and that it would be advisable if I left. As I got out I was met by Messrs Robert Mugabe, George Silundika, J. Z. Moyo and Robert

Marere who all said that I should leave the place. They all assured me their protection.'"

11. *Central African Daily News,* July 23, 1962, 1.

12. Editorial: "Youth Out of Hand," *Daily News,* August 20, 1962, 1. The same page ran a story directly under the Jamela story entitled "Mugabe Tipped as New No. 2 Man to Nkomo," which reported a controversy in ZAPU over who should replace Dr. Parirenyatwa as deputy president.

13. Geren continues: "Leaders of most of the SRTUC affiliates found themselves at complete odds with their memberships and cut off from any financial help because of Jamela's expenditures on thuggery. ZAPU pressure on Jamela's close supporters in the SRTUC grew, and by the first of September what had been a busy growing bumptious national center was a sullen gang of toughs guarding Jamela and a hard corps of trade unionists still believing in the principles of free trade unionism the SRTUC President had taught them but anxious to remove him because his name had been so besmirched by ZAPU." Geren to State, February 13, 1963, "Third Annual Labor Report," 8.

14. The article reports that the Court postponed passing sentence on the youth; if convicted he was to receive three years in prison. "Youth Had 'Kill' Leaflet," *Daily News,* November 7, 1962, 1.

15. Andrew Sardanis, *Africa: Another Side of the Coin: Northern Rhodesia's Final Years and Zambia's Nationhood* (London: I. B. Tauris, 2003), 91. Sardanis explains, "In typical Zambian folk humour it portrayed the people of Zambia dancing ChaChaCha and 'shaking' the Colonial Government out of office. One of the main streets of Lusaka has since been renamed from Livingstone to Chachacha Road" (91).

16. Geren to State, February 13, 1963, "Third Annual Labor Report," 8.

17. Geren to State, September 25, 1962, A-235, USNA RG 59 845c.062/9-2562, 2.

18. Shamuyarira, *Crisis in Rhodesia,* 140.

19. "ZNP 'Will Never Work with ZAPU,'" *Daily News,* June 22, 1962, 2.

20. Ibid.

21. Ibid.

22. *Daily News,* Weekend Edition, Saturday, September 22, 1962, p. 17 photo with caption.

23. "ZAPU Expels Jamela," *Zimbabwe News: ZAPU International Organ,* ed. Tasiana Mutizwavo, vol. 1 no. 3, Cairo, September 1962, Fox-Pitt Papers 6/6/4 Box 9 SOAS Archives.

24. Nkomo, *Nkomo,* 102. Nkomo worked with his Egyptian friend Mohammed Faiek to begin smuggling weapons into the country.

25. Geren to State, October 19, 1962, A-297, USNA RG 59 845c.062/10-1962, 4.

26. Jamela to S. Nedzynski, November 16, 1962, 2, George Meany Memorial Archives, RG 18-001, Irving Brown Papers, 1956–1962, Box 12 File 9.

27. Ibid. The full paragraph from Jamela's letter is cited in Raftopoulos, "Trade Union Movement in Southern Rhodesia," 68, based on a copy of the same letter in the ICFTU archives.

28. Geren to State, September 20, 1962, 3, A-216, USNA RG 59 845c.062/9-2062.

29. Geren to State, December 17, 1962, 3, A-502, USNA RG 59 845c.062/12-1762.

30. Geren to State, September 20, 1962.

31. Byrne to State, September 25, 1962, 1, A-174, USNA RG 59 845c.062/9-2562.

32. Geren to State, December 17, 1962.

33. Raftopoulos, "Trade Union Movement in Southern Rhodesia," in Ranger, *Democracy and Human Rights in Zimbabwe*, 2:67–69.

34. Enoch Dumbutshena to Maida Springer, November 16, 1962, George Meany Memorial Archives, RG 18-001, Irving Brown Papers, 1956–62, Box 12 File 9. Yvette Richards describes in wonderful detail the appeals of other Southern Rhodesian trade unionists to the AFL-CIO for funding after the splits in 1962. See Richards, *Maida Springer*, 226–33.

35. Geren to State, February 13, 1963, "Third Annual Labor Report," 10. The pro-ZAPU *Daily News* delighted in reporting the end of the SRTUC; for example: September 15, 1962, 3, SRTUC VP Phineas Sithole had his car set on fire in Bulawayo; September 15, 1962, 5, the Hotel and Catering Workers announce they have left Jamela's SRTUC. Paul Mushonga, who had formed the Zimbabwe National Party (ZNP), died in a car accident around this time.

36. Geren to State, February 13, 1963, "Third Annual Labor Report," 10.

37. Geren to State, "African Journalist's Comments on ZAPU Plans," August 17, 1962, A-109, USNA RG 59 845c.062/8-1762.

38. Ndabaningi Sithole, typescript, George Meany Memorial Archives RG 18-001 Rhodesia, 1956–62, Box 12 File 9.

39. Ibid., 2.

40. Southern Rhodesia Information Service, "Our Fight against Hooliganism and Thuggery."

41. Ibid.

42. City of Salisbury, Annual Report of the Director of African Administration, 1962, 40.

43. Vambe, *From Rhodesia to Zimbabwe*, 270–72.

44. Larry Bowman, *Politics in Rhodesia: White Power in an African State* (Cambridge: Harvard University Press, 1973), 58. The LOMA was particularly devastating to effective organizing. The act, as Bowman describes, included the following provisions: "the prohibition of meetings and of the right to attend meetings; police power to arrest and search without warrant; the banning of any publication; restriction without trial to any designated spot for up to five years; three-year prison sentences for intimidation; twenty-year sentences for possession of any 'offensive weapon or materials' (including a stone, acid, wire cutters, or inflammable substance); and sentences of up to five years for making subversive statements" (59). Sir Robert Tredgold described the LOMA thus: "as though someone had sat down with the Declaration of Human Rights and deliberately scrubbed out each in turn. . . . The cumulative effect of the security laws was to turn Rhodesia into a police state." Quoted in Dieter B. Scholz, "Robert Mugabe: Revolutionary or Rebel?" in David Harold-Barry, ed., *Zimbabwe: The Past Is the Future* (Harare: Weaver Press, 2004), 26 (originally from Sir Robert Tredgold, *The Rhodesia That Was My Life* [London: George Allen and Unwin, 1969], 229–33).

45. Department of State, Memorandum of Conversation July 16, 1963, "Inside View of ZAPU Split," participants: Herbert Chitepo, Director of Public Prosecutions, Tanganyika; William H. Brubeck, Executive Secretary, Department of State; J. Wayne Fredericks, Deputy Assistant Secretary, AF; and Edward W. Mulcahy, OIC Rhodesian

Affairs, AFE. USNA RG 59 Department of State Central Files, POL 13-9 RHOD & NYAS, Box 4023.

46. "Silundika Says Americans Deeply Involved in the Split among SR African Nationalists," Enclosure 1, July 30, 1963, from Salisbury, 1, A-105, USNA RG 59.

47. Ibid.

48. Ibid.

49. Department of State, Memorandum of Conversation "Call of Ndabaningi Sithole on Governor Williams," April 16, 1963, USNA RG 59 Department of State, Central Files, POL 12 RHOD & NYAS.

50. Ibid.

51. Ibid.

52. Martin and Johnson, *Struggle for Zimbabwe*, 69–71; Bowman, *Politics in Rhodesia*, 54–55.

53. Leonhart to Secretary of State, July 8, 1963, Secret Telegram 6026, USNA RG 59 Department of State, Central Files, POL RHOD & NYAS, Box 4023.

54. Ibid.

55. Ibid.

56. Bowman, *Politics in Rhodesia*, 55.

57. Geren to State, August 6, 1963, A-132, USNA RG 59.

58. Ibid. Shamuyarira explains the seriousness of events in July, claiming that Chikerema used ZAPU youth to "arrest" Edson Zvobgo after he had returned to Salisbury from Dar es Salaam. "As soon as Chikerema heard this, he went with ten youths and arrested him, took him to Nkomo and searched his clothes and suitcase, and found the letters. Nkomo read the truth in those letters about what was happening in Dar; for the letters said that the executive had lost confidence in Nkomo, and the people should prepare themselves for a new leadership and an entirely new movement." Shamuyarira, *Crisis in Rhodesia*, 181–82.

59. Geren to State, "Chikerema Reiterates ZAPU Plea for U.S. Support," April 25, 1963, A-1003, USNA RG 59 Department of State, Central Files, POL 12 RHOD & NYAS.

60. "Struggle for Leadership in the Zimbabwe African People's Union (ZAPU) of Southern Rhodesia," Memorandum for McGeorge Bundy, the White House, July 15, 1963, USNA RG 59 Department of State, Central Files, POL 12 RHOD & NYAS.

Chapter 7

1. Bowman, *Politics in Rhodesia*, 57.

2. Ibid., 60.

3. Geren to State, "Conversation with Robert Mugabe, Secretary-General of ZANU," Dar es Salaam, August 12, 1963, A-164 Airgram, 1, USNA RG 59 Department of State, Central Files, POL 12 RHOD & NYAS. Geren's optimistic reading of Mugabe's ambitions contrasted somewhat with the opinion expressed a month later by Leonhart, the American ambassador to Tanganyika, who cabled the following telegram to Washington: "Foregoing reflects of course version [of] SR scene, projected by Mugabe as ZANU Secretary General. I think he may however be beginning [to] consider [the] possibility [of] another role." Ambassador Leonhart to Secretary

of State, from Dar es Salaam, November 8, 1963, USNA RG 59 Department of State, Central Files, POL 13-9 RHOD & NYAS.

4. Geren to State, "Conversation with Robert Mugabe," August 12, 1963, 3.

5. Ibid., 4.

6. Geren to State, "Conversation with Robert Mugabe," August 14, 1963.

7. Nyagumbo, *With the People*, 181.

8. Ibid., 183.

9. Ibid.

10. Geren to State, A-164 Airgram, Salisbury, August 14, 1963, "Conversation with Robert Mugabe," August 12, 1963, 3.

11. Geren to State, April 6, 1963, USNA RG 59 Department of State, Central Files, POL 12 RHOD & NYAS, Box 4025.

12. Geren to State, August 5, 1963, USNA RG 59 Department of State, Central Files, POL 25 RHOD & NYAS, Box 4023.

13. Nyagumbo, *With the People*, 183.

14. Ibid, 180.

15. Geren to State, "Sithole's and Takawira's Reaction to Broadcast by Tranos Makombe in Peking," Airgram-317, September 26, 1963, USNA RG 59 Department of State, Central Files, POL 12 RHOD & NYAS, Box 4023.

16. Leonhart wrote the following cable: "ZAPU/ZANU prospects. Mugabe seemed satisfied ZANU making reasonable progress first months and ZAPU's early lead shrinking. He thought size of respective crowds at Nkomo and Sithole meetings misleading since ZAPU has funds for beer hall rallies, free food, and motorcades, while ZANU finances are scarce. He projected two lines (A) Increasing appeal ZANU in SR as only party with capacity and concepts for political change and (B) Growing disillusionment with ZAPU campaign of 'whipping up people' with no idea what to do next. He thought lines would converge about six months time when Nkomo would probably collapse. 'He has never worked so hard in his life; never gone so long without vacation from SR; can't stand the pace.' " Ambassador Leonhart to Secretary of State, Dar es Salaam, November 8, 1963, USNA RG 59 Department of State, Central Files, POL 13-9 RHOD & NYAS.

17. Ibid.

18. *Daily News*, August 14, 1963, 1.

19. Ibid.

20. "Todd Warns of Southern Rhodesian Strife: Bloodshed Could Follow Boycotts," *Daily News*, August 15, 1963, 1.

21. Ibid.

22. "ZANU Would Repeal Land Act: Sithole Assures Members," *Daily News*, August 22, 1963, 1.

23. American Embassy Dar es Salaam to State, September 5, 1963, USNA RG 59 Department of State, Central Files, POL 12 RHOD & NYAS. This source includes copies of press releases from ZAPU's Dar es Salaam representative, Benjamin Madlela, attacking the newly-organized ZANU. The most detailed of these ZAPU press releases is Madlela's "Information on the Men behind the Plot to Unseat Nkomo," n.d. (but likely August 19).

24. Madlela, "Information on the Men behind the Plot to Unseat Nkomo."

25. Geren to State, September 18, 1963, A-301, USNA RG 59.

26. Emphasis in the original. American Embassy Dar es Salaam to State, September 5, 1963.

27. Geren to State, September 10, 1963, A-263, USNA RG 59 Department of State, Central Files, POL 12 RHOD & NYAS.

28. Geren to State, December 3, 1963, Airgram-503, USNA RG 59 Department of State, Central Files, POL 12 RHOD & NYAS, Box 4023

29. Ibid.

30. Shamuyarira, *Crisis in Rhodesia*, 40.

31. Ibid., 45–46.

32. "ZANU Leaders Bribed £2 m—Jane Ngwenya," *Daily News*, September 14, 1963, 18. Ngwenya had joined township politics in Bulawayo and then joined the SRANC. See Barnes, "*We Women Worked So Hard*," 152.

33. "ZANU Leaders Bribed £2 m," 18.

34. American Consul, Salisbury, "Chikerema Calls Banda an Imperialist Agent," October 29, 1963, A-403, USNA RG 59 Department of State, Central Files, POL 13-9 RHOD & NYAS, Box 4025.

35. "First Killing in the ZANU-ZAPU Split," December 6, 1963, A-518, USNA RG 59 Department of State, Central Files, POL 13-2 RHOD & NYAS.

36. Geren to State, Telegram October 31, 1963, USNA RG 59 Department of State, Central Files, POL 25 RHOD & NYAS, Box 4027.

37. *Rhodesia Herald*, October 1964.

38. For a discussion of the difficulties faced by the ANC and PAC leadership in the early 1960s, see Edward Feit, *Urban Revolt in South Africa, 1960–1964: A Case Study* (Evanston: Northwestern University Press, 1971).

39. "Takawira Loses Appeal against Conviction," *Rhodesia Herald*, August 28, 1963, 5.

40. By 1964 the government had already arrested Takawira many times: in July 1960 after the Salisbury and Bulawayo riots, and a number of times in August 1963, during the split between ZAPU and ZANU. See "Takawira Refused Bail," *Daily News*, August 3, 1963, 5; Vambe, *From Rhodesia to Zimbabwe*, 88–90; and Richard Hughes, *Capricorn: David Stirling's Second African Campaign* (London: Radcliffe Press, 2003), 152–53.

41. Nkomo goes on to explain how Leo Baron, "his friend and legal advisor," built up a defense that argued the young officer had become disoriented upon entering the room and had fallen and hurt himself. They also claimed the police officer had not properly identified himself as a police officer when he entered, something the officer admitted to. "Quite wrongly, we were discharged after an appeal. This did not make the police any more sweet-tempered." Nkomo, *Nkomo*, 107.

42. The column points despairingly to the burning of the house of a Mr. A. Masawi at Mufakose, and the fear that it instilled in the community. He asks, "Will this get us independence? Hurting each other in the process only helps to set the clock back to 1923 and darkness." *Daily News*, November 30, 1963, 3.

43. Fay Chung, *Re-Living the Second Chimurenga: Memories from the Liberation Struggle in Zimbabwe* (Uppsala: Nordic Africa Institute, 2006), 60.

44. *Daily News*, January 17, 1964, 8. A few days later, when Nkomo returned to his home in Pelendaba, outside of Bulawayo, the police using tear gas dispersed his supporters. They fired a large amount of tear gas shells and some went into their house

and affected many people including Nkomo and his wife. Nkomo reportedly collapsed and his wife had to go to the hospital for treatment. The police denied having fired canisters into the house, but did admit, "one or two could have bounced into the house." *Daily News,* January 20, 1964, 1.

45. "Talk of the Week by the Tattler," *Daily News* Weekend Edition, February 1, 1964.

46. "S. Rhodesia Police Open Fire on Rioters," *Times* (London), January 29, 1964, 10.

47. *Daily News,* January 29, 1964, 1.

48. Ibid.

49. *Rhodesia Herald,* October 2, 1964; "4 Appear at Death Inquiry," *Rhodesia Herald,* October 3, 1964, 5.

50. "'Toughest Year for the Police': Brigadier A. Dunlop to SR Parliament," *Rhodesia Herald,* October 21, 1964.

51. Shamuyarira, *Crisis in Rhodesia,* 135.

52. On the same evening, "smash and grab thieves" broke into shops on Manica Road, Orr Street, and Sinoia Street, stealing food, a tape recorder, and clothing. *Daily News,* January 22, 1964, 9.

53. *Daily News,* January 28, 1964. In October 1964 a man was jailed for twelve months for contravening the LOMA "by intimidating Africans in the Magaba Beerhall on August 13." He allegedly told an off-duty African detective, "'Stand up and go. This is not the time to drink' or words to that effect." "Jailed for Intimidation," *Rhodesia Herald,* October 1, 1964.

54. Patrick O'Meara, *Rhodesia: Racial Conflict or Coexistence?* (Ithaca: Cornell University Press, 1975), 119; originally published in *Battle Cry,* March 27, 1964.

55. A similar process occurred in Dar es Salaam in the late 1960s; see Andrew M. Ivaska, *Cultured States: Gender, Youth, and Modern Style in 1960s Dar es Salaam* (Durham: Duke University Press, forthcoming).

56. "Thugs Warn Girls on Make-Up," *Daily News* Weekend Edition, Saturday, October 12, 1963, 1. The article reads: "One of the first victims of the latest terror campaign is pretty 22 year old Alice Ncube of Old Highfield. She was walking from the Machipisa shopping center to a friend's house in the Egypt section when six youths and a girl stopped her. They asked her why she was wearing perfume. She said she was not and they told her, 'You spend too much time putting on make-up instead of helping the country in the struggle.' She was then struck by one of the youths and she fell to the ground under a rain of blows. The youths ran off when a group of passers-by came to her aid. Her face was puffed and swollen when she spoke to me yesterday. . . . Twenty-four-year-old Violet Fambai—she works in a city store—said: 'It's a torture to travel by bus these days. Men insult us and threaten us for imitating European culture.' 'That's not our idea at all, we just want to look pretty.' 'They have warned us that any woman with a "brown" complexion will be beaten up next week because a light skin will indicate we have used make-up,' said Violet." Tim Burke has analyzed the significance of makeup as a marker of modernity, identity, and independence; see *Lifebuoy Men, Lux Women.* See also Lynn M. Thomas, "The Modern Girl and Racial Respectability in 1930s South Africa," *Journal of African History* 47 (August 2005): 461–90.

57. *Daily News* Weekend Edition, October 5, 1963. The editorial starts out: "The campaign, by gangs of thugs, against women and girls with above-the-knee skirts, is part of an intensive campaign of intimidation from which African townships now suffer."

58. "Why All This Fuss about Length of Dresses?" by Edna Mathende, Women's Page, *Daily News* Weekend Edition, October 12, 1963, 6.

59. "Rallying Call," *Daily News*, February 3, 1964, 7.

60. "Angry Women," *Central African Examiner*, May 1964, 4.

61. Cited in Barnes, "*We Women Worked So Hard*," 160 (original quote in Jean Davidson, *Gender, Lineage, and Ethnicity in Southern Africa* [Boulder, CO: Westview, 1997], 150).

62. Nkomo, *Nkomo*, 121.

63. "Is This Thuggery Helping Nationalism?" letter to the editor, *Daily News*, August 10, 1964, 14.

64. Shamuyarira, *Crisis in Rhodesia*, 123.

65. Shamuyarira goes on to say, "Politically-conscious young school-leavers are unwanted in commerce and industry, unwelcome in the Civil Service, and generally cast away by the controlling white society. Their plight will never end, until a popular government has been installed which can train them to play a full part in a society of equals, with ability alone, not colour, as the criterion for economic, social and political advancement. . . . Education for the barren streets of Highfield or Mpopoma township, is planned social suicide for the whole of Bulawayo and Salisbury." Ibid.

66. Interview with Mr. S. Z., by author and Joseph Seda, Engineering, Highfield, May 14, 1992, trans. Simba Handiseni.

67. Wason, *Banned*, 64–65.

68. Ibid., 65.

69. "Workers Defy the Thugs," *Daily News*, February 4, 1964, 1.

70. Chung, *Re-Living the Second Chimurenga*, 58–59.

71. "45 Arrests as Violence Again Sweeps the Suburbs," *Daily News*, January 27, 1964, 1.

72. Elaine Windrich, "Rhodesian Censorship: The Role of the Media in the Making of a One-Party State," *African Affairs* 78, no. 313 (October 1979): 523.

73. "Minister's Reason for Motion to Ban Paper," *Rhodesia Herald*, August 27, 1964, 1.

74. "House Endorses Ban," *Rhodesia Herald*, August 27, 1964, 2. Judith Todd has described the protest and subsequent arrests in her book *Rhodesia: An Act of Treason* (London: Panther, 1967), 115–19. See also Wason, *Banned*, 93–97.

75. Abrahamson went on to say, "I am not yet convinced that this paper has been guilty of subversion." "House Endorses Ban," 2.

76. Wason, *Banned*, 89–93.

77. Ibid., 532.

78. Windrich, "Rhodesian Censorship," 532 (quote originally from Southern Rhodesia Legislative Assembly, vol. 57, August 26, 1964, col. 1408).

79. N. Msemburi, the "under-secretary for legal defence and welfare" for ZANU, told the *Rhodesia Herald* on the morning of the ban, "The only members of the executive who are in Salisbury at the moment are Robert Mugabe, Stanlake Samkange,

Nathan Shamuyarira, and myself." "Guards on Offices," *Rhodesia Herald*, August 27, 1964, 5.

80. The *Rhodesia Herald* described the situation in a similar manner: "The police and troops ringed Highfield and all inhabitants were screened as they passed through the cordon." *Rhodesia Herald*, October 8, 1964.

81. Ibid.

82. *Rhodesia Herald*, August 27, 1964, 10.

83. "State of Emergency Declared in Harare as Police Make 4 am Swoop: 'Object Is to Round Up Thugs and Hooligans, Says Minister of Law and Order, Mr. Lardner-Burke," *Rhodesia Herald*, October 8, 1964.

84. For descriptions of this long period of imprisonment, see Nkomo, *Nkomo*, 120–42; Ndabaningi Sithole, *Letters from Salisbury Prison*; Ndabaningi Sithole, *African Nationalism*, 2nd ed.; and the numerous biographies of Robert Mugabe, such as David Blair, *Degrees in Violence*, 21–24, Martin Meredith, *Our Guns, Our Votes*, 33–37. Blair quotes a detention order similar to the one Mugabe and others would have received in 1964 signed by Minister of Justice Desmond Lardner-Burke. It reads: " 'Greetings. Whereas under the terms of Section 50 of the Law and Order (Maintenance) Act certain powers are vested in me and whereas certain information has been placed before me and whereas due to confidential information which I cannot reveal, I am satisfied you are likely to commit acts of violence throughout Rhodesia. Now, therefore, I herby direct that you be detained in Salisbury Maximum Security Prison until this order is revoked or otherwise varied by me. God save the Queen.' " Blair, *Degrees in Violence*, 21.

85. Norma Kriger, *Zimbabwe's Guerrilla War: Peasant Voices* (Cambridge: Cambridge University Press, 1992), 88. Kriger divides the war into chronological phases: a conventional phase from 1966 to 1970, and guerrilla warfare and negotiations from 1972 to 1979.

Conclusion

1. Clark, *Struggle for the Breeches*, 246.

2. Day, *International Nationalism*, 22.

3. An interesting comparison to this situation would be the similar politics of violence that had developed earlier in Nairobi, Kenya. See David Anderson, "Vigilantes, Violence, and the Politics of Public Order in Kenya," *African Affairs* 101, no. 405 (October 2002): 531–55; and David Anderson, *Histories of the Hanged: The Dirty War in Kenya and the End of Empire* (New York: W. W. Norton, 2005).

4. A very useful article covering the similarities of ZANU-PF's urban strategies and those of the RF in the early 1960s is Amanda Hammar's "The Making and Unma(s)king of Local Government in Zimbabwe," in *Zimbabwe's Unfinished Business: Rethinking Land, State, and Nation in the Context of Crisis*, ed. Amanda Hammar, Brian Raftopoulos, and Stig Jensen (Harare: Weaver Press, 2003), 119–54. I have also examined some of these similarities in "The 'Fascist Cycle' in Zimbabwe, 2000–2005," *Journal of Southern African Studies* 32, no. 2 (June 2006): 221–37. This issue of *Journal of Southern African Studies*, edited by David Simon, Deborah Gaitskell, and Lyn Schumaker, focuses on Zimbabwe.

5. For the importance of reading conflicting accusations and historical claims in Zimbabwean history, see Luise White, *The Assassination of Herbert Chitepo: Text and Politics in Zimbabwe* (Bloomington: Indiana University Press, 2003); and Ranger, "Nationalist Historiography, Patriotic History, 215–34.

6. "Go House to House, President Urges Party Youth," *Sunday Mail* (Harare), May 29, 1994 (quoted in Todd, *Through the Darkness*, 390–91). Thanks to Judith Todd for sending me the full text of the original article.

7. Norma Kriger, "ZANU(PF) Strategies in General Elections, 1980–2000: Discourse and Coercion," *African Affairs* 104, no. 414 (January 2005): 1–34.

8. Vesta Sithole, *My Life with an Unsung Hero* (New York: AuthorHouse, 2006).

9. Deborah Potts, "'Restoring Order'? Operation Murambatsvina and the Urban Crisis in Zimbabwe," *Journal of Southern African Studies* 32, no. 2 (June 2006): 276.

10. Enos Msindo, "Ethnicity and Nationalism in Urban Colonial Zimbabwe: Bulawayo, 1950 to 1963," *Journal of African History* 48 (2007): 267–90.

Selected Bibliography

Books and Articles

Alexander, Jocelyn, JoAnn McGregor, and Terence Ranger. *Violence and Memory: One Hundred Years in the "Dark Forests" of Matabeleland.* Portsmouth, NH: Hienemann, 2000.

Anderson, David. *Histories of the Hanged: The Dirty War in Kenya and the End of Empire.* New York: W. W. Norton, 2005.

———. "Vigilantes, Violence, and the Politics of Public Order in Kenya." *African Affairs* 101, no. 405 (October 2002): 531–555.

Arrighi, Giovanni. *The Political Economy of Rhodesia.* The Hague: Mouton, 1967.

Ashforth, Adam. *The Politics of Official Discourse in Twentieth-Century South Africa.* Oxford: Oxford University Press, 1990.

Baines, Gary. "The Contradictions of Community Politics: The African Petty Bourgeoisie and the New Brighton Advisory Board, c. 1937–1952." *Journal of African History* 35, no. 1 (1994): 79–97.

Barber, James. *Rhodesia: The Road to Rebellion.* Oxford: Oxford University Press, 1967.

Barnes, Teresa. "The Fight for Control of African Women's Mobility in Colonial Zimbabwe, 1900–1939." *Signs* 17 (1992): 586–609.

———. *"We Women Worked So Hard": Gender, Urbanization, and Social Reproduction in Colonial Harare, 1930–1956.* Portsmouth, NH: Heinemann, 1999.

Beinhart, William. "Political and Collective Violence in Southern African Historiography." *Journal of Southern African Studies* 18, no. 3 (September 1992): 453–86.

Beinhart, William, and Colin Bundy. *Hidden Struggles in Rural South Africa: Politics and Popular Movements in the Transkei and Eastern Cape, 1890–1930.* London: James Currey, 1987.

Bhebe, Ngwabi. *B. Burombo: African Politics in Zimbabwe, 1947–1958.* Harare: College Press, 1989.

Bowman, Larry. *Politics in Rhodesia: White Power in an African State.* Cambridge: Harvard University Press, 1973.

Bradford, Helen. *A Taste of Freedom: The ICU in Rural South Africa, 1924–1930.* New Haven: Yale University Press, 1987.

Burke, Timothy. *Lifebuoy Men, Lux Women: Commodification, Consumption, and Cleanliness in Modern Zimbabwe.* Durham: Duke University Press, 1996.

Campbell, Horace. *Reclaiming Zimbabwe: The Exhaustion of the Patriarchal Model of Liberation.* New York: African World Press, 2003.

Chadya, Joyce, and Koni Benson. "*Ukubhinya:* Gender and Sexual Violence in Bulawayo, Colonial Zimbabwe, 1946–1956." *Journal of Southern African Studies* 31, no. 3 (September 2005): 587–610.

Chan, Stephen. *Robert Mugabe: A Life of Power and Violence.* London, I. B. Tauris, 2003.

Chigwendere, Ignatius Takaidza. *White Aristocracy with a Black Proletariat.* Lusaka, 1975.

Clark, Anna. *The Struggle for the Breeches: Gender and the Making of the British Working Class.* Berkeley: University of California Press, 1995.

Cooper, Frederick. *Colonialism in Question: Theory, Knowledge, History.* Berkeley: University of California Press, 2005.

———. "Conflict and Connection: Rethinking Colonial African History." *American Historical Review* 99, no. 5 (December 1994): 1516–45.

———. *Decolonization and African Society: The Labor Question in French and British Africa.* Cambridge: Cambridge University Press, 1996.

———. *On the African Waterfront: Urban Disorder and the Transformation of Work in Colonial Mombasa.* New Haven: Yale University Press, 1987.

———. "Urban Space, Industrial Time, and Wage Labour in Africa." In *Struggle for the City: Migrant Labor, Capital, and the State in Urban Africa,* ed. Frederick Cooper, 7–50. Beverly Hills: Sage Publications, 1983.

Day, John. *International Nationalism: The Extra-Territorial Relations of Southern Rhodesian African Nationalism.* London: Routledge and Kegan Paul, 1967.

DeRoche, Andrew. *Black, White, and Chrome: The United States and Zimbabwe, 1953–1998.* Trenton: Africa World Press, 2001.

Elder, Glen. *Hostels, Sexuality, and the Apartheid Legacy: Malevolent Geographies.* Athens: Ohio University Press, 2003.

Eley, Geoff. *Forging Democracy: The History of the Left in Europe, 1850–2000.* New York: Oxford University Press, 2002.

Eley, Geoff, and Ronald Grigor Suny, eds. *Becoming National: A Reader.* New York: Oxford University Press, 1996.

Feit, Edward. *Urban Revolt in South Africa, 1960–1964: A Case Study.* Evanston: Northwestern University Press, 1971.

Frankel, Philip. *An Ordinary Atrocity: Sharpeville and Its Massacre.* New Haven: Yale University Press, 2001.

Geiger, Susan. *TANU Women: Gender and Culture in the Making of Tanganyikan Nationalism, 1955–1965.* Portsmouth, NH: Heinemann, 1997.

Gilroy, Paul. *Against Race: Imagining Political Culture beyond the Color Line.* Cambridge: Harvard University Press, 2000.

Glaser, Clive. "The Mark of Zorro: Sexuality and Gender Relations in the Tsotsi Subculture on the Witwatersrand." *African Studies* 51 (1992): 47–68.

Gray, Richard. *The Two Nations: Aspects of the Development of Race Relations in the Rhodesias and Nyasaland.* 1960. Reprint, Westport, CT: Greenwood Press, 1974.

Green, Miriam. "The Salisbury Bus Boycott, 1956." *History of Zambia* 13 (1983): 1–17.

Hammar, Amanda, Brian Raftopoulos, and Stig Jensen. *Zimbabwe's Unfinished Business: Rethinking Land, State, and Nation in the Context of Crisis.* Harare: Weaver Press, 2003.

Hancock, Ian. *White Liberals, Moderates, and Radicals in Rhodesia, 1953–1980.* London: Croom Helm, 1984.

Hannan, M. *Standard Shona Dictionary.* Rev. ed. Harare: College Press, 1984.

Holderness, Hardwicke. *Lost Chance: Southern Rhodesia, 1945–1958.* Harare: Zimbabwe Publishing House, 1985.

Houser, George. *No One Can Stop the Rain: Glimpses of Africa's Liberation Struggle.* New York: Pilgrim Press, 1989.

Iliffe, John. *Honour in African History.* Cambridge: Cambridge University Press, 2005.

Ivaska, Andrew M. *Cultured States: Gender, Youth, and Modern Style in 1960s Dar es Salaam.* Durham: Duke University Press, forthcoming.

Jeater, Diana. *Law, Language, and Science: The Invention of the "Native Mind" in Southern Rhodesia, 1890–1930.* Portsmouth, NH: Heinemann, 2007.

———. *Marriage, Perversion, and Power: The Construction of Moral Discourse in Southern Rhodesia.* Oxford: Clarendon Press, 1993.

———. "No Place for a Woman: Gwelo Town, Southern Rhodesia, 1894–1920." *Journal of Southern African Studies* 26, no. 1 (March 2000): 29–42.

Johnson, David. *World War II and the Scramble for Labour in Colonial Zimbabwe, 1939–1948.* Harare: University of Zimbabwe Press, 2000.

Kamete, Amin Y. *Governing the Poor in Harare, Zimbabwe: Shifting Perceptions and Changing Responses.* Uppsala: Nordiska Afrikainstitutet, 2002.

Kennedy, Dane. *Islands of White: Settler Society and Culture in Kenya and Southern Rhodesia, 1890–1939.* Durham: Duke University Press, 1980.

Kriger, Norma. "From Patriotic Memories to 'Patriotic History' in Zimbabwe, 1990–2005." *Third World Quarterly* 27, no. 6 (2006): 1151–69.

———. "ZANU(PF) Strategies in General Elections, 1980–2000: Discourse and Coercion." *African Affairs* 104, no. 414 (January 2005): 1–34.

———. *Zimbabwe's Guerrilla War: Peasant Voices.* Cambridge: Cambridge University Press, 1992.

La Hausse, Paul. "'The Cows of Nongoloza': Youth, Crime, and Amalaita Gangs in Durban, 1900–1936." *Journal of Southern African Studies* 16, no. 1 (1990): 79–111.

Leaver, John David. "Multiracialism and Nationalisms: A Political Retrospective on 1950s Southern Rhodesia ('Colonial Zimbabwe')." *Journal of Third World Studies,* Fall 2006.

Lessing, Doris May. *Going Home.* 1957. Reprint, London: Panther, 1968.

———. "Hunger." In *African Stories,* 404–519. New York: Simon and Schuster, 1951.

———. *Landlocked.* 1965. Reprint, New York: Plume, 1970.

Lessing, Doris May. *A Ripple from the Storm*. London: M. Joseph, 1958.
————. *Under My Skin: Volume One of My Autobiography to 1949*. New York: Harper Perennial, 1994.
Lindsay, Lisa. *Working with Gender: Wage Labor and Social Change in Southwestern Nigeria*. Portsmouth, NH: Heinemann, 2003.
Lodge, Tom. *Black Politics in South Africa since 1945*. London: Longman, 1983.
————. *Mandela: A Critical Life*. Oxford: Oxford University Press, 2006.
Lukhero, M. B. "The Social Characteristics of an Emergent Elite in Harare." In *The New Elites of Tropical Africa: Studies presented at the Sixth International African Seminar at the University of Ibadan, Nigeria, July 1964*, ed. P. C. Lloyd, 126–38. Oxford: Oxford University Press, 1966.
Makwenda, Joyce Jenye. *Zimbabwe Township Music*. Harare: Storytime Promotions, 2005.
Mann, Gregory. *Native Sons: West African Veterans in the Twentieth Century*. Durham: Duke University Press, 2006.
Martin, David, and Phyllis Johnson. *The Struggle for Zimbabwe: The Chimurenga War*. London: Faber and Faber, 1981.
McCracken, John. "Democracy and Nationalism in Historical Perspective: The Case of Malawi." In *The Historical Dimensions of Democracy and Human Rights in Zimbabwe*, vol. 2, *Nationalism, Democracy, and Human Rights*, ed. T. Ranger, 28–56. Harare: University of Zimbabwe Press, 2003.
Mlambo, A. S. *White Immigration into Rhodesia: From Occupation to Federation*. Harare: University of Zimbabwe Press, 2002.
Mlambo, Eshmael. *Rhodesia: The Struggle for a Birthright*. London: C. Hurst and Company, 1972.
Mnyanda, B. J. *In Search of Truth: A Commentary on Certain Aspects of Southern Rhodesia's Native Policy*. Bombay: Hind Kitabs, 1954.
Moore, David. "The Ideological Formation of the Zimbabwean Ruling Class." *Journal of Southern African Studies* 17 (September 1991): 484–85.
Mosely, Paul. *The Settler Economies: Studies in the Economic History of Kenya and Southern Rhodesia, 1900–1963*. Cambridge: Cambridge University Press, 1983.
Mothibe, T. H. "African Labour in Colonial Zimbabwe in the 1950s: Decline in Militancy or a Turn to Mass Struggle?" *Labour, Capital, and Society* 26, no. 2 (November 1993): 226–50.
Msindo, Enos. "Ethnicity and Nationalism in Urban Colonial Zimbabwe: Bulawayo, 1950 to 1963." *Journal of African History* 48 (2007): 267–90.
Mtshali, B. Vulindlela. *Rhodesia: Background to Conflict*. New York: Hawthorn Books, 1967.
Munger, Edwin S. "Charles Mzingeli, Leader of Southern Rhodesian Africans? A Letter from Edwin S. Munger." *American Universities Field Staff Reports, December 6, 1952, Central & Southern Africa Series* 1, no. 5 (Federation of Rhodesia and Nyasaland): 41–47. New York: American Universities Field Staff, 1956.
Murray, D. J. *The Government System in Southern Rhodesia*. Oxford: Oxford University Press, 1970.

Nhongo-Simbanegavi, Josephine. *For Better or Worse? Women and ZANLA in Zimbabwe's Liberation Struggle*. Harare: Weaver Press, 2000.

Noer, Thomas J. *Cold War and Black liberation: The United States and White Rule in Africa, 1948–1968*. Columbia: University of Missouri Press, 1985.

Nyagumbo, Maurice. *With the People: An Autobiography from the Zimbabwe Struggle*. London: Allison and Busby, 1980.

Nyangoni, Christopher, and Gideon Nyandoro. *Zimbabwe Independence Movements: Selected Documents*. New York: Harper and Row, 1979.

O'Meara, Patrick. *Rhodesia: Racial Conflict or Coexistence?* Ithaca: Cornell University Press, 1975.

Paton, Diana. *No Bond But the Law: Punishment, Race, and Gender in Jamaican State Formation, 1780–1870*. Durham: Duke University Press, 2004.

Phimister, Ian. *An Economic and Social History of Zimbabwe, 1890–1948*. London: Longman, 1988.

———. *Wangi Kolia: Coal, Capital, and Labour in Colonial Zimbabwe, 1894–1954*. Harare: Baobab Books, 1994.

Phimister, Ian, and Brian Raftopoulos. "'*Kana sora ratswa ngaritswe*' (If the grass is burning, let it burn): African Nationalists and Black Workers—the 1948 General Strike in Colonial Zimbabwe." *Journal of Historical Sociology* 13, no. 4 (August 2000): 289–324.

Potts, Deborah. "'Restoring Order'? Operation Murambatsvina and the Urban Crisis in Zimbabwe." *Journal of Southern African Studies* 32, no. 2 (June 2006): 273–91.

Raftopoulos, Brian. "Labour Internationalism and Problems of Autonomy and Democratisation in the Trade Union Movement in Southern Rhodesia, 1951–1975." In *The Historical Dimensions of Democracy and Human Rights in Zimbabwe*, vol. 2, *Nationalism, Democracy, and Human Rights*, ed. T. Ranger, 57–76. Harare: University of Zimbabwe Press, 2003.

———. "Nationalism and Labour in Salisbury, 1953–1965." *Journal of Southern African Studies* 21, no. 1 (March 1995): 79–93. Special Issue: Urban Studies and Urban Change in Southern Africa.

Raftopoulos, Brian, and Ian Phimister, eds. *Keep on Knocking: A History of the Labour Movement in Zimbabwe, 1990–97*. Harare: Baobab Books, 1997.

Raftopoulos, Brian, and Tsuneo Yoshikuni, eds. *Sites of Struggle: Essays in Zimbabwe's Urban History*. Harare: Weaver Press, 1999.

Ranger, Terence O. "African Politics in Twentieth-Century Southern Rhodesia." In *Aspects of Central African History*, ed. T. O. Ranger, 210–45. Evanston: Northwestern University Press, 1968

———. *The African Voice in Southern Rhodesia, 1898–1930*. Evanston: Northwestern University Press, 1970.

———. *"Are We Not Also Men?": The Samkange Family and African Politics in Zimbabwe, 1920–64*. Portsmouth, NH: Heinemann, 1995.

———, ed. *The Historical Dimensions of Democracy and Human Rights in Zimbabwe*. Vol. 2, *Nationalism, Democracy, and Human Rights*. Harare: University of Zimbabwe Press, 2003.

Ranger, Terence O. "The Meaning of Urban Violence in Africa: Bulawayo, Southern Rhodesia, 1890–1960." In *Cultural and Social History* 3, no. 2 (April 2006): 1–36.

———. "Missionaries, Migrants, and the Manyika: The Invention of Ethnicity in Zimbabwe." In *The Creation of Tribalism in Southern Africa*, ed. Leroy Vail, 118–50. Berkeley: University of California Press, 1991.

———. "Nationalist Historiography, Patriotic History, and the History of the Nation: The Struggle over the Past in Zimbabwe." *Journal of Southern African Studies* 30, no. 2 (June 2004): 215–34.

———. "The Terrible Mistake Policy." *Dissent*, no. 22 (October 20, 1960).

Richards, Yvette. *Conversations with Maida Springer: A Personal History of Labor, Race, and International Relations*. Pittsburgh: University of Pittsburgh Press, 2004.

———. *Maida Springer: Pan-Africanist and International Labor Leader*. Pittsburgh: University of Pittsburgh Press, 2004.

Roux, Edward. *Time Longer than Rope: A History of the Black Man's Struggle for Freedom in South Africa*. Madison: University of Wisconsin Press, 1964.

Saidi, William. *The Old Bricks Lives*. Gweru: Mambo Press, 1988.

Sardanis, Andrew. *Africa: Another Side of the Coin: Northern Rhodesia's Final Years and Zambia's Nationhood*. London: I. B. Tauris, 2003.

Scarnecchia, Timothy. "The 'Fascist Cycle' in Zimbabwe, 2000–2005." *Journal of Southern African Studies* 32, no. 2 (June 2006): 221–37.

Schmidt, Elizabeth. *Mobilizing the Masses: Gender, Ethnicity, and Class in the Nationalist Movement in Guinea, 1939–1958*. Portsmouth, NH: Heinemann, 2005.

———. *Peasants, Traders, and Wives: Shona Women in the History of Zimbabwe, 1870–1939*. Portsmouth, NH: Heinemann, 1992.

Sewell, William H., Jr. *A Rhetoric of Bourgeois Revolution: The Abbé Sieyes and What Is the Third Estate?* Durham: Duke University Press, 1994.

Shamuyarira, Nathan. *Crisis in Rhodesia*. London: A. Deutsch, 1965.

Shutt, Allison K. "'The Natives Are Getting Out of Hand': Legislating Manners, Insolence and Contemptuous Behaviour in Southern Rhodesia, c. 1910–1963." *Journal of Southern African Studies* 33, no. 3 (September 2007): 653–72.

———. "Purchase Area Farmers and the Middle Class of Southern Rhodesia, c. 1931–1952." *International Journal of African Historical Studies* 30, no. 3 (1997): 555–81.

Sithole, Masipula. *Zimbabwe: Struggles within the Struggle*. Salisbury: Rujeko, 1979.

Sithole, Ndabaningi. *African Nationalism*. 2nd ed. London: Oxford University Press, 1968.

———. *Roots of a Revolution*. Oxford: Oxford University Press, 1977.

Sithole, Vesta. *My Life with an Unsung Hero*. New York: AuthorHouse, 2006.

Stapleton, Timothy J. *No Insignificant Part: The Rhodesia Native Regiment and the East Africa Campaign of the First World War*. Waterloo: Wilfrid Laurier University Press, 2006.

Stoler, Ann, and Frederick Cooper, eds. *Tension of Empire: Colonial Cultures in a Bourgeois World*. Berkeley: University of California Press, 1997.

Summers, Carol. *Colonial Lessons: Africans' Education in Southern Rhodesia, 1918–1940.* Portsmouth, NH: Heinemann, 2002.

Thomas, Lynn M. "The Modern Girl and Racial Respectability in 1930s South Africa." *Journal of African History* 47 (August 2005): 461–90.

Todd, Judith. *Rhodesia: An Act of Treason.* Rev. ed. London: Panther, 1967.

———. *Through the Darkness: A Life in Zimbabwe.* Cape Town: Zebra Press, 2007.

Turino, Thomas. *Nationalists, Cosmopolitans, and Popular Music in Zimbabwe.* Chicago: Chicago University Press, 2000.

Vambe, Lawrence. *From Rhodesia to Zimbabwe.* Pittsburgh: University of Pittsburgh Press, 1976.

———. *An Ill-Fated People: Zimbabwe before and after Rhodes.* London: Heinemann, 1972.

van Onselen, Charles. *Chibaro: African Mine Labour in Southern Rhodesia, 1900–1933.* London: Pluto Press, 1976.

Vickery, Ken. "The Rhodesia Railways African Strike of 1945, Part 1: A Narrative Account." *Journal of Southern African Studies* 24, no. 3 (September 1998): 545–60.

———. "The Rhodesia Railways African Strike of 1945, Part 2: Causes, Consequence, Significance." *Journal of Southern African Studies* 25, no. 1 (March 1999): 49–71.

Von Eschen, Penny M. *Race against Empire: Black Americans and Anticolonialism, 1937–1957.* Ithaca: Cornell University Press, 1997.

Wason, Eugene. *Banned: The Story of the African Daily News, Southern Rhodesia, 1964.* London: Hamish Hamilton, 1976.

Weiss, Ruth, with Jane L. Parpart. *Sir Garfield Todd and the Making of Zimbabwe.* London: British Academic Press, 1999.

West, Michael O. "Liquor and Libido: 'Joint Drinking' and the Colonial Politics of Sexual Control in Colonial Zimbabwe." *Journal of Social History* 31, no. 3 (Spring 1997): 645–64.

———. *The Rise of an African Middle Class: Colonial Zimbabwe, 1898–1965.* Bloomington: Indiana University Press, 2002.

White, Luise. *The Assassination of Herbert Chitepo: Text and Politics in Zimbabwe.* Bloomington: Indiana University Press, 2004.

———. *The Comforts of Home: Prostitution in Colonial Nairobi.* Chicago: University of Chicago Press, 1990.

Windrich, Elaine. "Rhodesian Censorship: The Role of the Media in the Making of a One-Party State." *African Affairs* 78, no. 313 (October 1979): 523–34.

Yoshikuni, Tsuneo. "Gender and Urban History." Review of *"We Women Worked So Hard": Gender, Urbanisation, and Social Reproduction in Colonial Harare, 1930–1956,* by Teresa A. Barnes. *Journal of Southern African Studies* 27, no. 1 (March 2001): 172–74.

———. "Notes on the Influence of Town–Country Relations on African Urban History, before 1957: Experiences of Salisbury and Bulawayo." In *Sites of Struggle: Essays in Zimbabwe's Urban History,* ed. Brian Raftopoulos and Tsuneo Yoshikuni, 113–56. Harare: Weaver Press, 1999.

Index

Zimbabwe African People's Union
(ZAPU) (continued)
sellout politics of, 128, 132–33, 139–41,
160; strategy of, 125–26, 136; women's
wing, 141; youth wing, 10, 118–20,
126–27, 150–51. *See also* Chikerema,
James; Nkomo, Joshua
Zimbabwe Labour News, 112–13
Zimbabwe National Party (ZNP), 105,
120, 190n30

Zimbabwean; nationalism, 2–3, 5, 9; politi-
cal style, 84, 160–62; "purity" of political
parties, 122, 160
Zulu, B., 36
Zvinoyira, Mr., 130
Zvobgo, Edson, 129–30, 196n58
Zwimba Reserve, 75, 143

Rochester Studies in
African History and the Diaspora

Toyin Falola, Senior Editor
The Frances Higginbotham Nalle Centennial Professor in History
University of Texas at Austin
(ISSN: 1092–5228)

Not So Plain as Black and White:
Afro-German Culture and History, 1890–2000
Edited by Patricia Mazón and
Reinhild Steingröver

Writing African History
Edited by John Edward Philips

African Urban Spaces in
Historical Perspective
Edited by Steven J. Salm and
Toyin Falola

Yorùbá Identity and Power Politics
Edited by Toyin Falola and Ann Genova

Constructions of Belonging:
Igbo Communities and the Nigerian
State in the Twentieth Century
Axel Harneit-Sievers

Sufi City: Urban Design and
Archetypes in Touba
Eric Ross

A Political History of
The Gambia, 1816–1994
Arnold Hughes and David Perfect

The Abolition of the Slave Trade in
Southeastern Nigeria, 1885–1950
A. E. Afigbo

HIV/AIDS, Illness, and
African Well-Being
Edited by Toyin Falola and
Matthew M. Heaton

Ira Aldridge: The African Roscius
Edited by Bernth Lindfors

Natural Resources and
Conflict in Africa:
The Tragedy of Endowment
Abiodun Alao

Crafting Identity in Zimbabwe and
Mozambique
Elizabeth MacGonagle

Locality, Mobility, and "Nation":
Periurban Colonialism in Togo's Eweland,
1900–1960
Benjamin N. Lawrance

Sufism and Jihad in Modern Senegal:
The Murid Order
John Glover

Indirect Rule in South Africa:
Tradition, Modernity, and the Costuming
of Political Power
J. C. Myers

The United States and West Africa:
Interactions and Relations
Edited by Alusine Jalloh and Toyin Falola

The Urban Roots of Democracy and Political
Violence in Zimbabwe:
Harare and Highfield, 1940–1964
Timothy Scarnecchia

The Urban Roots of Democracy and Political Violence in Zimbabwe details a democratic tradition developed in the 1940s and 1950s, and a movement that would fall victim to an increasingly elitist and divisive political culture by the 1960s. Providing biographical sketches of key personalities within the genealogy of nationalist politics, Timothy Scarnecchia weaves an intricate narrative that traces the trajectories of earlier democratic traditions in Zimbabwe, including women's political movements, township organizations, and trade unions. This work suggests that intense rivalries for control of the nationalist leadership after 1960, the "sellout" politics of that period, and Cold War funding for rival groups contributed to a unique political impasse, ultimately resulting in the largely autocratic and violent political state today. The author further proposes that this recourse to political violence, "top-down" nationalism, and the abandonment of urban democratic traditions are all hallmarks of a particular type of nationalism equally unsustainable in Zimbabwe then as it is now.

Timothy Scarnecchia is assistant professor of African history at Kent State University in Kent, Ohio.

"Scarnecchia lays down a challenge to those who would have us believe that contemporary Zimbabwe was forged in the struggle between African nationalists and white supremacists. With painstaking research, Scarnecchia shows how the troubled politics of Zimbabwe have their roots in the African politics of the 1940s and beyond, when Africans were able to manipulate, and be manipulated by, the imperial retreat, decolonization, and Cold War rivalries. Scarnecchia recuperates the politics and struggles within the townships of Southern Rhodesia, where trade unionists and politicians, youth leagues and women's organizations, created democratic spaces for themselves, and, almost as often, deployed violence to destroy the populist spaces of their rivals."

—Luise White, Professor of History, University of Florida

"Tim Scarnecchia's study of the urban roots of Zimbabwean nationalism offers an important and original exploration of the ways in which violence, generation, and gender shape political mobilization and political culture. He traces the carefully negotiated rise of demands for 'imperial citizenship' among working class men and women of the 1950s, and their displacement in the 1960s by a violent politics in which the quest for power and loyalty placed the language of the sell-out and young men center stage. This latter version of nationalism won out, and continues powerfully to shape Zimbabwe today."

—Jocelyn Alexander, University Lecturer in Commonwealth Studies, University of Oxford

Printed and bound by CPI Group (UK) Ltd, Croydon, CR0 4YY
09/06/2025
14685716-0001